A Heaven of Words

A Heaven of Words

Last Journals, 1956–1984

GLENWAY WESCOTT

*Edited and with an introduction
by Jerry Rosco*

THE UNIVERSITY OF WISCONSIN PRESS

The University of Wisconsin Press
1930 Monroe Street, 3rd Floor
Madison, Wisconsin 53711-2059
uwpress.wisc.edu

3 Henrietta Street
London WC2E 8LU, England
eurospanbookstore.com

Printed in the United States of America

Library of Congress Cataloging-in-Publication Data

Wescott, Glenway, 1901–1987.
A heaven of words : last journals, 1956–1984 / Glenway Wescott ; edited
and with an introduction by Jerry Rosco.
p. cm.
Includes bibliographical references and index.
ISBN 978-0-299-29424-3 (pbk. : alk. paper) — ISBN 978-0-299-29423-6 (e-book)
1. Wescott, Glenway, 1901–1987—Diaries. 2. Authors, American—
20th century—Diaries. I. Rosco, Jerry. II. Title.
PS3545.E827Z46 2013
813′.52—dc23
[B]
2012037076

Contents

Preface

Originally, there were supposed to be several volumes of Wescott journals, according to a contract signed in 1972. The man who agreed to take on this task was the wonderful literary editor Robert Phelps (1922–89). A graduate of Oberlin College, Phelps was the author of one novel, *Heroes and Orators*. After that he dedicated himself to the most ambitious literary projects, including editing autobiographical works of Colette and Jean Cocteau. He was married to artist Rosemarie Beck (Becki) and had a son, Roger (Phelps's bisexuality was merely a complication to his married life). Often he supported himself by writing endless magazine articles and reviews so that he could complete the literary books. The purity of his passion earned him a great friend: novelist and screenwriter James Salter. An inspiring book of their correspondence, *Memorable Days*, was recently published.

Robert Phelps's love of literature culminated in his devotion to a writer's writer, Glenway Wescott. The formal elegance of Wescott's prose hooked him, as did the sensitivity and humanity in his novels. The fact that Wescott was very famous in his youth and yet stopped writing fiction in mid-life added mystery. Phelps found that he also loved Wescott's short stories and his essays about art, as well as his literary criticism. When Phelps heard that Wescott had massive journal materials in three-ring binders, his mission became clear. However, the journals faced many delays.

After Glenway died in 1987, Phelps and the publisher agreed to com-press several volumes into one big book, *Continual Lessons: 1937–1955*. A little more than a year later Phelps's health failed, and he had the pub-lisher bring me in to finish the work. It finally appeared in 1990 and was well received and quoted everywhere.

Ten years later I completed my biography of Wescott. Then, gradu-ally, the ambition of Robert and the voice of Glenway drew me back to the journals. This is a smaller book than *Continual Lessons*, less dreamy perhaps, but intense and just as rich in life and love. Unlike the earlier journals, most entries are dated. Where there is a blank space between entries it is the same day but different documents. Ornaments indicate undated entries; they are placed where they belong, or seem to belong. A few entries from the earlier 1950s were repeated, but I respect perfec-tionist Wescott's placement. Text within square brackets is my own—it reflects the many "visuals," such as clippings, photos, and scratch-notes, that I found with entries. No doubt Wescott would have preferred many images with entries—he did create some scrapbooks like that. He also liked to invent nouns, verbs, and adjectives, often in humor, and copy-editors should stand back.

As Glenway would wish, this book is dedicated to the memory of Monroe Wheeler. Thanks to executor Anatole Pohorilenko for permis-sion to select and edit the Wescott journals. Four photos here are repro-duced with the permission of John Stevenson. One photo is reproduced with the permission of Roger D. Phelps and another with the permis-sion of John Connolly. All other photos are reproduced with the per-mission of Anatole Pohorilenko for the estates of Glenway Wescott and Monroe Wheeler, and three of those photos with the additional permis-sion of the estate of George Platt Lynes.

Thanks one more time to archivist/curator Timothy Young and every-one at Yale's Beinecke Library, and to the staff of the Berg Collection of the New York Public Library. Thanks to artist Kim Kasow. And finally, thanks very much to editor Raphael Kadushin and the University of Wis-consin Press staff.

A Heaven of Words

Introduction

A S A WRITER AND PUBLIC FIGURE, Glenway Wescott (1901–87) doesn't fit neatly into the categories of either literature or celebrity. While the high art of his four novels assures that he'll be remembered, four aborted novels make him something of an enigma, so that it's best to say simply that he was a major talent. One of the most famous American writers during the 1920s era of the expatriates in Paris, by midlife he was less well known as he turned to essays, his long-suppressed journals, and decades of literary work for the American Academy and Institute of Arts and Letters. Yet throughout his life many of the century's top writers, artists, and social figures cherished his friendship, including Isadora Duncan, Jean Cocteau, William Somerset Maugham, the Sitwells, Katherine Anne Porter, Dr. Alfred Kinsey, Joseph Campbell, and the Rothschilds. As a thinker, conversationalist, public speaker, and activist for the arts and social progress, he was an extraordinary man, not just a writer.

Yet language and literature meant more to him than anything, and friends such as Porter and Marianne Moore chastised him for putting others' work before his own. Early on he wrote beautifully of his native Midwest, yet his elegant lyrical prose seems more Continental than American. Some readers appreciate this style, others don't; but Wescott himself explains (in his February 13, 1957, entry) that his slow, lyrical approach to writing is tied to his beginnings as a poet. As for the piercing sensitivity and humanity of his prose, that is a matter of the heart or soul.

Born on a poor farm in Wisconsin, Wescott made it to the University of Chicago on a scholarship at age sixteen—his professors were stunned that he'd done far more reading than most graduate students. The deadly Spanish Flu cut short his college years but, influenced by Yvor Winters and the Chicago poets, he was soon publishing Imagist poems and book reviews. At that point, in 1919, he met a dynamic young man, Monroe Wheeler, who was interested in the arts and creating beautiful books. One of the great gay relationships of the century followed. It was Wheeler who published Wescott's first book of poems, encouraged him to move east to New York, to visit Europe, and to dedicate himself to writing. *The Apple of the Eye* (1924), a haunting poetic novel of the impoverished Midwest he knew, was very well received. Wheeler then encouraged Wescott to join the expatriates in France, and the popular, award-winning *The Grandmothers* (1927) followed, an influential chronicle-style novel that remains an example of the ambitious great American novel. Admittedly envious of this success, and disliking Wescott personally, Ernest Hemingway parodied him in chapter 3 of *The Sun Also Rises.*

Wescott then published *Goodbye, Wisconsin* (1928), a book of short stories about the Midwest. Meanwhile, Monroe Wheeler continued publishing a line of beautiful small books, and when he and Wescott befriended a wealthy young American heiress, Barbara Harrison, they created Harrison of Paris, one of the great deluxe book presses of the early 1930s.

After a last story of the Midwest—the bound, deluxe *The Babe's Bed* (1930)—Wescott's career took a detour. A collection of prophetic essays of the coming European war, *Fear and Trembling* (1932), was too high style for most readers (Wescott was speaking and reading French fluently). *A Calendar of Saints for Unbelievers* that same year was a very humorous little work but it wasn't the big book he needed to get back on track.

When Wescott, Wheeler, and Harrison returned to New York, Harrison met and married Glenway's brother Lloyd, and they bought a large farm in Hampton, New Jersey. A house and surrounding acres reserved for Glenway and Monroe was called Stone-blossom. Beginning in 1937, they had the country home and Wheeler's city apartment for the rest of Glenway's life. Wheeler's career took off as director of publications for the Museum of Modern Art, where he would revolutionize museum books and catalogs in quality, design, and size. Over the decades he became invaluable in setting up exhibitions for MoMA, traveling to Europe and around the world. (In 1951 he received France's Legion of Honor award for introducing French artists to America.) Likewise, there was the major success of the young fashion and portrait photographer George Platt Lynes. Lynes lived with Wescott and Wheeler in a triangular relationship—closer to Monroe—beginning in the late twenties, remaining friends with them even after their 1943 breakup.

During the thirties Wescott felt stifled, producing two aborted novels ("The Dream of Mrs. Cleveland" and "The Deadly Friend"), but in 1938 he found his voice with the erotic and introspective long story "A Visit to Priapus." It remained unpublished during his lifetime (Ned Rorem called it "a posthumous masterpiece"), but its autobiographical first-person narrator, Alwyn Tower, led the way to what is perhaps Wescott's greatest achievement. Included in anthologies of the best short novels, *The Pilgrim Hawk* (1940) is believed by many—including William Maxwell, Susan Sontag, and Samuel R. Delaney—to be one of the great short novels in English. Inspired by an afternoon at Barbara's home outside of Paris, it is rich in double meaning—of the artist's struggle to create and each person's painful search for love.

Wescott made a good start on another novel, called "A Fortune in Jewels," about the war in Europe. But because he couldn't put his Alwyn Tower character at the center of the story, it came to a halt. However, when he heard a true story about a family in Nazi-occupied Greece, he quickly wrote *An Apartment in Athens*. Unlike anything he'd done before, this psychological novel was a Book of the Month Club bestseller.

In the 1950s, Wescott made another good start with "Children of This World," using material from his early Chicago years, but eventually gave up on it. At Monroe's request, he wrote an illustrated little MoMA bookshop favorite, *Twelve Fables of Aesop: Newly Narrated by Glenway Wescott*, which sold continuously for over twenty years. An example of one of his rewritten fables, one not used in the book, appears here in the July 29, 1956, entry. His admirable book of essays, *Images of Truth* (1962), about six novelist friends, is a tribute to the art of literature. Other worthwhile nonfiction books were started and abandoned, such as a memoir of W. Somerset Maugham and a volume of late personal essays.

However, from the late 1930s on, Glenway had been saving short journal notes and potential journal material, such as parts of letters. By the early 1960s, a young editor named Robert Phelps convinced him that his journals could compose an important work that would put his uneven career in perspective. By 1972 they had a multivolume contract, but delays and disagreements postponed the work indefinitely. It wasn't until Glenway died in early 1987 that the contract was changed to require a single large volume of selected journals from 1937 to 1955. When Robert Phelps fell ill, he suggested that the work be finished by me—as someone who knew and published essays about Wescott. *Continual Lessons* finally appeared in early 1991, giving Wescott's voice to matters of art, literature, nature, events of the day, sexual freedom, famous friends, and so much more. In a later *Washington Post* piece, Rick Whitaker wrote, "*Continual Lessons* . . . is miraculously good, as if the gods were determined to give their favored boy one last benediction."

Since then I devoted a decade to writing the biography *Glenway Wescott Personally*. After a few years away, I returned to Yale's Beinecke Library and began to read and select material from the Wescott Papers for Wescott's last journals. Most of the entries have dates, and undated material is placed where it almost surely belongs. This is a smaller book than the voluptuous *Continual Lessons*, simply because Wescott was writing less in those late decades. The reader must remember that when Wescott refers to his journals here, he means all of them. However, in December of 1969 he wrote, "*A Heaven of Words*. This is my presumptive title for the final volume of my journals: the time of my life when I hope to enjoy writing more than ever before."

1956–1959

GLENWAY WESCOTT'S EARLIER COLLECTION of journals, titled *Continual Lessons*, ends in December 1955 with the death of photographer George Platt Lynes at the age of forty-eight. Lynes had remained a close friend after the breakup of the three-way relationship between himself, Wescott, and Monroe Wheeler in 1943. As this journal begins in 1956, Wescott is dealing with the details of that untimely passing. He's also concerned with the health of his friend Dr. Alfred Kinsey at the Institute for Sex Research in Indiana, and in June he travels to the Institute (as well as to Utah, to give college lectures). His last serious attempt at a new novel, "Children of This World," ended a few years earlier—good autobiographical fiction that came to a dead end. In the late 1950s he is frustrated again in his writing projects, with literary essays being one outlet.

As always, his social life is often too rich for writing discipline, with friends such as Baroness Pauline de Rothschild (formerly the famous American fashion designer Pauline Potter), novelist Katherine Anne Porter, *New Yorker* writers Janet Flanner and William Maxwell, *Sunday Times* critic Raymond Mortimer, poets Marianne Moore, Louise Bogan and the Sitwells, author William Somerset Maugham, and many others. His grants and awards work for the National Institute of Arts and Letters takes up more and more of his time, and he is elected president at the end of the decade. Wescott's partner, Monroe Wheeler, is at the height of his career as director of publications and exhibitions at the Museum of Modern Art. The two bring together their fascinating worlds during the evenings at Wheeler's 410 Park Avenue apartment, a classic art and literary salon.

Away from the city, they have their Stone-blossom home on the large gentleman's farm of Glenway's brother Lloyd and his wife Barbara ("Baba") in Hampton, New Jersey. Glenway spends more time there while Monroe works in the city and travels to arrange exhibits. By the end of the 1950s, the Wescott clan will be forced to leave their land for another farm—as the state plans to turn the valley into a reservoir—and Wheeler will change his city home in another move. One constant is the relationship of Wescott and Wheeler, even with younger lovers in the picture—John Connolly (an ex-Marine) for Glenway, and first Bill Miller (formerly "handsomest man of the forties") and then poet and artist Ralph Pomeroy for Monroe. (The pseudonym for John Connolly in the earlier *Continual Lessons* journals was Ronald Neil.) Wescott also has a relationship with Will Chandlee, who becomes a loyal friend.

Toward the end of the decade, the young writer and editor Robert Phelps convinces Wescott to plan a collection of his shorter works called "A Windfall." This leads to years of collaboration, and while "A Windfall" is endlessly postponed, other books emerge for both men. Country, city, family, and literature continue to be Wescott's great concerns. In the months after Lynes's death, Wescott is involved with his friend's legacy, securing photos and negatives for Lynes's executor, artist Bernard Perlin (a longtime friend of Wescott), and helping Lincoln Kirstein plan a book of Lynes's ballet photography.

1956

JANUARY 1956

George Platt Lynes: The erotic dreams he always had at daybreak—I was always ashamed to ask about them. The worst of death: the unaskable questions.

∾

Mother: She is, I think, like one of the great queens. Which one? Perhaps Catherine the Great. The simplicity, the subtlety, the amorousness, the autocracy. I wonder if others who know her, even her other children, think or feel any such thing.

Maurice Chevalier, explaining to a reporter the fact that he is on the wagon these days, said, "On the verge of my 67th year"—I think in fact he is older than that—"I sing wine and I drink water."

"Mary Butts' Image of Me." When I lived in Villefranche I disobeyed and bitterly disappointed the English fiction-writer Mary Butts [GW slept with her brother Tony], who had been my friend for years, so that her friendship turned to witchcraft. For quite a while after she returned to England, perhaps until she died, she thrust needles into a wax image of me. Friends that we had in common used to report this anxiously; and I would brag that my personal magic was more potent than all the nonsense she had learned from the Rosicrucians and from Aleister Crowley. Then she died suddenly, untimely—oh, half a lifetime before me—which made me shiver; the nearest I ever came to believing in such things.

Overheard: Religious old American lady reminiscing: "I am so grateful to Doctor Bachman. He introduced me to Jesus Christ, and also to the Queen of Romania."

FEBRUARY 25

Anna Braake: One of the drawings in the dining room broke its wire and fell with a clatter. No harm done, but Anna and I hurried from our respective sides of the house to investigate.

"Spooks," she said, "spooks!"

"It's what the Germans call a poltergeist," I said.

"Yes, we had it in one place I worked in Newark, in the kitchen. Oh, it moved things, it broke things, until we had a priest come and sprinkle it with holy water; then it stopped. I don't believe in things like that, but they're true."

MARCH 31

Sent to Monroe in London: my memorandum supplementary to his will—how strange! No, not strange; partings have to be a rehearsal for the great aloneness.

Sometimes one's love of a person is like an attachment to a place—it is the scene of some great part of one's life; it is the chief abode of one's home sweet home.

APRIL 10

[Re auction of the late George Platt Lynes's possessions.]

I telephoned the Beverly Storage to enquire whether or not George's things might be seen in the late afternoon, before the sale. "Oh, it's terrible," said Mr. Beverly, central European. "We got so much stuff now, we try to put some out in the halls but there's too much. Maybe we sell some Lynes stuff tomorrow, maybe Wednesday; but maybe we have a better idea, to get a couple of dealers, and sell some stuff in lots all together, then we have more room."

This worried me, so in a very tactful and careful way I confided to him that I was an old friend, only interested in some papers, some letters, some snapshot albums, etc. To which he responded most sympathetically, "Oh, you know, we're not interested in that kind of stuff . . ."

I told him that I might try to come to the auction at the time previously specified . . . I telephoned Bernard [Perlin], whom all this irritated extremely, of course. He undertook to call Russell [Lynes, brother of George].

If we challenge Russell or inconvenience him too much, perhaps he will just not give Bernard the portrait negatives prior to 1952, or not for a good long while. He told me that he intended to do so, when he was asking me for salable nude negatives—but he has not specified any such intentions to Bernard. It is a dilemma. It is a kind of Balzac plot— *Le Cousin Pons?* No, *Cesar Birrotteau.*

This is the last day of my fifty-fifth year. Certain sorrowful and fascinating things which preoccupy me seem a matter of chance, mischance, not of wear and tear. Thus I see no reason not to wish to live forever. If permitted, I could still solve my problems, justify my pretensions, procrastinations, and other eccentricities.

APRIL 18

Anna Braake: I showed her Monroe's itinerary on a map and what impressed her most was Tokyo, Jakarta, Melbourne and Auckland, Fiji, Honolulu and San Francisco. "Oh, there's a terrible lot of water all around there, that's the trouble! It's a wonder the countries aren't all drowned."

APRIL 24

George [Platt Lynes] once told me that Alfred Kinsey expressed some surprise at the fact that Tex Smutney and Buddy Stanley never got erections while posing for him, despite the warmth of the bright lights, and the proximities, and voluptuous atmosphere.

But here—about a half dozen photographs with a sand pile in a studio, intended for some assignment of bathing suits and beach fashion— Buddy has an erection. The erotic effect is very poignant and odd.

The greater poignancy for me is the mystery of George's having made the above statement to me. Mystery forever, now that he is dead.

Upon the death of any longtime and intimate friend, this must be one of the strangest of the ways in which we feel the loss, and the fear of death in general. There are questions that no one except the departed could ever answer. We all have things to tell that no one else can ever be expected to understand or to take an interest in. We begin to formulate one of these questions, our minds start practicing one of these tales in order to tell it well at our next meeting—suddenly we catch ourselves at it; we are facing the abyss of bereavement, of oblivion.

JUNE 5

What a combination of pride and amusement I should feel if I could hybridize a new iris! Likewise, if I could coin a word. (The verb "belittle" was an invention of Thomas Jefferson's.)

JUNE 7

Leaving New York for Chicago this Saturday. I shall leave Mother to the bear-hugs of the Jacobs family, lunch at the airport with perhaps Hugh Wilson and a university interviewer; then to spend the night with Monroe's parents. On to Salt Lake City next day—and extremely occupied there, with eight 90-minute talks to my students, ten obligatory half-hour "coffee breaks," one obligatory banquet, goodness knows how many novels to peruse and to criticize in tête-à-tête conferences, one public reading of my own fiction (I am inclined to rebel against this, or to play tricks when the time comes), one symposium on the "market" for manuscripts, and my public lecture with slides.

On to Bloomington [the Institute for Sex Research], from June 23–26. A.C.K. [Alfred Kinsey] keeps complaining almost petulantly of my not giving them more time.

∾

When Kinsey preaches happiness and the right and proper pursuit in all this matter of love and sex, I wonder about us artists, etc., and I daresay so does he. But for two men to survive together stimulatingly, constructively, they must be well matched; and sameness of age is one of the great factors. Also they must have some mutual interest or enterprise: something more at stake than their pleasure and pride. Then if they are good enough, stoic enough, they stand a chance of outgrowing most of the painfulness and instability in due course, in a conjugal kind of friendship, like mine and Monroe's.

∾

Kinsey isn't old, nevertheless he is nearing the end, with terrible cardiac deterioration. Perhaps the circulation of his blood in his brain is irregular, causing lapses of memory, or recurrences of old patterns, devices, prejudices, fears—it is so in my mother's case.

But also the aged develop a new and particular ruthlessness, because they are in such a hurry, with so little time left, with no more of the luck of life—they expect us to forgive them, afterward, when we look back and conceive what they were feeling; and so we shall do, no doubt.

I am haunted by Willy [W. Somerset Maugham], by the portrait I might do of him. They say he has forbidden us all to do anything of the kind. Does he feel so powerful?

JUNE 8

George Platt Lynes: Strange bad news: Bernard has now taken possession of all of his inheritance—and has found only select portrait negatives: only the Lynes family, the dancers, the celebrities, and George's intimates—none of the ordinary commissioned portraiture; nothing for poor Bernard to sell. Monroe and myself in quantity, for example—but nothing of Lloyd and Barbara and Debo [GW's niece]. The Tichenors and Chuck [Howard]—not Henry McIlhenny or even J. Wisner. To be interpreted two-fold, of course—bitterness against the bourgeoisie—and intense concern for what will interest posterity. Oh, one of Monroe's lessons he learned well.

Ralph Pomeroy is another foolish youth made self-conscious by poetry writing, who therefore is going to have trouble, or make trouble for myself, when it comes to writing prose. In his case the trouble is mainly that he writes verse with exceptional facility, and expects prose to flow still more facilely. In a way, free verse is easier—as Shaw once pointed out—because you can leave little difficulties, freakish syntax, riddlesomeness, ellipses, etc.

JUNE 10

Salt Lake City, University of Utah. Yesterday I began the day with a reading, almost a "performance" of *The Pilgrim Hawk*, abridged to an hour's length—and I was proud of it. The tragedy of a life like mine is that years pass without producing any such work.

In Evanston, Monroe's parents seemed to be happy—their thoughts turn to him with a little flutter, wonderment, and indeed raison d'etre, every few minutes.

JUNE 14

University of Utah. The evening is long and lonely—perfect for reading and annotating the poor insignificant typescripts. I haven't the head or heart for it. Waiting for the evening breeze from the little canyon—it has been 98 again today—I have come up to a bench on the golf course: the green is a comfort.

This afternoon a bright little rag of a boy who writes poetry helped me bring a shelf full of books up from the lower campus, as I have made a point of hoping that my writers will read a little; and I complained in a mild clever way of the fact that the university does not have [K. A. Porter's] *Noon Wine* (I bought a copy for them) or *The Pilgrim Hawk* or Hemingway's *Green Hills of Africa* or Osbert [Sitwell]'s memoirs. A little later, as he arranged the others of my selection in the conference secretary's office, the boy said, "It is surprising how many of these books I or friends of mine happen to own."

"That is a comfort to me," I said.

"Yes, that is why I told you."

"Yes, I know, thank you."

～

Notes on Hemingway. "Father and Son": Nick Adams—a boy's loss of virginity with Indian girl, her little brother standing by. *Green Hills of Africa*: Mainly about killing wild animals, beautifully written—technique extraordinarily suggestive of sexual pornography. *Death in the Afternoon*: Brief ugly paragraph—anti-homosexuality in re Cocteau and Radiguet.

To Have and Have Not: Moving account of a widow's grief, with reminiscences. "The Sea Change": Lesbian love. Janet Flanner has referred
to this as a fine piece of fiction on the subject. *The Sun Also Rises*: Crass,
self-centered mentality, fantasy of castration, misunderstanding of the
heroine.

JUNE 18

University of Utah. This is my worst day here (I feel)—perhaps
because I am angry at certain persons. I have been spoiling them. The
Maugham lecture this morning. Two novels added to my schedule
of reading, annotating and consultation—both by *important* professors'
wives; nice women. Tomorrow Katherine Anne [Porter] in the morning,
and the art lecture in the evening—a double-decker day, in order to leave
early Friday.

JUNE 28

Anna Braake: Our old fool of a crabapple tree, one third of which
broke down years ago with excessive weight of apples, over-produced
again this year. But fortunately the heat and the drought have weakened
the stems, and bushels have already fallen, with a reek of ill-concocted
cider. This morning Anna raked them up, to be transported by me to the
back fence. "What a terrible lot!" she kept exclaiming. "Poor old tree,
she certainly has done her best.

"I'll give the Dalrymple's cows some over the back fence, they're
starved for some green food, but just a few shovels." She enjoyed our
working together. "Your mother should see us corporate. We make a
good corporation."

⁓

Sayings of Anna Braake: "The communists is just like an act-o-pus,
you know what I mean, an act-o-pus. It grabs all over the world. Oh, oh,
Mr. Wescott, I hate war. You can't buy noth'n.'"

JULY

Bill C. angered me, getting Monroe to agree with him as erroneously about some aspect of my sexual morals, so that I picked up one of the little iron tables with murderous impulse—which astonished him, and Mike L., but not me, not Monroe, not much.

JULY 29

"Death and the Weary Old Woodcutter." (New writing of Aesop fable, prompted by Chagall's etching; finished for Monroe.) An old woodcutter with too great a burden of wood on his back trudged along homeward but still had a long way to go when a stick loosened from the lot and fell, and trying to pick that stick up he let another fall, and in anger and exhaustion threw down the entire load and lay down beside it and wept.

"I wish I were dead. I cannot bear my burden any more. It is time to die. O death, come and get me. There isn't any other solution."

Down swooped the great angel thus called upon, favorably inclined, like other divinities, toward any sort of prayer we may address to him. Of course he cannot grant them all, but he listens.

With his old opaque and tearful eyes the woodcutter failed to recognize him. But the mere apparition of a person of such consequence, seemingly interested in his situation, did him a world of good. Perhaps also, while he lay in the path in despair, he had rested a little.

He said to Death, "Please, sir, help me get my load back up on my shoulders. My home isn't so very far now. I can make it all right, with just a helping hand."

Moral: The death-wish is often only loneliness, and needing to be helped, and wanting a helper.

AUGUST 3

Today in the bus there was a beauty: perhaps eighteen or nineteen, sunburned, with Venetian-red hair—a fine straight neck, fine high cheekbones, eyes like a child's, lips like a girl's, but a great nose, almost coarse, and heavy sexual-looking hands.

[August 25: Dr. Kinsey dies of heart failure. Wescott and Wheeler attend the funeral in Indiana.]

Language is a god, sex is a god, time is a god.
Fate is a convocation or combination of gods, an entire Olympus.

OCTOBER 1

It was delectable here last night. Monroe's 410 Park Avenue late dinner for Pauline de Rothschild and Diana Vreeland and her husband—the only happy (I mean consequential, future-full) part of the day.

I want less of everything—and the vacuum to myself for objective retrospection or purely poetical or sensual work.

OCTOBER 26

[To Lincoln Kirstein on proposed George Platt Lynes book of ballet photos.]

My dear Lincoln: Of course I am deeply touched, most favorably impressed, indeed thrilled, by your concept of an anniversary-and-memorial publication as stated (insufficiently) by Monroe . . . One thing I am especially glad about: the not-funereal aspect of it—George's death not a finis, only a chapter-ending, part of the continuing ballet record.

(Alexander) Jensen Yow is one of the young friends whom I especially appreciate—no sexual responsiveness or even compatibility. His attachment to Lincoln Kirstein and Lincoln's disapproval or mistrust of me has kept us from much frequentation. Not a really impressive person, except for his good looks, perhaps Scandinavian, pink-skinned and golden-haired—not very friendly, maintaining a detachment, rather cat-like. Still he suits the old-fashioned American idea of gentlemanliness: polite with a sort of ardor; never self-assertive but on the other hand not shy. He is an artist, with some aptitude, inclined to the conventional—though perhaps he hasn't worked hard enough to have proved or disproved anything.

Presently he attached himself to Lincoln Kirstein. He thinks of it and sometimes refers to it as a sort of marriage, and certainly some of his feeling toward Lincoln is filial. He lives in the house but bypasses some of the sociability. Lincoln's wife, by a characteristic seeming ingenuousness or shamelessness, has given the relationship respectability in a way. Everyone thinks it has been good for Lincoln, in his worrisome career and public life, perhaps not specifically influential, but steadying, comforting.

CHRISTMAS NOTE, 1956

[Re a MS draft.]

For my dearest Monroe, this last fruit of a lean year, upon a broken branch but with a deep and live root, and with my true love. Glenway.

1957

JANUARY

[About Marlene Dietrich, 410 Park Avenue neighbor.]

"Do you see?" said Miss Dietrich when our taxi slowed up in the West 30s on our way to Penn Station, making me look as we stopped amid truckloads of ready-made dresses in the garment district. "There is the little church of my patron saint."

"Which is your patron saint?"

"Foolish, don't you know? Mary Magdalen."

JANUARY 15

As I sometimes tell surprised college boys and girls in a lecture, one reason for the decline of the forms of fiction is that this has become a period of letter writing. It was one thing that Maugham used to raise hell with me about.

~

The essential of the aphoristic form: It shall be terse, brief, neat, and shall give pleasure by the way it is expressed—and arouse in the reader's mind a good many more examples than it specifies.

JANUARY 18

To Paul Gebhard, re Sam Steward: My last important conversation with Dr. Kinsey was about Thornton Wilder—more disapproving, or perhaps I should say more disillusioned, than I remember his having been about any other friend of mine. That same evening I went to Chicago and dined with Sam Steward, and to my surprise (of course I had not reported the K. conversation with him) he gave me an amusing, resentful tale of his having had sex with Wilder passingly in Paris some years ago; no one else has ever told me any such thing.

JANUARY 21

Our time as creators falls into seasons. Immaturity is a season; even senescence is a season and can be made to flower somewhat and to bear particular fruit, strange tasting perhaps, but enjoyable by someone, good for something.

FEBRUARY 1

What pain is to the body, shame is to the mind.

FEBRUARY 3

Always, I have found, a thing to do to alleviate boredom: educate yourself a little about something.

FEBRUARY 5

Note: A basic difference between homosexual and heterosexual. Double maleness emboldens, and makes the enactment of erotic fantasy more extreme. Doubtless, the heterosexual male is stimulated by indecency—but the female keeps checking it by her relative disinclination, her sense of desire to be respected etc., whereas males egg one another on, the voyeur encounters the exhibitionist, etc.

FEBRUARY 7

There has been a mysterious lull in Thornton Wilder's fiction-writing in the last ten years, as indeed my own. Oughtn't I to understand it? Yes, but creativity bewilders one, even a little creativity. I do seem to see him more objectively than I see myself, but all in chiaroscuro, as in certain portraits by Rembrandt, golden in the center and either very profound or strangely empty in the corners of the canvas. A part of what I take to be his problem is ever present in my mind, about my own writing, in the way of my daily and hourly fits and starts, my endless planning and re-planning.

∾

There is nothing stranger than life, unless it is literature.

FEBRUARY 8

"Are there not lovely books forgotten—perhaps buried alive by accident?" Somerset Maugham's terrible bit of worldly wisdom about best sellers and posterity. Indeed, not all best sellers last—but almost all the books that are not best sellers are forgotten, out of print, unread—except *Wuthering Heights*.

∾

Johann Adolph Hasse, the Saxon composer, Bach's friend, and as famous in his century as Handel and Gluck: how great was he? Perhaps it is hard to tell: for all the work of two-thirds of his lifetime was destroyed in the siege of Dresden in 1760, as he was preparing it for publication.

FEBRUARY 13

A little airy snowstorm. All the air is pallid with it. Black fruit of birds in or on the old thorn-hedge . . . This is one of my little exercises in image-making; a kind of thing that I begin innocently enough, just jotting something down, but that then fascinates me for half an hour, half an hour wasted. A kind of thing that is quite worthless until it has been made perfect, if possible. Thus, in the realm of poetry rather than prose; or on the borderline, which is risky, arid, and un-remunerative.

FEBRUARY 15

GW and Monroe Wheeler: We construct our lives, each of us his own, and both of us one another's, little by little, straw by straw, because bricks can't be made without straw, and then brick by brick. Likewise our self-destruction and mutual destructiveness.

FEBRUARY 20

Do you know what a "gaze hound" is? I have learned today, in *Newsweek*'s report of the Westminster Kennel Show: It is the Afghan, and the meaning is literal: it hunts by sight, not scent.

MARCH 1

My old house is precarious, and the way of life in it, numerous and disorderly—partly in rebellion against the number of little problems that are arbitrarily assigned to me by so many people, against the flattery and self-flattery that must have been involved all these years in my willingness to try to be helpful in so many instances and to give so much advice. Even to speak about things, even to hear about them, even to know and think, seems to distract me from my literature, to tire me and embitter me.

At a poetry recital arranged by the Poet Laureate, Edith Sitwell and T. S. Eliot were seated directly behind Queen Elizabeth. Among other readings on the program, John Gielgud undertook Marvell's "To His Coy Mistress," and did it badly. Afterward Mr. Eliot said to Edith, "I wished to give you a nudge, but I dared not, for fear of catching my cuff-links in the Queen's pearls."

Re Osbert and Edith Sitwell. Spoonerism: Yes, it is in the dictionary, I looked it up. It is the reversal of syllables by slip of the tongue, constant and pathological in some cases. It happens to me once in a while. I wonder what brings it on. This morning, in casual reference to our dear

Sitwells, I called them Oddith and Eesbert. At which my guests laughed, thinking it a witticism.

~

In 1923, at twenty-two, I was taken to Edith's flat in Bayswater at tea-time. I left behind a walking stick of cherry wood that I was fond of. Next afternoon, without notice, I returned and knocked on the door; a solecism. The tall poetess in a tone of apology, haughty and insincere, told me that she had already presented it to another transatlantic visitor even younger than I, to get it out of the way. Standing there in the hallway as briefly as possible for purposes of farewell, I felt sure that I could see my dear cherry wood in a corner behind some umbrellas.

One memory arouses another, adjacent in the mind which is always half asleep. During World War II, she and one or both of her brothers, perhaps partly for fun, brought a law suit against an unfavorable book reviewer, arguing that as they were professional poets, it affected their livelihood. And indeed they were accorded damages, not much but an outrage, I thought.

This angered me, despite the quantity of worse things going on in the world, and I solemnly swore that I would not resume our slight but protracted friendship if occasion arose after the war.

Night before last, dining at Monroe's apartment, basking in Edith and Osbert's obvious but well-circumscribed affection, smiling through and through at their powers of entertainment—even their looks and grand attire were humorous—suddenly I recalled that vow and gave a shiver. How weak my character is, almost always!

Strange names are a part of their notorious charm, which exasperates some people. In (I think) the eighteenth century, one of them was Sir Sitwell Sitwell. They have charmed one another down through several centuries.

MARCH 22

I went to town with Baba yesterday and she came within an inch of committing another of her follies: a Pissarro at Sam Salz's gallery. Then she gave a dinner party at the Astor, and took us all to see the preview of Tennessee Williams' new play, "Orpheus Descending," by way of a benefit for the Karen Horney clinic. The play is more important than his previous plays, I think, because it embraces more of the historic reality of the South, not just freakish misbehaving individuals. Miss [Maureen] Stapleton, with a wonderfully pleasing young leading man named Cliff Robertson: the love scene plausible and tender, so that one longed for a happy ending.

Last Friday at Flemington Junction I caught my foot in some switch contraption and fell and gashed my head and loosened my principal tooth—nine stitches, and who knows what dentistry.

Good News from Bloomington [the Kinsey Institute] yesterday: the U.S. Public Health Service is underwriting them for three years—specifically unafraid of Congressional investigation, etc.—isn't that good to know? Not enough money, but maintenance and continuance, and (I suppose) a most respectable endorsement and new prestige.

Georg von Ihring, "My German" of 1924, protagonist of a never written story, telephoned last week; and with perhaps self-protective instinct I have lost his telephone number. I haven't seen him since 1933 or heard from him since the war.

Life is too much, and I have been too sad, and have lived too much in detail, and made mistakes.

MARCH 26

Almost three hours in the bus, yielding to Francois [Reichenbach]'s insistence that I see his film at a special showing in a rented studio. It excited and embittered me, because he goes so far, almost to the point of excellence and originality. How can I give him the necessary extra push, teach him the pre-graduate lesson? A talent without aesthetic, a genius with not enough meaning.

He forces me to go through the motions of advising and helping him, but in vain, in vanity. Vanity on my part also as to my having the power to advise or help.

APRIL

Cynicism is rather an ugly state of mind, but it is a weakness to be incapable of it.

APRIL 11

Sorrow and excitement on my birthday. All seems in the dark—my many failures and continuing difficulties—though only yesterday I seemed to see my life and vocation more clearly than ever. The dark—just after it has been visited by lightning flashes.

This is my 56th birthday. No celebration. I have made certain resolutions in re literature and personal life, perhaps more realistically than in other years, certainly more solemn. The day itself has vexed me: income tax bother again; and two hours with Bernard Perlin who says that he wants to be influenced by me, but then resists all my suggestions; and then the National Institute dinner meeting, with old Mrs. Frank Lloyd Wright sermonizing, John O'Hara embarrassed by our old inimicality, my dear and sometimes inspiring Louise Bogan enjoying my jokes. Only one hour of intense pleasure: the nineteenth and twentieth century French pictures from the Sao Paolo Museum on loan at the Metropolitan, especially Cezanne's great tree, and Madame Cezanne in the raspberry-red dress bathed in blue light.

APRIL 14

New Jersey is a-thirst, a-thirst. No help for it now, so Lloyd says and Bruce says: Spruce Run and the Mulhocaway rivers are going to be dammed, just above the village of Clinton, just below their confluence, which will drown us out . . . It will drown us out, all our fools' paradise, Lloyd's farm and Baba's Mill and Stone-blossom . . . I wish it were an individual, personal, human need. It isn't even collectively human . . . nothing of the kind—the need is for "industrial" water, for Johnson & Johnson, and Johns-Manville, and American Cyanide, *et tutti quanti*.

APRIL 18

To Raymond Mortimer: It is a basic misery of my life, misery and mystery—underneath all the joie de vivre, the prosperity and sensuality and nature worship and music, etc.—in the last decade I must surely have written more letters than literature; and I am not a first-rate letter writer.

APRIL 19

I have decided on a life expectancy of ten years. How important this is! How for example it conditions my thinking as to the possibility of the state's taking all of our valley and submerging it for a water reservoir in (they say) three or four years.

MAY 1

The industrial-water prospect and Mother: I approached it so carefully, anxious not to have hidden from her so grave a development, afraid that someone else would spill the beans in the wrong way—whereupon I found that Lloyd had told her some time ago, and she has been "thinking it up and down, up and down." Her conclusion: that she and I had better move into New York, so that I won't have to waste so much time and money on buses, etc., and so that her daughters can drop in every few days, and Baba and Lloyd when they come to the city.

MAY 3

In his narrow, peculiar aesthetic way, George [Platt Lynes] seems to have had a stronger character than the rest of us—certainly he has the strongest ghost, in my experience.

MAY 11

My thoughts in response to Janet Flanner's saying that I have been cursed with perfectionism: My main difficulty is that I have learned to write as a poet. I compose prose as though it were verse, beginning with the word, the phrase, the image, the cadence—see my last lecture at the University of Utah, "The Great Flaubertian Fallacy." I am slow, slow,

slow. And in the circumstances of my life, every hour, every day, every week, every month, every year, frittered away by little interests, temptations, inconveniences, senses of duty, interrupting self-secretary-ship, letter-writing, conversation, and my attachment to persons of stronger character than my own, I never have enough time.

The other great factor is my universality of interest and sympathy. Promiscuity of the mind. I have never been wedded to any one kind of subject matter.

MAY 13

I am an aging genius, with an insufficient talent; now pregnant with certain books that I have been gradually laboring at for years; in extremely unhappy circumstances in some ways; extraordinarily independent but with very little liberty; kept in extraordinary luxury here at home but penniless otherwise; perhaps due to be famous before long, perhaps more apt to fail, to sicken, to disappear from the picture. Yet there are a few things I know more about than anyone else alive.

Two children talking: "Do you believe in God?" There was a half minute's pause and the word "Yes," with a little hesitation, the syllable extended downward. "It's just like Santa Claus."

Let me occasionally write a letter to Santa Claus, thinking of myself as my own Christmas benefactor, no matter when.

MAY 26

In a dream last night something happened to my hand and/or my brain so that I could only write initial letters. Again and again I made a capital R with my fingers tightly gripping my pen, and kept endeavoring to go further, to make the rest of a word beginning with R. When I tried to think what word, I came up with several at the same time— rose, riot, rage—and I kept hoping to make a sentence, but I couldn't. R, R, R. R,R,R,R. Only R, R, R. Only R—R—R!

[Stone-blossom.]

Maximum iris, about a week earlier than usual . . . Hedgerows and wild meadows and hilltops strewn with blackberry, the bramble blossoming in such quantity that its delicate faint scent fills the air.

JUNE

Last evening after sunset I went with Lloyd to his wood-lot, the abode of deer: densely wooded acres but narrow, so that from the center of it we could still see the golden evening light, intensified by a field of wheat on one side, and of barley on the other.

He also had me look at his corn, without one sprig of weed, and smell his perfect hay, some in green swatches, some cured and raked, some in bales. Because I always have to forgive him for thinking his farming is more important than my literature, now and then he likes me to see his ecstatic pleasure in hill and dale. And observation of pleasure is my religion.

JUNE 10

[Re Carl Malouf's 1940s sex parties.]

An evening with Carl Malouf, whom a god once inhabited to change my life—or, more exactly, who recognized the lifelong but hitherto unavailing pattern of my sex life.

Remembrance of one of the last parties we gave together which included certain old friends of mine. They were like sleepwalkers, walking not to any doom of great importance, but to the breakdown of relationships with me, the point of farewell.

Bill Miller. His unsteady erection, untimely ejaculation, and all the little effects of somewhat dolorous self-consciousness, and so forth, are of interest along with all the rest of sexual reality—vain pursuits, mistaken arrangements, frustrations, waste of time and energy and money, are as significant a part of the picture, as the fulfillment, the marvel, the ecstasy.

JUNE 15

Names to remember: darlings of the great Grecians: Atthis, the teen-age girl whom Sappho loved. Antilochus, Nestor's son, dear to Achilles and Patroclus, buried in the same grave with them. Lais, who Apelles seduced and made a courtesan of.

JUNE 30

Homeward bound. At the entrance to the early morning train there stood in farewell position the tag-end of a homosexual connection of some kind: a stout youngish middleclass Manhattanite man of the Madison Avenue type, and a really young, somewhat stoop-shouldered boy. The latter spoke with a kind of unenthusiastic good will, and I caught the tone of his voice, low-class, pessimistic, obedient. Sadness detracted from his good looks, a teenage sad-sack.

Then in the train the boy gave me a glance, recognizing my homo-sexuality, which I fancy he might not have done except for his night's experience, whetting his mind about the matter, wondering if I would be more fun or less fun, more generous, etc. And probably he was also anxiously wondering whether I could recognize his novice, little, ten-tative, perhaps remediable, homosexuality—hoping and fearing I was sorry for him. I did not like his looks.

JULY 9

At the Institute for Sex Research: Erotic dream at 3 a.m.—how rarely I have erotic dreams!—A.C.K. [Alfred Kinsey] and Michael [Miksche] and two girls. A.C.K. exactly as in reality. Not the least perversion or even impropriety—as in Section XX of the *Female* volume.

JULY 28

This is the most mysterious time of my entire life: some shrouded fate constantly perceptible but never quite comprehensible; some sense of everything changing, well or woe, foreboding or euphoria, pregnancy or malignancy . . . I am holding my breath, I am afraid even to be pessi-mistic. It is as though I were in a prison cell, in the darkest hour before

dawn—I keep hearing footsteps, I keep hearing keys—and I have no way
of knowing if it is my executioner or my rescuer.

JULY 30

Gore Vidal, ever the same odd character: intelligent but inaccurate;
virtuous in a way but cheap; with the great pusillanimity of wanting to
have, trying to have, even succeeding in having, his cake, while at the
same time eating it; and with the bothering question of whether he does
not sometimes simply lie. He used to pretend to be younger than he
actually was. In the suggestion of his having had to earn a living by his
pen, also pretended? Monroe thinks he has a little independent income.

AUGUST I

[Re the death of Tchelitchev.]
Pavlik died last night. I am afraid. I am weary.

AUGUST 8

An image of old age as I can imagine experiencing it myself: Walt
Whitman, old, was sitting by himself on his porch; there were a number
of young people in the house, and one of them suggested his coming in
and joining them. "No, dearie," he said, "I love to hear your laughter, but
I don't care for your talk."

AUGUST 9

Two types of humanity: Those who are lunatically faithful to another,
self-neglecting, though often harmful to others, and those who are lunatically devoted to themselves—instinct ridden, incorrigible. Of course I
am thinking of the extremes—degrees of unreasonable devotedness that
is often destructive to the beloved, and degrees of selfishness that is
ruinous to one's interests and hopes, and defeats even its own ends.

AUGUST 27

[To Pauline de Rothschild.]
Barbara thinks me some sort of saint: "the most Christian man on
earth," she said the other evening, and did not understand that my

blushing signified anger. In Monroe's opinion I am not a saint but a martyr. Neither of them, I'm afraid, takes me very seriously as a philosopher.

AUGUST 30

Old Misia Sert, in her foolish, proud forgetful memoirs, expresses her regret that when Renoir was painting her she would never let him look at her breasts.

"Open your dress a little more, oh, please. Good Lord, it's a crime not to let your breast be seen," said Renoir. She says that more than once he was on the verge of weeping. Prudery and silliness and stupidity, she explained. Perhaps also a kind of intimate stinginess, I should have thought. How many less fortunate women have been more generous, women and men and boys.

This brought tears to my eyes—tears of gratitude.

"The Boy from Hackettstown." I had a date with John and when I took the precaution of telephoning him from the corner I could tell by his veiled tone of voice that he was having intercourse. I said, "Shall I go and do some shopping before I come up?"

"No, no, come right away. Hurry."

He opened the door sideways, naked as I expected, somewhat covering his erection, and in the middle of the room stood a ravishing boy of extraordinary beauty. The beauty of his face, with rather pouting lips, was like one of the female movie stars of the twenties, the more feminine because of the confused emotions: lust, lust just consummated, and the lust still to come, and the surprise of my arrival. The body of a boy but not immature, and a tremendous tapering phallus, swinging out in front of him, and standing up superbly without provocation or touch.

"This is Don," John said.

OCTOBER 8

I live here in luxury, perhaps even more enjoyable for those who visit me, than for permanent and over-domesticated me. My dear family has pauperized me grandly, and for love of literature as well as of me, and not entirely in vain. It is a golden, not just a gilded cage. But now not only have I wearied of it, but I am no longer managing well.

It seems to me that I might give it all up, except that it would mean forcing my aged mother, no less spoiled than I, to go and live in a poor nursing home. As it is at present, I owe my dentist eight hundred dollars; I have just borrowed one hundred and fifty dollars from my best friend; I have not bought a phonograph record for six months; I am tired of my old clothes, etc. I am purposely not explaining one or two things in a more pathetic category, concerning one or two persons whom I dearly love. But the chief grievance of my life is that I can never travel. Only once since the war have I been out of my New York-New Jersey runway for more than a fortnight. Only once since the war have I voyaged to Europe, and then I had to work while there, and to come back sooner than I wished.

OCTOBER 15

The fire of my life has been a little too flaring, and with too many irons in it. Monroe is in bad health, in constant pain. Perhaps it may be one of those nervous inflammations like the shingles he had in 1953, but this time it is mainly in his chest. I haven't been able to get him to the Medical Center for fundamental tests. Sometimes stoicism is a form of fear—he stands the pain in order not to think of the danger.

At seven a.m., the incomparable colors of leaves due to the long draught—yellow and gold and vermillion maroon and red and pink, drowned in mist like the milkiest opal with the most wondrous fires within.

OCTOBER 21

[To Louise Bogan.]

A solemnity: I have failed you, as a horse you put your money on at *The New Yorker*, though the inspiration still holds good for me . . . It has been a bad year and continues in the same way. The trouble is that I can't

find time to write, or do I mean energy? I write more letters than anything else, most of them dutiful or compulsive. Doubtless I read more
than is virtuous for me to do, in my circumstances; I rationalize that.

NOVEMBER 4

Censorship: Gogol in a letter, in 1833: "My pen keeps writing things
the censorship will never pass . . . All that remains for me to do is to
think of a subject so innocent that it will not hurt the feelings even of
a policeman. My mind seems paralyzed."

One of my favorite bits of literary legend: As Guillaume Apollinaire
lay dying, a multitude came down his street shouting, "Mort a Guillaume!" This struck terror to the sick man's mind. Had he in his singular
career outraged public opinion more than he knew? Or could these be
spirits of the damned, delegated to get him and escort him to his damna-
tion? In fact, that day was November 9, 1918, and the outcry was against
another Guillaume: the Kaiser Guillaume II.

NOVEMBER 22

Barbara's father: "Francis B. Harrison Dies; Ex-Governor of the
Philippines" (New York Herald Tribune).

DECEMBER 6

Old Letter Found: When we were moving out of 410 Park Avenue
today, December 6, 1957, I found this in Monroe's large closet, behind
the wardrobe: "Dearest of all, only worthy: All this is an illusion, as mys-
tics say—what matters is what lasts.

"I want to remind you of *me* (as I am always reminded of *you*)—not
the episodic present; but me as a grubby, sickly, deathly, bluffing farm-
boy as I came to Evanston in 1919, or (if you like) me as a cold, talented,
rich, trustworthy, illustrative old man, as I may be before long if you will
keep serene for me, to our joint advantage. That fascinates—the rest is
just a matter of 'chic,' of romantic social sense, of pastime.—Your Gl"

1958

JANUARY 20

My talent—oh, there ought to be a less pretentious word for it!—
is like some deplorable sort of shrub or vine that blossoms only on last
year's wood; but meanwhile its new growth is so incessant and fast that
it all lies in its own shadow and tangle. I can't keep up with it. Year after
year before I get the necessary pruning done, autumn comes, winter
comes.

Perhaps in my case genius would be a less pretentious word than
talent. Remember Paul Valéry's grim epigram: "Talent without genius
isn't much. Genius without talent is nothing at all."

FEBRUARY 1

Cold War: For us Americans nowadays the death's head at the feast
is a terrific appetizer. Doom that we foresee and resign ourselves to—
what is to be done about it anyway?—justifies us in our headlong enjoy-
ments, our cult of leisure.

The trouble with hope is that it entails hard work.

FEBRUARY 5

410 Park Avenue has been demolished and Monroe has moved to 215
East 79 Street—which has been hard, as he has had acute spinal arthritis
all winter. We shall have another year of Stone-blossom [before the
valley is turned into a reservoir]; probably not longer, as things are now
moving. Young engineers fuss around our hilltops, drilling down to
where they think there may be caves, and exploding little charges of
dynamite in the depths.

FEBRUARY 12

I have been unhappy but peaceable—only not peaceable with my poor
beloved Monroe. The move to 215 East 79 Street demoralized him,
although as his friends come there and admire the art and the bibelots
against the white walls, everything clean and tidy, he reconciles himself

bit by bit—O great mirror of worldliness! Fatigue is the worst of it—no taxis around the Museum at the end of the day, the buses too full even to stop, the subway crowd clenching around his arthritic back like a huge fist.

I seem to have given up sex, not just circumstantially, frustrated, in the maze of my nature, with the hindrances and the shortcomings, and too many rules of the game—all of which is an old story—but now also by a certain decisiveness arrived at in my head and/or my heart, as it has seemed almost suddenly—which is new. Loss of courage; due mainly to the miserable experiences of several friends; perhaps due to age, chilling and weakening—a feeling (not without its component of rejoicing, or at least thanksgiving) that I have used up my share of good luck; and very great concern for Monroe—one more misfortune or disillusionment at this point would floor him.

~

In re the onset of old age—non-hope and wisdom: Lord Byron: "'Tis time this heart should be unmoved / Since others it has ceased to move."

FEBRUARY 21

What castrates perhaps more than anything? The superior woman's judging of her man, disapproving, disrespecting, but persisting in loving him, as though disqualification did not matter.

Blame without rejection constitutes ownership. To be given pleasure or comfort or help from—to give pleasure, etc. to—one who judges you, with incessant indefinite reprieve instead of punishment.

~

Forster's great general shortcoming: A kind of absent-mindedness amid his brilliance—as though bemused by his own figures of speech and mixed feelings—shifting from an almost frivolous realism to an almost irresponsible mysticism. He whisks away from things that happen not to inspire him—or are they things that he doesn't know, hasn't in mind any experience to refer to and build on?

MARCH I

John and Joseph S. arrived by the late train. Love-making in front of the fire. I was inhibited by not wanting to spoil J's pleasure. Anxiety about his shyness. I came away before the last act of their copulation. A good many young men who are manly and—in spite of passivity and eroticism—who think of themselves that way, mind being watched while being fucked.

MARCH 18

My dear John is now employed by our most prosperous playwright, William Inge, as secretary, majordomo, chauffeur, and solitude-dispeller—nothing to be read between the lines—and they are in Florida this week.

Shadow lives only in light. There are delicate pangs of vulnerability and self-criticism which occur only amid the joyousness of being in love.

MARCH 21

A Hustler: At Ed Jorgerson's very large party of muscle-builders, Fire Islanders, giddy boys, and old friends, there were two hustlers, pointed out to me as such. One was of singular beauty, Aubrey Beardsley-like, but husky, and a little crazy with narcissism, who went away with Blair Rogers; the other a great big dark low-class boy, so coarse and soft that he seemed blurred, as though due to a defect in one's eyesight. He was well enough dressed in the conventional fashion of the evening: chino cloth trousers and tee-shirt, with a jumbo dragon tattoo on his thick right biceps. He said to me in his spongy, shapeless voice, scarcely more than a consonant per word, "Don' I know you? Din'nh you pi' me up one night a' t'huh Wagon Wheel? You look jus' like the guy. I made fifty bucks tha' night. Jeez, it was crazy."

MARCH 31

I think that relations between men usually have some time limit, a certain number of years beyond which it is not naturally for them to run, unless they are based on something other than the romance and the sexual enjoyment—mutual vocation, or economics, or sometimes society, something regarded as more important than happiness. As to the romantic quarrelings and separations, our analysis is apt to cover the how; not the why.

APRIL 2

At Monroe's apartment. I have begun to believe that I shall never get any more important writing done. My main reason for coming to town was to have lunch with William Maxwell, for whom I promised to write three or four stories for *The New Yorker* as soon as I could clear my desk of the Wilder essay and other erroneous enterprises. That was more than a year ago and my desk is still unclear.

I sometimes deliberately mislead editors about work in progress, or work not progressing, because their interest may have an abortive effect.

APRIL 7

Barbara has exchanged the not-strong Pissarro, plus a Picasso plus a Renoir drawing plus a tiny Bonnard plus a Soutine plus the Kirchner that I thought of as "mine," for a Gauguin portrait of a little boy priced at $100,000, worth about half that. Now she has a notion of re-swapping it.

Miniature: Audubon. On the back of Audubon's watercolor of the cottontail rabbit, he noted that it was his only solace on the day his little daughter died. (I found this in Julian Huxley's review of *Audubon's Annals*, edited by Alice Ford.)

MAY 20

On my birthday my mother had another little stroke. Her speech was affected; also one foot or perhaps I should say one leg, a rather lurching step. She has recovered admirably, but of course it frightened her, and made her more dependent, with tears and new problems—it has made work for me, as psychiatrist as well as lady's maid.

Then on May 12, Baba had a coronary thrombosis—almost half the heart muscle affected, and she must lie abed in the hospital and elsewhere for many months. She has always had great recuperative powers . . . Just now she is acting rather like a general shot in the leg during a battle, wildly giving orders from a stretcher-cot in the rear.

JUNE

News clipping: "Maugham Revisits Boyhood School, Canterbury, England" (UPI). Somerset Maugham, the author, now 84, revisited yesterday King's School, where he once attended, and told the pupils: 'I am very, very old and I shall never see you again.'"

[Newspaper photo of] Somerset Maugham: A face of the utmost interest as to the mask-like form and fine texture, brushwork strokes of experience and length of life.

Something Japanese about it, kabuki theater? Only in the dark draughtsman of wrinkles deeply incised, with emotional significance not always recognized. The Japanese characterize their dramatic personae by spasms and grimaces, and they aim to affright or to amaze (perhaps also in a way to amuse). In Maugham's case the emotions have settled; the expression on his face is a residence; his will-power has become habitual.

"Scarlet tanagers." Just as I woke up this very cloudy morning, two extreme rednesses in my window made me blink; upon the pale green foliage of the sycamore tree fiery-red coals. I could not believe my eyes— only three or four yards from my bed, it was a pair of scarlet tanagers. For years and years I have not seen any. Like flames borne through the air on black plumed wings.

JULY 28

A great many things about me and my everyday life, morning, noon and night, month after month, year in and year out, manifest or at least indicate fictive talent, novelist's temperament—but preclude my accomplishing anything along that line in any large continuous form.

Most of the time in my little world I am the one most able to imagine what needs doing or saying, therefore I almost always have something to do or say, or at least to begin or attempt. I do not love my dear ones as much as they love me but I understand them better than they understand me; therefore I am the chief sufferer from our various contestations of will-power, confrontations of our respective points of view. *Tout comprendre est tout pardonner.* My feeling of emotional, sensual, and (sentimental) loneliness is like an itch, a goad, a scourge; I am restlessness personified. I cannot sit still long enough to accomplish anything; furthermore, in point of fact, I am never alone enough, long enough. I am the slowest worker in the world, but if I am ever to succeed I must do as much in an hour or two before daybreak as the average writer does in a day. I must do as much in a day, when I happen to have peace of mind and no houseguests, as the average writer does in a week.

What is the worst thought in the dead of night, or in depression during the day? It is time leaking away into eternity, lifetime going to waste.

AUGUST 29

Katherine Anne [Porter] is in a happy mood—in town to have herself photographed for the jacket of *Ship of Fools*. She now says the novel is *done, done*—"only it has to be copied, in triplicate, and of course I have to put in little bits here and there, and I really can't do more than six or seven pages a day." Suspense—but of course when a work of art approaches its completion, one can devise some strength and health from it.

SEPTEMBER 10

The strangest evening with Paul Gebhard [of the Institute for Sex Research]. He came at 6:30 and we talked alone until 8 when Will Chandlee arrived to dine with us—and then we talked until 2! So shy and modest, almost dull, until he had his dinner and drink; then inquisitive, mysterious, mercurial—questioning me a great deal. I think he expects some great preachment or uplift from me—and I do know some things that he needs to hear.

OCTOBER 17

Chickens have a language consisting of 13 sayings, but some of it is rooster talk, some hen talk; only eight phrases are common to both sexes. It is all instinctive, non-learned, inborn. Indeed at least two of their utterances are prenatal. You can hear them inside the egg, just before it hatches, holding your ear to the cracked shell: something about the horror of feeling cold, something about the delight of the temperature going up. But, I must say, I detect a certain sentimentality in calling this language—it is an audible exteriorization of emotions. The essence of language is insincerity—the possibility of it, the means of it.

OCTOBER 29

Monroe had a very successful journey around Europe, not only got his museum work done but visited twenty rococo churches in Bavaria, and saw Cyril Connolly and Graham Sutherland and Mr. Forster and Edgar and Margaret Wind and Mr. Maugham and Osbert and Edith Sitwell at Remshaw and Pauline at Mouton-Rothschild.

Now Lloyd has settled with the state for the sale of the valley—for much less than he had hoped—and bought the Paul Whiteman property at Rosemont.

∼

The great objection to television—as indeed previously to motion pictures and even to radio broadcasting—the terrible cost of new inventions. Half-invented in the first place; perfected at the expense of the purchasing public; at the general mass expense; with the patents kept under control as they may be most profitably exploited; re-invented when the invention might become cheap—like the sealed envelope of Mr. Singer.

When things cost too much the bankers become the most powerful collaborators.

The police in New York are arresting all the improper younger generation around town night after night. Thus far, in spite of dungarees and tee-shirts, none of my youngsters has been mistaken for a hustler or anything else illegal. Very strange when you read further than the headlines: the city needs seven thousand more cops and they must have increased pay; and by this crusade the mayor and the commissioner intend maximum publicity, until something is voted. Do you suppose we might have political power?

Graffiti: I have never noticed any obscene inscriptions in the men's room of the Dixie bus station, but now there is one on a large scale. Over the width of the four urinals, just above eye level, there is a large-sized cock and balls, and then two sentences plainly printed: "This is no police station. Get out, you cops."

I have never really liked Mr. Frost. He has the appearance of a small man enlarged and coarsened, and he seems damp somehow. His manner is fatherly to everyone, perhaps not an affectation, but certainly a habit. I sense (or I fancy) unkindness. The work also suggests this, particularly his sexual puritanism, as though it were something to be proud of.

But how agreeably he expresses everything, even wrongness and eccentricity, with an effect of wealth and sparkle!

1959

JANUARY 26

Marianne Moore praises me for "your taking time, your compartmental competence, your sunny attitude despite annoyances and burdens" which, she thinks, if I become an "impresario," that is, president of the Institute [of Arts and Letters], "augur happy days."

Last night I had a long comical nightmare about the Institute election. A great many women's club women came en masse, disrupted the meeting, prevented Karen Blixen [Isak Dinesen] from speaking, and wouldn't let me be elected. What a funny animal the subconscious is!

JANUARY 28

I scarcely enjoyed the Maria Callas concert at Carnegie Hall. She sang as loud as possible almost all the time, like a buzz-saw, with a slow tremolo. Manner and appearance of a teenager. Leo Lerman introduced me to her father! He was with Baroness Blixen who wore a tight turban, and looked like the Pharaoh Rameses. I managed to get Baba up the aisle for a few words with her, which pleased her.

Very gratifying note from Douglas Moore: "Ever since I have had anything to do with the Institute you have always been an unfailing direction-finder. Whatever progress we have made has usually come from Wescott inspiration. It is high time you should give up this leadership by proxy and take command."

FEBRUARY 9

Lunch at Monroe's with Christopher [Isherwood] and Don [Bachardy], handsome and enthusiastic. Christopher scandalized to hear that Isak Dinesen has even been considered for the Nobel Prize. Huxley should have it, he feels, though he scarcely admires the novels.

FEBRUARY 13

Suddenly I remembered how, before his final operation, I had to get my father to sign the paper absolving the hospital from blame in the event of death on the operating table; and he seemed to be making difficulty about it, impatient awkwardness in his hand as I placed the pen in it. And then he found his voice in spite of his vexation and said,

"Oh, my dear son, you have lived with me for fifty years, and still you don't know which hand I write with." I had been trying to get him to sign with his right hand. This remembrance gave me a lump in the throat . . . for I delight in and believe in all the emotions that ride from memory— the greatest of which are bound up in love.

MARCH 1

After lunch I stopped at the Mill [Barbara and Lloyd's house] to pay my respects to Debo [his niece on her engagement to marry], and on the way home somehow—unimaginably—lost my glasses. I walked all the way down again, and back again, peering along the side of the road—no. So now I must use a pair several years old that make my head ache.

MARCH 4

BBC radio program on American expatriates in Paris after the first World War: A good deal of foolishness has been talked and indeed written about the reasons for our expatriation in the twenties. I especially deride the theory that we were dissatisfied with our native land, as a place that was morally repressed or arid, or that we were maladjusted in the matrix culture, or felt easier or more forceful somewhere abroad.

Hemingway, Katherine Anne Porter, Dos Passos, the composers Virgil Thomson, Roger Sessions, Henry Cowell—poor Fitzgerald is the exception, but he was extremely unlucky, if not accursed, wherever he lived— our subsequent careers back at home show, I think, that we got on well with our compatriots. Indeed we have maintained rather more prominence and power than one might think desirable. The successive younger generations have not pressed us very hard. I wonder why.

My poor mother went all to pieces in my absence—failure of her speech (it is getting worse all the time, and she worsens it by panic), fits of weeping, very hard on Anna, and Lloyd's secretary, and Baba. I'm afraid I did wrong to commit myself to the lectures in Utah.

MARCH 9

My mother's speech has been deteriorating—complicated somewhat by an odd choking cough. She is 83. My brother and I were given the confidential report yesterday. Her heart and lungs and other vital organs are in excellent shape—but something less common: a dying of the ninth nerve, which governs all of the mouth and tongue. She will become entirely speechless, and then she will cease to be able to swallow. I shall cancel Utah. Perhaps she cannot go to the new house at all. In any case I shall be the last person to understand what she says, and probably the only person who can steady her as the ordeal develops, so that her behavior at the end shall not be unworthy of her.

MARCH 24

Russell Lynes wants me to point up, amplify—or perhaps clarify without amplifying—my little Isak Dinesen speech, for *Harper's Magazine.* He'll make me work more than it's worth—but I love to have an editor wanting something—which has been one of my weaknesses, but which might be a strength, if an editor caught on.

APRIL 16

Anna, mopping up under a leaky bit of plumbing: "Water always had been my enemy somehow. It gets the better of my nerves quicker than anything. I'm not kidding, but I don't know why it is."

To Robert Phelps: I can't think when I have received a letter that interested me so much, or gratified me so intensely, in the way of my self-interest. Putting your finger on the mannerism of my writing; seeing through it or beyond it, seeing something in it . . . You know, until middle age, and after painful experience of inability, it never occurred to me that I was not a novelist of latent power. Then, to confuse me and other interested parties, suddenly I was able to produce *Apartment in Athens* in six months.

MAY 25

I have been much concerned about the house in Rosemont. I went over there with Monroe, my housekeeper Anna, and John Connolly and a friend of his—we worked hard for four hours, drawing rooms on squared-off paper with measurements. It is time to assign the work to a building contractor. Tomorrow I must go back again with poor Mother, to consider the rooms we call hers.

MAY 30

I am glad to have carbon copies of some letters to post in my three-ring binder notebooks, as of the date of writing, and someday perhaps chop out a lovely paragraph here and there. It's one thing I am proud of and zealous to teach: my desk methods—I never had any until I was a post-mature man.

JUNE

We are told that Joyce only dreamed once in his lifetime, or only remembered one dream, in which he was the ace of diamonds walking up stairs.

JUNE 5

Forgetfulness is one of the forms my modesty about my writing takes—be it justified or morbid or both—and sometimes it keeps me from productivity. I forget to write, and virtually never forget anything else.

JULY 7

I am inclined to name the new home "Hay-meadows."

JULY 12

The carpenters and electricians and plumbers have begun work in the stone house at Rosemont (Haymeadows), and three times in the past week I have gone with them at 6:45 a.m. and worked with them most of the day. Today I got John Connolly to take down the running horse weathervane from the spring house—the beginning of the move.

AUGUST 18

Our houses past and future: On Sunday, with a hired local young man and John in the afternoon, I moved five hollies, two azaleas, one large syringa, four little hemlocks, one small Japanese maple, and one dogwood. It was 90 degrees—no time for moving shrubs, but they were in the way of my brother's bulldozer. I have also transplanted 85 varieties of iris.

Half a dozen lovely postcards from Monroe in Hawaii. He rented a bright yellow car and drove Raymond Mortimer all around Kauai.

AUGUST 19

I told Mother that Elizabeth intended to spend next Saturday at Beulah's in New York [GW's sisters]. A violent little expression of sadness passed over her face, and she reached out and scribbled, "I was going to ask Beulah to come out for the weekend." I gave a good many reasons in a vague way why it would have been hard for her to do so. "I'll be alone," she wrote. This I denied with some affectionate asperity. "What do you mean, alone? I will be here. John will be here. Anna will be here."

"No one to baby me, I guess." And with her half-dead lips she managed to smile a little.

AUGUST 26

The summer passes blessedly, beautifully; all is well, except the irremediable things; we are sad.

SEPTEMBER 5

All the humidity wafted away last night, and it has been one of those days that you worship, cloudless and fresh, with all the foliage and the grasses greener than ever because of the past rainy month.

Mother had a bad day, choking worse than usual, so I did not dine with the others, but stayed and read to her.

SEPTEMBER 7

A young hawk visited me, not gyring for food but flying straight across very like a speed-boat, but in magical silence, just over the roof-tops—I loved him.

SEPTEMBER 15

[Re Robert Phelps's plan for a collection of Wescott works, "A Windfall."]

Eminent fellow-writers the world over have honored me with affection, esteem, etc., but not one of them has taken it into his head to write about me. I must be glad of what the gods provide.

Last night, Mother had slipped on a new bath matt and lay there on the floor for almost an hour, afraid that she'd fall again. I must say she took it all very well—always at her best in any emergency or ordeal—and wrote the entire incident down for me on a series of slips of paper. But at the end she began to point mysteriously across the room, and wrote: "Two or three weeks ago I had a spell of seeing shapes of people out of the corner of my eyes." I expressed interest, with equanimity. "I didn't let it bother me then," she wrote, and then added, pointing again, "Now there is a small woman dusting at the foot of my bed." Hallucinating but not fooled by it.

SEPTEMBER 20

Baba caught Charles in the act of swiping money from her purse. Charles apologized. My brother hopes that oil can somehow be poured on this wildly troubled water and that Charles can be kept on. Lloyd's extraordinary, almost universal compassion—like cynicism in reverse.

My mother now seems to be fading rapidly. Every day seems to count now. Lloyd and I have decided that we don't want to leave her alone with

Anna. He proposes to spend the night or to ask Elizabeth to do so, when I need to be away. It will be hard for him and intolerable to Elizabeth— but fortunately I haven't many departures in prospect.

SEPTEMBER 27

Dostoyevsky: "What is hell, oh my brothers? Is it anything but this: that one has become incapable of love?"

It is not love but the lack of love that is blind.

SEPTEMBER 28

[Dr.] Pauline Goger thinks mother not likely to live more than three or four days. She has the Medical Center's beautiful room, 515, and three handsome affectionate nurses around the clock. Lloyd and I told her that it was necessary to insert a tube in order to feed her, she nodded understandingly, and the fantastic will-power by which she has been living seemed to give way. But then the doctors found themselves unable to do what they had undertaken.

OCTOBER 5

Mother has had a dull day, scarcely noticing anything except the vicissitudes of her dying. I am so sorry for the poor little thing, it's unspeakable. We are all as nervous as cats about it, including the tired nurses and Dr. Goger. She now gets a massive dose of Thorazine every four hours, and still the one dim angry eye opens, still she raps on the metal fence of the bed with her wedding ring.

OCTOBER 6

I wish mother's end were gentler, or let me say instead, swifter. But death is a beast; even in an ideal little hospital, which we practically own, it's rather like the middle ages.

OCTOBER 29

Janet Flanner and Natalia Murray spent last weekend here and we were fond and boisterous, disputatious and humorous. Next week I must be very official—at Cooper Union's hundredth anniversary convocation, and at the Institute's Gold Medal dinner meeting; and Monroe is giving a party for Sir Kenneth Clark; and I am squiring Marianne Moore to the Academy of Poets banquet; and, in-between, wooing my publisher and my agent a bit.

Mother remained indomitable, though the hospital thought her at death's door for days . . . Tonight I am on duty in her hospital room. In ten days we are going to be able to move her to a luxurious nursing home nearby. And of course it is all to do over again, back to the dark gate which in our modern way we try to keep locked and to get through at the same time.

NOVEMBER 2

Chinese man's response to an American missionary's account of the Trinity: "Oh, I see, it is very American. The deity is a committee."

Re: Journals. What about volume two? Cross that bridge when we come to it. The great overall problem is to enable the shifting, forgetful reader to recall the previous volume, if he has read it—or if he hasn't, to start with the one just offered him.

A Hundred Affections [a possible book project]: Note: "The press of my foot to the earth springs a hundred affections. They scorn the best I can do to relate them."—Walt Whitman.

Poor Glenway's Almanac: Diderot said: "No one steals my life from me. I give it." Yes, I say, think, this is true of me, for better and worse.

NOVEMBER 14

The past week or ten days have been very difficult or distracted. My poor mother is headed back to the underworld again. Baba and Lloyd are to move to Rosemont on Wednesday and I have promised to help her hang pictures in the great new room there on Sunday. Also, my chief female friend, Pauline de Rothschild, is making her brief annual visit to her native land—she is weekending here now—and it is the first time we have seen her alone since she married the good proprietor at Mouton.

DECEMBER

[Re the four aborted novels.]

I invented some great American plot and form, and often signed a contract, and in due course found myself incapable, and wore myself out or, more important, wore my plot and subject matter out. Thus "The Dream of Mrs. Cleveland," "The Deadly Friend," "A Fortune in Jewels," and "Children of This World." And to this day I have never been allowed (except by unconstructive old William Maugham) to plead insufficient ability, to ask for "A" for effort.

The other night at the Institute my guest of honor, old Edna Ferber, said, "I suppose that you may want to tell me to mind my own business, but I really would like to know why you haven't written more novels." And I answered, "In so far as I understand the matter myself, it is because I have not had the talent required." Whereupon she flew into a temper, so that I had to change the subject to official, Institute business. Everyone does, each according to his prejudice, blaming me for my sex life, or for not having had a university education, or having allowed my family to support me, or for not having been psycho-analyzed, or for having taken my mother to live with me, or something.

It seems to me that Robert Phelps and Bill Maxwell, and some others of the younger generation have asked me for just a little more of what I have already done—what comes easily and naturally.

DECEMBER 25

I am having to spend this entire day at the nursing home. We have two nurses in eight hour shifts, besides the staff of the establishment. But two of them are feuding, in consequence of which the day shifts have gone unscheduled; and Mother has caught cold and her strength and morale have sunk very low. The Christmas confusion is no time for hammering and chiseling my Thomas Mann essay, so I have been reviewing "A Windfall" and pondering the arrangement . . . I got Monroe to read "The Stallions"—in fact Ralph Pomeroy read it aloud to him—and he says it is admirable, thinks it will not shock anyone unduly.

[At the top of a loose page above eight indecipherable penciled words.] Mother's last words perhaps—Christmas week 1959.

1960–1964

THE NEW DECADE IS FIRST MARKED by the death of Josephine Wescott on January 4, and then by the move from Stoneblossom to Haymeadows, which is completed in April. In the city, Wheeler finds a more suitable apartment, number 8M at 251 East Fifty-First Street at Second Avenue, where he and Wescott will host their memorable gatherings for almost three more decades.

As president of the National Institute of Arts and Letters, Wescott becomes increasingly involved in high-profile literary politics and in the business of awards and grants. Despite endless planning with Robert Phelps for a retrospective collection, "A Windfall," he postpones the volume in February 1961, partly because he wants to use some material in a 1962 book of literary essays and reminiscences. *Images of Truth* is a well-received work on the art of fiction, with personal perspectives on the life and work of Katherine Anne Porter, W. Somerset Maugham, Isak Dinesen, Colette, Thornton Wilder, and Thomas Mann. This leads to book tours and television appearances, sometimes with Katherine Anne Porter, who has her great success with *Ship of Fools*.

Wescott promises his publisher to follow up with a reshuffled "A Windfall" anthology, but when it involves finishing a long-delayed story, "The Stallions," fiction once more becomes a stumbling block and a dead end. Still, Robert Phelps, whose own career blossoms with works on Colette and Cocteau, remains devoted to Wescott's work and eventually will edit the first book of journals, up to 1955.

Among the post-1955 journals on these pages are interesting comments on the passing of such notables as Hemingway, Cocteau, Marilyn Monroe, and John F. Kennedy. Wescott's articles in *Life* and *Atlantic Monthly* and frequent 1963–65 *New York Herald Tribune* book reviews keep him in the public eye. Also, he's included in a July 1963 *Esquire* issue on the American literary scene, photographed with contemporaries such as Dawn Powell, Malcolm Cowley, Virgil Thomson, Carl Van Vechten, and Man Ray.

Family and farm life, as well as the New York social world, absorb most of his time. Meanwhile, Barbara is an important patron of the arts, and Lloyd Wescott takes on appointed positions for New Jersey's succession of Democratic governors. As president of the State Board of Control for prisons, he sometimes finds work for released convicts from a nearby women's prison. One colorful and permanent farmhand is Ethel "Bunny" Sohl, who dresses as a man and who, in 1938 with a girlfriend-accomplice, had robbed and murdered a bus driver. A behavioral problem at first, Ethel's loyalty is won over by a few private pages written by Glenway. He sometimes refers to her as "our transvestite murderess." Influenced by his younger friends, he re-visits the gay enclaves of Fire Island, where his crowd sunbathed nude in the twenties. He also becomes angered to the point of "cop hatred" by police harassment of young gays in the pre-Stonewall years.

Despite his urban celebrity and his comfortable country life at Haymeadows, he remains "a bird in a golden cage." Any income from writing is quickly claimed by needs and debt. As a cosmopolitan man who speaks French, has many British friends, and loves the museums of Europe, it is a shame how little he travels—only one European trip since 1938! His sympathy for writers down on their luck influences grants he proposes at the Institute, and he tries to interest the federal government in small pensions for retired writers in need. In the October–November 1962 *Authors Guild Bulletin* he writes of the indifferent reception his idea got at the Wingspread Foundation arts conference that June—where he realized he was speaking to an audience of well-salaried professors. He also states that literature is not helped by mountains of critical academic books written in academic language.

1960

JANUARY 18

Mother's deathbed, and the strain of not being able to help her in any way, has confused me in my relations and connections with the rest of the world.

FEBRUARY 7

I miss her painfully, though of course I forbid myself to grieve, because her life was nothing but a heroism and a sorrow at the last. But now I am impatient to move to the new house in Rosemont.

She seemed to have very little concept of a heaven, but sometimes I thought that her spirit longed to get back to Wisconsin. She wearied of all of us here because we could not help her.

APRIL 6

From Seneca, as quoted by Montaigne: "Why do we never make a frank declaration of our vices? Because we are still too much absorbed in them. One has to be wide-awake in order to tell one's dream."

APRIL 7

This weekend, with John C[onnolly] and a boy with one of those box-like Volkswagen delivery-wagons and Lloyd's Ethel with a small truck, we shall move the pictures and vases and the contents of my study. Next Tuesday and Wednesday I work with a packer: books, dishes, etc. Next Thursday, a van and four men will take the furniture. Next Friday, a van and three men will empty the attics. Thus, on April 20 I'll be resident at Haymeadows, Rosemont, New Jersey.

JUNE 23

Haymeadows. My farcical insolvency (I really cannot regard it as tragical) continues bumpety-bump. Lloyd undertook to question Baba about her having pulled the skids out from under me. Meanwhile he said that he would cover the overdraft—and for this or that reason left a part of it uncovered. More angry-looking yellow slips from my bank, and more unpaid bills including Anna's wages. I have one dollar. I gave Anna a simplified account of the situation—I couldn't not do so.

Meanwhile the Wescott show goes on, as it must, I suppose. Lloyd had four hundred farmers at the barn last night; over the plush-green weedless forage crops bejeweled with fireflies I could hear his beautiful voice, making a speech, the point of which was that you cannot make money farming without a large investment. Monroe, broken-backed still but braver than in New York, paces around the lawn with me, arguing about the placement of trees. Tomorrow John is bringing a husky Southern boy to help me lay some more flagstones; and tomorrow there is to be a picnic for sixteen beside the swimming pool—Leon and Debo's farewell party. [Niece Debo at age 18 married Dr. Leon Prockop.]

I try to imagine putting it in a novel form—like what? Like Balzac, for the play of passions and the desperate theme of money? Like Jane Austen, for the pettiness and the pleasant manner (except between Monroe and me), for the terrible family togetherness, and the domination of beautiful, over-flattered, opinionated, philanthropic women. But neither Balzac nor Austen could have coped with it, or even understood it.

I live novels instead of writing them.

JULY 13

Fire Island: Laurie Douglas and Tennessee Williams and Bill Flores and Martin Snyder were there, among others. I found myself conscious of being a sort of celebrity, with amiable handsome young persons paying me attention; and I played the part for them: tolerant, a little startling, fatherly, humorous.

Friday evening we dined somewhat grandly at Peggy Fears' in the Pines. The combination of Miss Fears and me, veterans of the twenties, drinking champagne together, amused Bill Miller.

Meanwhile what I loved, as always—since 1924—was the island itself— the ancient hollies with gray and white bark; the dunes by moonlight like mountains in the pseudo distance; the spaces of almost sterile sand seemingly afloat here and there like clouds amid the dark blueberries—Shakespeare-like, *Tempest*-like.

Haymeadows: Never any news here except the wild life: a fox with three cubs, a quail with five chicks, a doe with two spotted fawns. Ethel found an infant corn snake in their deep freeze. The mocking bird no longer vocalizes on Baba's aerial, but when I go down there to dine, it comes to meet me, half way up the road, and escorts me with its odd helicopter-like flight from post to post.

A lovely weasel considered living with us in the spring: a Least Weasel (Mustela rixosa)—dancing slowly along, holding his head up like a snake; of the softest umber color, with a cream-white bib. It dug a small round hole by the doorway. Then it went away forever.

JULY 20

Last night after a late dinner in Lambertville, we came upon a rehearsal and drill of a bugle corps at the large playground, about thirty buglers and a half dozen drummers and a violent unimaginative drillmaster putting them through extraordinarily complex marching patterns with sudden silences, then sudden ear-splitting silvery outbursts, up and down and to and fro in the warm half light—a thunderstorm in the offing—husky small town youngish bodies, some stripped to the waist, one pitch-black. In the background in muggy warm darkness, little children (their children, no doubt) ecstatic in swings. A sort of heaven, with cherubim, I thought.

JULY 21

Robert Phelps came to see me night before last, and stayed until this morning. He and his wife are half-separating; he is going to Yaddo and she to Rome. I gather that he is in love with a young poet, but he confided nothing in detail. I talked wisely about all that sort of thing in general. I didn't want to talk much about my writing or my problematic economics. A strange relationship.

AUGUST 22

I went to the Medical Center for my annual checkup . . . and Dr. Goger put me on a thousand calorie diet until I have lost fifteen pounds. In one week I have lost ten pounds. As my brother said last night: "more self-indulgent than anyone, more self-disciplining than anyone." I wish I could manage my talent as well as my vices.

AUGUST 24

The other morning I came down for my caffeineless coffee and hard-boiled egg before Anna arose, and stood gazing out from the kitchen. There descended five or six blue jays, onto the flagstone terrace and into the overhanging maple tree. And to my amazement the kestrel whom I have seen in the air at some distance dive-bombed them twice, first by himself, then with his female; and having cleared the place, sat for a while on the great ash stump. I have never been so close to a hawk not caged, and he is one of the loveliest-looking, with his tail feathers of burning brown, and blue-gray shoulders, and fantastic little mask.

AUGUST 30

Tennessee Williams: I have known him only slightly but for many years, and I like him. My impression is that he is a rugged and rather happy-natured man, certainly not a sufferer—except now and then from exhaustion, and perhaps from drinking too much and taking the usual pick-up pills and calm-down pills when he has been working himself to death. The habit of over-working is not, to my way of thinking, a psychopathological trait in a creative man. He is not a self-expressive creative man, but somewhat like Maugham and G. B. Shaw and such, audience-minded. When he holds these press conferences about his psychology and his inspiration, etc., though I suppose he speaks sincerely, according to his lights, the point is to promote whatever play he has coming up.

ELECTION DAY, NOVEMBER 8

Monroe sweet-talked his way out of the Medical Center sooner than expected, and is to be here for a fortnight, for medication and repose. Evidently no cancer. Slight hepatitis, which cleared up immediately . . . So now he is pretending to have retired, and (I note) if he ever does retire with as much energy as he has now, he'll be the death of me. For example, he insisted on painting the fore-edges of all the bookshelves white. In consequence, now I have all my books on the floor, to be put back before I forget which heap is which.

NOVEMBER 13

I dined at [William] Inge's [apartment] with the little movie star Sal Mineo, a sort of pocket version of Mark Pagano [a GW intimate], but with complexities instead of mystery; a devotee of Carroll Righter as well as other occultisms, and just lately an aficionado of bullfighting. He has been in the *Exodus* film in Palestine, and returned via the high spots of Europe. In Rome he had clothes made. "Aren't you making the trousers too tight?" he asked the tailor. "But why not? If you've got it, why not show it?" was the tailor's retort. So the little star, with something to show indeed, went for a walk up and down the Via Veneto, and returned in laughing enthusiasm. "Make me a dozen pair, as fast as you can." He told us all this with a delicate touch-me-not air, and occasional heterosexual references; wonderfully funny—but I am afraid that Hollywood society would make me nervous.

THANKSGIVING DAY, NOVEMBER 24

Last week I had an erotic dream of John Cheever; very surprising choice of partner. When I hindered him from sucking me, he exclaimed in his rather scornful, chuckling voice (unmistakably his), "Oh. Ha, ha! I have long suspected that you were a self-satisfier!" He had a brawny, difficult, yet enjoyable penis. But a couple of foolish young women arrived and, though without seeming to take notice of our activity, interrupted it. It was a long dream, with a good many supernumeraries, of that same raffish type, Greenwich Villagers, etc., and everything that happened seemed a little comic.

DECEMBER 7

My lecture, "Memories of the Twenties," at City College seemed somehow the hardest work in the world—I hated having to cut it down to the time allotted, between two clanging academic bells.

I stayed at Monroe's new apartment, 251 East 51st Street, in order to move furniture this way and that, to rearrange his books, and to hang some pictures—partly to give handsomeness to our dinner party, partly to lure poor Monroe into reconciling himself to staying there . . . this will be the equivalent of a housewarming.

DECEMBER 13

The humorousness of our modern American vulgarity: "New York News, Sunday Coloroto Magazine": Jayne Mansfield, an actress with celebrated breasts, and her Hungarian-born husband, Mickey Hargitay, a former Mr. Universe, have a Romeo and Juliet balcony projecting from the bedroom floor of their Sunset Boulevard house into the "palatial" living room. This means a great deal to them because they are still lovers. She lies face down on the floor with a Chihuahua, kicking up her heels, while he reads aloud to her, with his shoes off.

DECEMBER 14

Americans: Alger Hiss still looks familiar to people who encounter him on the street and now and then someone speaks to him. For example: "Pardon me, but aren't you Charles Van Doren?"

DECEMBER 25

To Monroe: I am ashamed to offer you a promise to work harder and better—I have done that so many times, in vain. What I will offer now is a sacrifice of pride—I am going to try for quantity (in a way), that is, to resign myself to a more modest, easier level of work. Perhaps the muses will grant me more inspiration than I deserve, for your sake. It brings tears to my eyes to think of it.

DECEMBER 31

I am one of those unreasonable persons who desires to live forever—and therefore, having had the greater part of my share of time, I no longer exactly enjoy changes of date, anniversaries, etc. Instead I delight in any sort of feeling that existence, for me, is all of a piece; that the Now reflects and echoes and answers and illuminates the Then.

1961

JANUARY 1

"Happy New Year, dearest," said my dearest. I replied courageously, "What I want is a productive year. I have had my share of happiness."

JANUARY 3

The Christmas snow has melted just a little and refrozen. Before sunrise, soft clouds in the southeast turned bright pink, and suddenly the entire lawn and the meadow reflected it, pale glassy pink and shiny, attracting my attention at the kitchen table where I sat at work.

JANUARY 6

In Portland with John Yeon and his friend Jim Gamwell. We're going to the ocean this noon, to Cannon Beach near Seaside about eighty miles from this city. In about a week's time we plan to go to San Francisco for a long weekend . . . Then on January 17 to Evanston, chez Monroe's parents, 639 Forest Avenue—and on January 19 to Bloomington [Indiana, to visit Mrs. Kinsey].

JANUARY 10

Cannon Beach: No spark of eroticism among us, evidently, alas. We are all three shy, and if one of us were not, we might enjoy each other, but the relationships are too delicate and the situation too cloistral and rigid, for any experimentation and impulsiveness.

JANUARY 11

Cannon Beach: The first clear evening since I got here—an inspiring sunset. There were ten rows of slow breakers with great stripes of lavender and pale green between them, and they brushed themselves out very thinly up the moist beach, lace-edged. After, the sun settled into a long cloud almost indistinguishable from the distant sea, a powerful brightness spewing along it, like a serpent, like a fallen thunderbolt.

One reason I came, I suppose—a deep buried-reason—is that in 1932 Baba invited me to go to China with her and Monroe, and I declined because I was homesick for America, and because I had resolved once more to write another novel. In fact I got almost no work done, and was dismal. And now perhaps I shall never see that great part of the world, and I have always been ashamed of my proud would-be virtuousness.

But the moral of it all I'm afraid is that I must try to have more money and plan my own vacations. However, this has been wonderfully pleasant and affectionate, and it has been good for me to be away from my desk, perhaps also to be away from those I most love—to whet my appetite, to give me perspective. My heart is very full.

JANUARY 22

[After visiting the Kinsey Institute.]

An especially beloved professor was arrested last week for having engaged in some indecent "pen pal" correspondence, and he attempted suicide in a terrible and grotesque way. I felt the importance of the research as much as ever, and the great courage of this going on without Alfred. I missed him bitterly.

JANUARY 24

[To Paul Gebhard, of the Kinsey Institute.]

In re "pen pal" correspondence: Lytton Strachey used to like to write fanciful obscene letters to certain friends. After his death, Alan Searle (now William Maugham's secretary) destroyed a packet of them. He told me this and I reproached him for having done so.

FEBRUARY 18

Do not ask yourself whether or not you are happy. As a rule the answer is no. Only admit to yourself that someone or something is giving you pleasure, that you are proud of this or that ability or effort, and then your unhappiness will be mitigated, perhaps forgotten.

FEBRUARY 19

For Baba's sake even more than his own, Monroe invited Lincoln Kirstein here yesterday. It was a great success, but I found it rather a hardship when I arrived by the early morning train and bus, tired of New York, to find that personification of the great city, storming and joking, irrepressible though pessimistic.

FEBRUARY 20

I enjoyed my two hours with Michael Miksche. He was so happy; he seems exactly corresponding to the concept of himself that he likes best: beautiful baby, beautiful wife, beautiful old ex-lover, even beautiful plump young Irish nurse, concubine-style. Oh, my life was complicated enough without his picking his way back into it. As Monroe once said, "He has a displacement like the *Queen Mary!*"

Jim Lord lunched here today, in his best form, telling stories of the life abroad, especially the wonderful story of his peasant lover whose heart he broke, who became a monk.

FEBRUARY 22

To Robert Phelps: I feel honor-bound to let you know that I am now inspired not to publish *A Windfall* as we planned it last year; certainly not at this time. I want to do something else instead . . . The very thing that appealed to your imagination in your first concept of *A Windfall*, its constituting a kind of cumulative self-portrait, has come to be absolutely disheartening to me. It is going to be necessary for me to change myself in some ways, soon; therefore this is not a time for me to be exhibiting myself, or even looking at myself in any kind of mirror.

MARCH 7

Spring-song. This year's first real concert of the birds: orchestral grackles and starlings and various sparrows, and lovely continuous solo of the mocking bird *mimus polyglottus*, our little dear savage, our "Castro." Not a hint of his pugnacity in the tone of his voice. In all the arts, even that of birds, style is a strange thing.

APRIL 12

At Institute of Arts and Letters dinner: Robert Frost said, "You're now one of my oldest friends," which, I may say, gave me a different feeling of my age than I have ever had before. He explained to the meeting: "I've followed him ever since Mrs. Vaughan Moody sent him to see me when he was a 21-year-old boy."

MAY 1

Washington, DC. Frost's reading in the State Department auditorium, one of his regular performances, paid for by the members of the President's cabinet—not worth coming down for, at some expense to the Institute . . . Our governing class (of which presumably this audience was representative) impressed me as amazingly handsome. Frost was not at his best; he seemed shy—is that possible?—although the audience responded cordially enough . . . Mr. Udall called him, "Our poet laureate, without portfolio."

MAY 17

A little letter from Mr. Udall, handwritten in a boyish scrawl, on his Secretary [of the Interior] stationary, with a buffalo in the upper left-hand corner. I copy it exactly: "Dear Glenway, It was a pleasure to get acquainted. We're moving in the right direction. Who knows, maybe we'll achieve one of Robert's goals soon. Regards, Stewart." Just in case anyone fancies that the Administration is all Harvard or Harvardesque.

MAY 27

One of the profoundest truths about me is that my life is too rich. If I had as many arms as the god Siva and a fountain pen in each hand, it seems to me that I could write six books at once—simultaneously, not just concurrently—easier than I now write one.

MAY 29

I don't suppose that I shall ever feel sure of the safety of my mss. and letter files again. The burning of Aldous Huxley's house with all his unpublished work, the image of the firemen having to restrain him by force, as he wept and begged to be allowed to go into the flames to rescue as much as possible, has alarmed me absolutely, permanently.

JUNE 11

Monroe has been rather unwell this weekend but stoically up and about. Jet plane travel gives him bronchitis almost invariably, and at the same time the arthritis gripped his poor back. I wish he could have tiny injections of Novocain like the President.

JUNE 21

Lloyd says that he has never seen hay so heavy as this year's first cutting in the east and south fields here at Haymeadows. They disappointed him last year; he gave them potash as well as manure.

JUNE 23

The strangest little things remind me of my mother, with realistic evocation and true bereavement: for example, reading in W. S. Lewis's Walpole lectures that Mary Queen of Scots, the night before her capital punishment, treated one of her feet with a salve. A lump in my throat . . .

AUGUST 10

I spent two or three days with my dear Felicia Geffen of the Institute, a day and a half with blessed Will Chandlee at Harvard, the inside of a week at old Mrs. Josephine Crane's at Woods Hole (along with

Monroe), an annual event of the past 18 years or so, for sentiment rather than the fun of it.

Before leaving for New England I gave my "Memories of the Twenties" lecture at Columbia. Then *Esquire* heard of it and wheedled me into correcting and typing the entire 35 pages in two days. Great hurry; for their Christmas issue perhaps. They have declined it, William Morris Agency now informs me.

Pennsylvania Station, early morning. The two vast clocks at the north and south ends of the waiting room labeled in red, "Timed by Benrus"— fourteen minutes apart, south 7:12, north 6:58. No wonder the railroads go bankrupt; the wonder is that there aren't more train wrecks.

SEPTEMBER 18

In the absence from home of neighbor Reul Tunley, someone entered and stole little objects of art, souvenirs of his world travel, and other belongings. My brother and sister-in-law have never bothered to keep their house locked or even to have proper locks or to carry keys. Baba dined here on Friday night—Lloyd had gone to Boston—and I read to her the report of Tunley's misfortune in *The Democrat*. When she got back home later that evening there lay in her bathroom on the tile floor a man's handkerchief, unidentifiable and inexplicable. Her servants who had been in the kitchen, but not all evening, testified plausibly that neither they nor anyone known to them had entered Baba's part of the house. It planted seeds of fear—reminiscent of the seeds of jealousy that resulted from the murder of Desdemona by Othello. Would that she could be kept just a little fearful, just enough to motivate her to lock up her glamorous house, jewels, various valuables, and half a million dollars worth of paintings.

OCTOBER 3

The literary life: In the Register of Copyright's report dated July 1961, the average age of authors at death is 68, the average age of authors at publication of first book, 32, and at their last book, 64.

OCTOBER 11

My first novel, *The Apple of the Eye*: For a good while I have been struck by the fact that young people who I meet, who take an interest in what I have written, often prefer it to the rest of my fiction . . . Is this because they like to discover the less familiar title, less often remembered by their elders? My style in it is more sensuous, and, one might say, more "modern," less educated, less French; and much of the plot as such is romantic, with Bad Han as an earth-mother, the triangularity of the youngsters, the re-burial in the swamp, etc. It made my reputation overnight.

NOVEMBER 16

Elderly appearance: I take a keen interest in the way literary men and women of my generation have been aging. Even what I see in the mirror interests me, although I am not sure that I can interpret that properly: rather like the sort of North British or Scottish country gentleman, ruddy and silvery, jovial or at least genial, with a look of hot temper gradually mollified by pleasure and gratitude and affection.

There was the change in the late Hemingway's appearance so recently, the sportsman-dandy giving fond, vain glances over that unique great fan of beard, as tense as a peacock's tail, suddenly softened by his several irreversible illnesses, but still ever bravely posing for photographers in Spain last summer, like one of Dostoyevsky's sufferers at the vulgarized bullfights. It scarcely bears thinking of; it is too sad.

Thornton Wilder, like an exalted or inspired army officer. He could play the part of a demagogue or a dictator—in a play on stage; oh, not in reality.

Katherine Anne Porter, the texture of her skin not youthful but with a vivid sort of paleness, and her lustrous, dark, rather melancholy eyes.

Monday Class [lectures at the city home of Josephine Crane]. J. D. Salinger: I should like to say some things to him, as to his plight in the narrative art, between the two stools: his Hemingway-like colloquialism on the one hand, and his high-brow loquaciousness and desperate self-criticism on the other hand, influenced by Henry James.

NOVEMBER 19

One cannot approve the risks that many of my generation have been running in the matter of letting time elapse; feeling everlastingly youthful and mistaking that feeling for a true and probable life expectancy. It is a folly and perhaps a psychopathology. Examining myself severely I realize that I have been pampered by my family, dispensed from having to write for a living; that I have never had any sense of vocation or of genius in the literary way. But when I apply the same criteria to fellow writers, I find that my wonderment only increases.

Poor Katherine Anne Porter, except for the hospitality of writers' colonies, various grants and fellowships, and teaching courses in creative writing at slave-driving universities, has been dependent on her mere writing talent for a living. Hemingway was obviously a genius type, and a dynamo in the way of energy and vitality as well as ego. Yet, according to Mrs. Hemingway, he left behind thousands of typewritten pages that he had not troubled to put in publishable order, as though he did expect to live forever.

DECEMBER 4

Books I have delighted in during 1961: *The Chateau* by William Maxwell, *Sermons and Soda Water* by John O'Hara, and *An Only Child* by Frank O'Connor. To which let me add an adorable masterpiece of 1960 which I read belatedly, *The Leopard* by Lampedusa, and another not yet published in this country, *The Fox in the Attic* by Richard Hughes.

1962

JANUARY

From William Blake: "Everything possible to be believed is an image of the truth."

JANUARY 2

According to [Harley] Granville-Barker, Shakespeare's preoccupation in all the late plays, implicit in *Hamlet* and *Measure for Measure*, explicit after that: "the problem of the re-valuing of good and evil in the light of self-knowledge"—a beautiful and profound statement.

JANUARY 12

First visit to the Barnes collection—incomparable. An effect of adorable good taste and of strange unity or coherence. A love of boldness, of going all out. The Cezannes greater than the Renoirs. The Matisses and Modiglianis supreme.

FEBRUARY 1

A black woman on the bus: "Just let me have enough money to make ends meet. Oh, I tell you, I'd not care about a surplus, not a bit. Someday, yes, someday. But, honey, it won't be on this earth, not for me." A sweet virtuous voice; no pathos.

FEBRUARY 17

6 a.m., Ridgefield, CT. At bedtime—my bed in Bernard's room—blissful triangularity, with an orgasm, though I was at my wit's end with fatigue. Phallic worship of Bernard a factor in my life for more than twenty years, a factor now (so to speak) reduced to happiness.

The thrilling early daylight is gradually filling Bernard's wild valley; a cloud recumbent in the swampy woodlot, pitch black tree trunks heavily edged with snow.

When I get caught up in my work for publication, I propose to keep more to journal writing. My small-scale everyday subject matter is more interesting intrinsically than the material I have in mind for books. Also it seems I now have the necessary technique (better late than never) for journal writing.

Hemingway: A little while before his death it was reported in the newspapers that his publishers, Charles Scribner's Sons, had seen a first draft of a volume of his reminiscences of Paris in the twenties; and a little thrill of apprehension ran through the (not) Lost Generation, along with the prospective pleasure of reading anything by him, even perhaps second-best work.

I hope the work exists—and I hope the Scribners and Mrs. Hemingway will not withhold it too long, even if it is in an incomplete state. Oh, I want to live long enough to read it.

Presumably in this work he will get some things wrong, but he has always been apt to immortalize things as he has conceived them. While his judgments of psychology and morality and social relationships were never very perceptive, he wrote like a veritable necromancer, mirroring his phantoms to the life, echoing their utterances; even if sometimes fictitious and unjust, his small talk was hallucinating and unforgettable.

MARCH 19

I am in a productive fit (high time). During the years and years of my supposed indolence or incompetence, I have been piling up drafts and scribbles and notebooks and letter-files, out of which I now can mine and quarry some books.

APRIL 1

Read first half of my Thomas Mann essay aloud to Baba, Earl and Freddie: It is repetitious because it is argumentative—if I had done it in the light, flashing style of my Colette, Porter, and Wilder essays it would not have been convincing. If it would not have been pompous and grand-eloquent it would have seemed carping and tedious. I am somewhat proud of it but I do not like it. It corresponds too closely to his work, philosophizing and elaborate and ironic. Never again will I let anyone assign a subject to me. My last critical criticism? Probably. I hope so.

APRIL 9

From my interview in *Milwaukee Sentinel*: "I believe there is more precise truth in a story than in philosophy, preaching and teaching. Stories pacify our wild hearts. Samuel Johnson said, 'The only end of writing is to enable readers better to enjoy life, or better to endure it.'"

APRIL 10

[Re his lecture at the Central Library, Milwaukee.]

In the front row sat a big lug of a teenager with eyebrows like Santiago's, in elegant skin-tight workpants and sweater, who amazingly delighted in my long Burke-like sentences. When I started one he would lean forward with his lips parted, watching it as though it were a tennis match, and when I got through the syntax without mishap, he would grin from ear to ear, and lean back in his chair, spread his legs with fine basket displayed. A budding writer, I suspect—syntactical sense is one of the signs. I didn't get a chance to talk to him.

Overheard from a girl in Madison:

"He's in the army now, but he sends me tape recordings, and I weep buckets about his verbalizations."

APRIL 12

[To Monroe Wheeler, after visiting Wheeler's elderly parents in Evanston.]

Dearest of all: I forgot to tell you last night that I have what I think of as a birthday present, discovered on a bookshelf in your old room, brought away without asking your father's permission: *Madame Bovary* in French, but published in Vienna, very yellowed paper and fragile casing, inscribed to me by you in September 1922 with an expression of your belief that I would do something still finer. A formula for heartbreak but a motivation for hard work. In fact I don't think that I should have accomplished anything if I had not aimed beyond my ability, and aimed optimistically.

APRIL 23

[Visiting the Kinsey Institute for Sex Research, Bloomington, Indiana.]

Back at my cubicle in the library of the I.S.R. having had only four hours sleep, the buzz hum of fluorescent light tubes, the love-song moaning of pigeons, and the hard whirr of lawn mowers.

I long for a little pleasure, as I always do, especially when I have been confined to my intellect for a long while. I wish I could get into the film archives as well as the bookshelves. But here, more than anywhere else perhaps, I have to act my age.

MAY

My "Talks with Thornton Wilder" retyped in order to let Thornton and Isabel read it on their transatlantic liner. They never wrote me about it. Isabel insisted on my inserting four or five lines about his shrinking from publicity (vide *Images of Truth*, page 255).

MAY 14

K.A.P. [Katherine Anne Porter] and I were *very good* on television yesterday—an entire hour, with only one moderator, and no buttinskis.

≈

K.A.P.'s favorite quotation: "It doth make a difference whence cometh a man's joy."—St. Augustine.

JUNE 21

Haymeadows, 5 a.m.: For two or three days I have had three mocking birds fighting a good deal of the time, with great snappings-out of their white edged fans, like Kabuki actors. Now one of them is singing in competition with my brown thrushes, making noise enough for me to hear through the door and above the radio.

JUNE 30

Mrs. Lesser, the little 85-year-old German bluestocking who has been the principle translator for the Institute for Sex Research all these years, confided to me that she hadn't read my books until this year—obliged to rest her eyes when not earning a living—and they made her suffer at the same time that they aroused her admiration and gave her pleasure. "There are always such horrible things in your books. I keep wondering, why, why?" I wanted to know what horrible things: the burial of Rosalia, the feeding of Lucy, the feeble-mindedness of little Leda. Her daughter the psychiatrist's wife, protested, "But, mother, how can you be shocked by things like that, when you have been dealing with real horrors for Dr. Kinsey for so many years?" She brushed this aside: "Oh, my dear, all that really isn't very bad."

JULY 14

Chez Felicia Geffen, Pawling, New York. Literary life in Fairfield County: The Cheevers and Philip Roth at the Cowleys' last night. The Harold Strausses and the John Herseys and the Matthew Josephsons and Charles Miller tonight.

Love life and writing: I wrote the second half of *The Apple of the Eye* and all of *The Grandmothers* during an ideal conjugality; *The Pilgrim Hawk* in an interval of a love affair that was thrilling in intercourse but humiliating and boring in every other way. But *Apartment in Athens* came at the end of a desert in my life, eighteen months of only grief and masturbation. Good work is more to be relied on to lead to good sex than vice versa.

AUGUST

Marilyn Monroe, born Norma Jeane Baker, in Los Angeles, June 1, 1926; died August 4, 1962. The cause of her death apparently was accidental. Having become extremely addicted to Nembutal, she took a maximum dose of presumably fifteen or twenty capsules; then she was awakened by a phone call, couldn't get back to sleep, and befuddled by the first lot, perhaps also by champagne, forgot and took another fifteen or twenty; perhaps tried to call for help, died with the telephone in her hand. She had had great misfortunes earlier that year: *The Misfits*, the cruel film that her husband Arthur Miller wrote for her and about her; her loss of him to another woman, Cartier Brésson's friend, Inge Morath; suspension by the studio in the midst of a film, charged with malingering—she had misfortune all her life (vide the *Time* profile) but just before her death her career had taken an upward turn, and she seemed optimistic.

AUGUST 14

[Re *A Windfall.*]

My anthology as re-planned with editor Walter Bradbury: "The Babe's Bed"; "The Rescuer"; "The Sight of a Dead Body"; "A Feeling about Henry James"; "The Moral of F. Scott Fitzgerald"; "A Trans-atlantic Glance"; "A Series of Letters"; "Fifteen Fables"; "A Writer's Collection of Paintings"; "Pissarro's Paris"; "Poor Greuse"; "Mr. Auer-bach in Paris"; "The Frenchman Six Feet Three"; "The Love of New York"; "A Picture of Country Life"; "A Dust-Basket"; "The Stallions"; "The Valley Submerged."

Hemingway and I were never friends; only friendly acquaintances, less and less friendly. Though proud and somewhat spoiled, on the crest of the wave of youthful success—my family chronicle, *The Grandmothers*, got the Harper Prize in 1927—I ardently admired the epoch-making artistry of *In Our Time* and *The Sun Also Rises* . . . a master stylist in his way—extreme colloquialism, make-believe illiteracy—he charmed a generation of educators, and is partly responsible for the damage that lexicographers and specialists in linguistics have been doing to our language in recent years.

AUGUST 15

The Penn Station men's room: As I went across to pee, a man behind me said, "Come on, Glenway, let me help you." I turned, surprised, and saw that it was a young father with a very small son, almost too small for the urinal . . . I had never known or heard anyone named Glenway, except the grandson of my father's civil war buddy who was named after me, and who killed someone in his teens and had to serve a prison sentence. Perhaps the father of this manly little fellow is one of my readers, I was too shy to ask him.

My sister Katherine and her husband drove here from Wisconsin for a farewell visit before moving to San Francisco, and my other sisters fore-gathered—the entire complement of siblings and remaining in-laws and

Bruce and Dorothy and Monroe. You can imagine the noise, etc.; and of course I had to cook, and everyone followed me into the kitchen to talk or be talked to.

An occasion in another way as well, in that Beulah brought the first copy of *Images of Truth*. And for two days I have been laboring over my address books to assemble a list of illustrious authors and another list of perhaps influential professors and a vast list of out-of-town people to whom Harpers will send announcements. Furthermore, they want to give me a promotion party, which they almost never do nowadays. But surely it is good for the morale of the house—all the long term Harper employees who have had to explain to all and sundry why I haven't been producing books all the time. This is the season when the extinct volcanoes have begun to erupt fire and brimstone and honey and perhaps even money: Porter, Hughes, et al.

Small Boy in Borrowed Plumage: It has been a blissful pleasure to write *Images of Truth* (except the Mann)—like a small child, an imaginative, self-dramatizing child, who has got into the family clothes closet, and paraded up and down in his father's top hat, his mother's feathers and furs, his sister's high heels—that is, the pearls of K.A.P.'s condesa, the pearls of Colette's Lea, the red tights of Mann's Mephistopheles, Thornton Wilder's trench coat, the toga of Julius Caesar. I have never had so much fun writing a book.

SEPT. 4

[Cape Cod, to K. A. Porter in Washington, D.C.]

Dearest Porter: On our way Capeward for the traditional weekend with Mrs. Crane, we found Cyrilly Abels and her husband in the train, and they gave us the awful news of your trouble and broken bones . . . Oh, my poor blessed bothered tired genius-ridden friend, the good fairies bringing you the recompense for so many years' endeavor [*Ship of Fools*] have really behaved worse than harpies; harpies in reverse!

SEPTEMBER 6

E. E. Cummings' death oppresses me. Katherine Anne fell down her Southern-type stairway and broke seven ribs, perhaps due to having tried to drown her sorrows one day last week. Are we perhaps turning out to be a lost generation after all?

SEPT. 7

Isak Dinesen's death, announced to me on the telephone by Beulah. It made me cry; with a backlog of grief due to Porter's falling downstairs, the deaths of Cummings and Faulkner, even Marilyn Monroe's solemn cautionary events, symbolic of deadly bad luck.

OCTOBER 26

[With K. A. Porter in Washington, D.C.]

Katherine Anne kept asking me last night: "How much money am I going to have: is it thirty-six hundred a month or thirty-six thousand a year?"—and at one point she misspoke: "thirty-six thousand a month." Money matters are not real to her, that is, not factual. Her making fun of herself for not being allowed to get hold of all the money that *Ship of Fools* is making for her: "Whine, whine, whine! Now I'm going to stop it. If I ever say one more word about money, you just slap me."

When I got back from luncheon she was fast asleep and I had to cancel her dentist appointment. Presently she came downstairs, got me to agree to drink a little champagne with our dinner. She of course did all the drinking, scarcely any of the eating; repeatedly transferring spoonfuls of chicken and rice from her plate to my plate.

OCTOBER 30

[A note from publicist Tom Sullivan.]

"The WOR telecast 'Meet the Author: Glenway Wescott with Katherine Anne Porter,' screened October 7, attracted a remarkable half million viewers in New York."

NOVEMBER

Portland. No one on earth is as affected as the immature American male. The way our boys, and many of our homosexuals old enough to know better, arrange their genitals in tight denim trousers corresponds almost exactly to the wearing of cod pieces at the end of the middle ages when they no longer served any useful purpose.

NOVEMBER 29

James Thurber: "Let us not look back in anger, nor forward in fear, but around in awareness."

NOVEMBER 30

Milwaukee. Reading selections from Whitman in Wisconsin: Magical, purely poetical gift, like Tennyson's. It means less than I used to read into it—only his courage about eroticism is very admirable, and that based (I suppose) on his self-assurance of relative innocence, that is, scarcely having done anything. For probably he was a masturbator for the most part, like Henry James, like Thoreau.

DECEMBER 1

Night before last, having missed my train to Milwaukee by four minutes (the ladies having hung onto my coattails too long, then driven too slow), and I was sitting in the Union Station, two and half hours to wait for the next train, there came a deaf mute boy, handing out cards to everyone on the waiting room benches, returning a few minutes later to take them back or to receive one's contribution—poorly but neatly dressed, sturdy but not fleshy, pink-cheeked, blue-eyed, self-respecting, lonely-looking.

The only enemy of quality in this country these days is, I believe, quantity. The number of books—400 a year at Harpers—the high rental of book store real estate, ditto book warehouse space—everyone concerned naturally eager to get one's book out of the way.

DECEMBER 3

Madison, Wisconsin. Paul Engle, introducing me, read the first two paragraphs of *The Grandmothers*: Alwyn's trying to discern a trace, amid the melon vines, of the foundation of the house in which his father had been born. He added, "I think that, all his life, Glenway has been looking for his birthplace."

I replied: "Paul Engle's introduction stirs my mind and touches my heart. As to the deeper implications of what I suppose he meant to imply, there is a coincidence that may interest you. Last week when I lectured in Milwaukee, I spoke of wanting to drive up to Kewaskum, in Washington County, to Farmington Township, to Orchard Grove, to Valley Farm, to revisit the house I was born in, which I last visited in 1935. I was told that it lately had burned to the ground. I offer this as a matter of fact and sentiment and coincidence, not as a symbol. Nothing really symbolic about it—I think."

The America of DC3's, never seen from the road or the train or the jet plane. Someday I'd enjoy traversing the entire continent in little hops, sitting in the tail seat as to see under the wings.

Pretty hill country around Ottumwa, Iowa, breaking up the great fertile rectangles of black earth, tawny stubble, winter grains, dark thistle, strong little water courses, eroded pastures, contour planting. Further on, as we crossed into Missouri, noble old woodlots reduced to noble groves with brown and golden winter sod in the vacant spaces. Lorraine-like.

DECEMBER 8

Paul G. reports that a large part of the respectable male population of Bloomington gave a stag dinner party to raise money for the Boy Scouts, with obscene motion pictures after dinner. All concerned, or almost all, would favor rigid censorship of books and pictures and the performing arts, indeed, inhumane prison sentences for purveyors and performers of erotica.

DECEMBER 27

Strange as it may seem, El Greco had a friend familiar enough to criticize him for spending all his life brooding, pondering and perhaps sulking in a dirty, stuffy, dark-curtained room, and to propose his coming out for a walk. "No," said the great visionary painter, "No, the sunlight would disturb the light that is shining within me."

I should not have stayed away quite so long. I couldn't resist Bloomington and Charlottesville, favorite universities. Now I have exactly four months to produce a book-length text [*A Windfall*]—and my strong perceptive bossy new editor is insisting on seeing an incomplete, unfinished version of "The Stallions" within a couple of weeks, so that, if we decide against it for our immediate purposes of autumn publishing, there may still be time for me to produce something else. What else? Since I got back I have been having nightmares about this—I mean, literally; bad dreams.

How far back one could trace my almost incapacitating self-consciousness, fits of vanity interspersed if not offset by painful slumps.

1963

JANUARY

On May 8, 1932, the *New York Herald Tribune* "Books" published a review of my *Fear and Trembling* by Isabel Patterson, the only respectful review it had, and they illustrated it with Cocteau's flattering drawing of me, made in 1926.

Last week, a neighbor lady, moving into an old house in Rosemont, found those yellowed pages on the floor of the attic, recognized me, and brought them to me.

JANUARY 5

Against the urgency brought to bear upon young university professors to "publish." It tends to lower standards or to imply, in the application of strict criteria to the work of main extra-academic body of contemporary literature, a certain insincerity.

As their publications are not, as a rule, successful in book form, it is conducive to the envious, almost paranoid disposition which is one of the worst features of university life, at least in the area of literature and the arts—conducive also to provincialism.

Teachers should be encouraged to feel that education is the greatest of all intellectual activities, as indeed it is the most fundamental.

JANUARY 20

The most obvious thing in the world about me, my life, my work: I am not going to have time enough to write all I could and should write; I am not going to have energy enough to work as many hours a day as I should like.

FEBRUARY

Stories of Pavlik [Tchelitchev]: Our quarrel about George Platt Lynes (1943); our quarrel about Peter Watson (1947); his peacemaking letter and gift of a 1925 portrait drawing, after George died.

FEBRUARY 1

A good kind of scientist: Wilson Alwyn Bentley, the snowflake man, 1865–1934, a Vermont farmer's son, poor and celibate, who devoted his life to the study of snow-crystals, accumulating evidence that they are almost all hexagonal and no two are exactly alike.

One storm in 1928 brought him a hundred new types of crystal formation snowflakes. In 1931 the American Meteorological Society subsidized the publication of his lifework, *Snow Crystals*, whereupon he died.

In late afternoon light a fine partridge sat amid the black twigs of the apple tree closest to the house, silhouetted against the pallor of the snow. At twilight, a horned owl in flight swept softly from tree to tree.

FEBRUARY 4

Elizabeth, New Jersey looks rather like a suburb of Paris, that is to say, like certain paintings by Utrillo.

FEBRUARY 6

William Inge, after extreme adverse criticism and a brief run of his "Natural Affection," went charging around the country, demoralized. My dear John Connolly, employed as his secretary-chauffeur, sent me a picture postcard of the Old Slave Mart in Charleston, now a museum, with this message: "If I were put up on the block here, I wouldn't be at all surprised. Plans have changed five times so far."

FEBRUARY 18

There is this equation in post-mature sexuality: The effect of asking, and getting a negative answer, is a youthful feeling, however sorrowful. *Not* asking is what ages one.

FEBRUARY 19

I blithely committed myself to delivering my story of animal love, "The Stallions," not later than May 1st and presently I grow creative about it, perhaps too creative. It got longer, took in some additional characters and episodes, and now I am behind schedule.

MARCH 1

[Philadelphia.]

A birthday dinner for Stephen Spender at Henry McIlhenny's. I sat on Lady Diana Cooper's left. Beautiful still, though masked-looking. Beautiful soft voice. She has just returned from Washington. The president's favorite sister, Mrs. Shriver, guided her through the White House, and later in the week he himself came to dinner with her at the [Joseph] Alsops'.

She dotes on the president and covers all the family with a blanket fondness, even the attorney general and his wife. (Come to think of it, she didn't mention the president's wife.)

MARCH 6

I despise the administrators of the Noble Prize, not only for certain frivolities and sentimentalities in their selection of men of letters, but for not giving the Peace Prize to Jean Monnet, just now.

I rage against our conceited, hypocritical participation in the war in Vietnam. Detestable, disgraceful double standard in all these areas where the cold war erupts into warfare.

MARCH 19

Who do you suppose invented the sonnet? Pier della Vigna, the life-long lover and/or beloved of the very virile, ambisexual Emperor Frederick II. This sex-appealing poet seems not to have been well-born and began life as a lawyer.

MARCH 22

[To Raymond Mortimer.]

Fiction, especially any sort of love story, is bound to be most troublesome for the emancipated, that is to say, free-thinking homosexual man . . . There aren't any important homosexual factors in the theme or the action of my story ["The Stallions"]. But with regard to sexual morality in general, according to the life that I have lived, I disagree absolutely and uncompromisingly with the majority of men and women about almost everything.

MARCH 23

The second day of spring. Rosy sunrise. The first jubilant exclamations of a robin. There have been two or three at Baba's all week; this is the first here at Haymeadows.

Uncommon sight: six deer lying down, in the midst of the meadow, as calm as cattle. I saw them stretch sleepily.

APRIL

An almost summery spring, but, this morning, frost and a wind, a wolf
of a wind. It seems to me that I have been more neurotic this spring, in
the strict precise meaning of the word, than ever before in my life.

APRIL 5

Citing Richard Hughes upon his election to honorary membership of
the Academy-Institute of Arts and Letters: Playwright and fiction-writer,
the author of three novels, *A High Wind in Jamaica*, *In Hazard*, and *The Fox
in the Attic*—all three transcending the area of experience that they cover,
as important fiction should do, sending the mind backward in time, as
on an errand or a pilgrimage, and winging the imagination upward and
onward into the future.

APRIL 26

I remember a story that Paul Robeson's wife Essie used to tell about
her mother who was almost white (of Jewish extraction with a Sephar-
dim name). She could "pass" and one fine day, when she was a girl, she
took it into her head to try it, in a Jim Crow streetcar. Bold little minx,
up she went to a seat in front. The darker people seated at the back all
recognized her for who she was, but somehow sympathized. They flick-
ered their eyes at her and one another, but without a word or even a smile.

Essie herself had a friend who really had passed; moved away from
Harlem, settled in Brooklyn, married a well-to-do white man. At the
time of Paul's successful concerts, she wanted to visit him backstage at
Carnegie Hall, and desperately communicated to Essie, asking not to be
recognized, and Paul and Essie let her get away with it.

This came to my mind when I was thinking of Auden. Now as a
Christian, now as a homosexual, he behaves like that, and expects the rest
of us to take it kindly, like the darker Negroes at the back of the bus.

MAY

[From GW's foreword in the Catherine Vivano Gallery catalog for the
Bernard Perlin exhibit.]

In the prime of life one has less free will than in younger years, and an increase of the subconscious factor in whatever one undertakes, and by the same token, more power. Certainly if a mature artist is to say anything in his art, it must be something that he has in him, something actually experienced, previously revealed, meditated at leisure: a feast of remembrance.

MAY 30

My dear bold thresher (or thresheress) brought his (or her) infant up on the terrace just now, perhaps because I gave them leftover bread yesterday—a long-legged tail-less chick, with tasseled breast already.

Often I feel that the best of the literary life, in human value and intellectual interest, is to be found in the character and behavior of men and women of letters of the second rank. Geniuses as a rule are too mysterious, too compulsive; idiosyncratic and therefore uninspiring and un-instructive.

JUNE 15

[Re Isak Dinesen obituary book.]
In the contemporary literary life what a lot of work one does for nothing—in vanity of talent, in delusion of its serving some purpose, or in mere fondness for someone.

JUNE 19

[To Monroe Wheeler re Ralph Ginzburg.]
The editor/publisher of *Eros*, convicted of obscenity on 28 counts, exposing him to a possible sentence of a hundred years in jail, hundreds of thousands of dollars in fines, quoted Blake: "Children of the future Age / Reading this indignant page, / Know that in a former time / Love! Sweet Love! was thought a crime."

Composing my novelette about stallions and mares and boys and girls, behind schedule, I have to let my correspondence lapse; I long for sexual intercourse, or at least some proximity of other's pleasures, but I make no move; life glides away.

JUNE 21

Thrilling obscurities of history: Why did the population of Ireland increase fantastically, by 150 percent, in the half century preceding the famine? In the census year of 1841, it was denser than any other country in Europe. A sort of collective Liebestad. (*The Great Hunger*, Cecil Woodham-Smith.)

JUNE 23

O fragrant world! The hay in the acreage north of the house dying, curing; and south of the house, a very different odor, like a citrus fruit, the hay there only now yielding to the great mower. Elderberry blossoming along the road, and milkweed in the bud, just beginning to attract the butterflies. The honeysuckle has ended, and the clover is going to seed.

All of this more overpowering as it breathes its farewell than at the peak of sweetness, in full force. Like our own sex life when we have begun to feel our age.

JUNE 24

Never has so attractive and sympathetic a man proved so disappointing as our president. His enlightened domestic policies ineffectual against the oligarchy of the Senate; his foreign policies (I'm afraid) just foolish and still, for the most part, Dulles-like.

JUNE 25

Ralph Pomeroy's friend Edward Field very handsome in *The Herald Tribune* upon publication of his Lamont Prize poems. John said, "Wow!"

JULY

I must lunch with Walter Bradbury on Monday, to explain my failure to produce "The Stallions" in time. Of course I shall not pretend that my depression and indolence have all been due to their weak handling of *Images of Truth*; but I have a point to make. More and more the business of publishing has become a matter of finding ways to spend less and less on authors. As they handled *Images* in the trade edition, it was really only a build-up for their paperback edition next spring. And for Signet's *Goodbye, Wisconsin* paperback next year, of which Harper & Row takes half. Doubtless I'll not be powerful enough to have better terms in my new contract in the autumn. In a house like H&R, a writer like me is a sort of loss-leader, chargeable in some measure to their institutional advertising.

JULY 4

At peace on this historic day, traumatic in my life by coincidence. Certainly in 1915, when, in dread of degeneracy, I bade farewell to E.R.K. [a high school lover], I didn't think of it as Independence Day; and in 1949 when I screeched and kicked at Lloyd and Monroe on the lawn at Stone-blossom, I had nothing in mind except infuriation against the theories of Dr. Horney applied to me by Baba—I wasn't aware of being on the verge of new patterns of sex life more comfortable for me than the old hopeless romanticism. . . .

If E.R.K. had been the seductive, coercive sort of young male, if my wanting to detach myself from him had challenged and aroused him to exercise all his sex appeal, to have me and to hold me against my will and my better judgment, I think it might have changed my character somewhat. As it happened, in all my misery in the five years after that, I thought of it as deriving from a decision of my own, relevant to a general social injustice and folly—it wasn't a thing that someone beloved had done *to* me. And in due course, when Monroe understood the direction of my life, he too made me responsible for my own morality.

An enchanting evening with Baba last night. We dined by ourselves at the Lambertville House, and talked of the importance of feeling that one is needed by someone: her theory. "Even you yourself," she said, "although your literary vocation gives you a sense of justification and identity, I think you would feel lost if Monroe and I and John did not depend on you in so many ways." The great factors in my life, I tried to explain to her—the bases of my value-judgments of people close to me—are my admiration and gratitude.

Then in twilight we drove up through the woods on the far side of the river, where all the vast rhododendrons are in bloom, ghostly unflickering candle-flames, and on our way back, parked the car and walked down the tow-path toward Center Bridge, where the canal too is banked with great foliage and gray-pink flowers. Then I read to her for an hour, the first four of [Francis] Bacon's *Essays*—my old interest in them revived by Kitty Bowen's new biography.

JULY 17

As I left Monroe's apartment on my way to Pennsylvania Station, homeward bound, I saw and heard a couple of handsome, immoral-looking policemen in the lobby, tormenting the doorman with questions. Whatever the matter was, the doorman kept miserably assuring that he knew nothing about it, he hadn't seen anyone or heard anything.

I winced at their presence, not only with my usual feeling of cop hatred but because I had under my arm a large conspicuous portfolio containing our Tchelitchev erotic drawings: Tchelitchev at his best and worst.

JULY 22

Higher education in the United States constitutes a new vested interest, indeed a new bourgeoisie, against which those of us who love the arts and are determined to live according to creative insights now must defend ourselves.

With reference to our literary and artistic situation, I said, "The chief enemy of quality is quantity." "No," Monroe said, "the chief enemy of quality is novelty."

Bernard and I got to talking of our respective household problems, and of the shocking amount of money we spend on our hospitality, food and drink, etc., deploring it but concluding that all things considered, it was worthwhile. "Pleasure lasts on and on," he said, "in one's mind, one's remembrance, one's art. Nothing else does."

AUGUST 2–4

Notes on weekend with Homer Price: Narcissism, one of the most grievous orientations of the psyche. One may dread involvement with beauties because other people have spoiled them all their lives—but I don't think that this is the main trouble.

Extreme subjectivity, self-consciousness, self-absorption, keeps one from the intent observation of others, the intense responses to others. They are disastrously isolated and lonely.

Objectivity is the third dimension of character.

AUGUST 9–11

In re the weekend with Lou: I really personify enlightened selfishness. No one is so obstinate and single-minded in pursuit of his heart's desire. On the other hand, not many are so enlightened.

I have got to an age when one is apt to be lonely in company, and not likely to be lonely when alone.

AUGUST 11

En route to N.Y. from Woods Hole, Cape Cod: Neither Monroe nor I brought money enough; Josephine Crane no longer keeps cash on hand because she can't keep her mind on anything; and the Falmouth bank yesterday closed at 2:00 rather than 3:00.

Our entire visit has been worrisome, demoralized and futile—except for certain beauties of Nantucket architectural and geographical, and Padraic Colum's new one-act play [*Cloughoughter*] which he read aloud to us yesterday. Padraic is 82. His first play was produced in Dublin the year I was born, and I think the latest play may well be his most important work, though it is too learnedly historical, too profound in the way it philosophizes, to be successfully performed, even in Ireland. It is mostly about Roger Casement, the patriot whom the British not only hanged for treason but put to shame for homosexuality. He wrote one about Oscar Wilde's father last year, and intends to do another about Parnell; a trilogy about scandal and the failure of leadership. "That will complete my lifework," he said yesterday.

[Re publicity photo of GW on *TV Guide* page listing the program "Ex Libris," Channel 4.]

TV Guide—circulation 400,000—the farthest flung publicity I have ever had.

SEPTEMBER 3

[To Monroe.]

My dearest, for fifteen minutes I have been staring at these envelopes, wondering what is in them, thinking of you, of us both. Forgive me once more.

I can't bear to say "I forgive you," because I can't bear the thought of blaming you; in a sense I never do—though I suppose my wearying of my life and dread of the future must seem a reproach to you.

When I harangue you bitterly it is a desperate hope of inducing you to help me out of my unhappiness, to persuade you to bypass my terrible pride and anger. O incommunicable humanity! When I shout it deafens you; when I speak softly you don't feel that you have to pay attention to my little plans, woes, foibles.

One thing I am sure of: it is of the utmost urgency for us to develop and practice certain new courtesies and indeed amenities before we get any older, based especially on a recognition of our separateness, our differences of need, of nervous system, of criteria, of habit, and on strict observance of little areas of right and predominance within our co-residence, here or wherever we may be. If we don't, we're going to end up like some hateful play by Beckett or Albee or the like: two old codgers down a well or in a mine shaft; their love disgraced, their remaining strength wasted.

I love you always.

OCTOBER 11

What a commotion, in my mind, and on the telephone, with Cocteau's death, and in the middle of the night, last night, Debo's second
baby girl!

Monroe has been seeing Tchelitchev's sister, on my behalf; and of
course Cocteau's friendship goes further back in our lives than any other
relationship still surviving.

Now I must try to apply my mind to my Colette review—if I can get
Cocteau out of my mind. The most multifarious man who ever lived—
which is not quite the same thing as an *huomo universalo*—he buzzes in
one's thoughts like a swarm of bees.

OCTOBER 12

[Letter to Monroe Wheeler.]

One of the strangest things about Jean [Cocteau]: Self-concerned
though he was, like a sort of prima-donna lawyer in self defense, hawk-
ing his work in the way of an old fashioned street vendor with a pushcart
full of mixed vegetables (mixed indeed!), living or pretending to live one
continuous, lifelong, public or semi-public, pseudo-narcissistic plot, and
surely narcissistic enough to be preserved from the very worst, the very
greatest excesses of love—still he was not egocentric; in fact extraordinarily extrovert. All his life he kept discovering, "protecting," tutoring,
introducing, championing, promoting, one creative person after another.

No letter from my dearest—only two small communications from
the lover of a young person with whom I may be said to have fallen
somewhat in love. How terrible it would be, if this true statement were
to be taken as literal truth!

My brother sometimes speaks interestingly of the relaxed, released,
ennobled sensuality of women who have had their change of life; that is,
who no longer dread impregnation. Something corresponding to that in
my case, because I am not afraid of falling in love, and of being found
inadequate, of being made jealous.

Post-mature state of mind, or perhaps I should say, state of heart, founded on lifelong love that has outlasted desire, and on the above-mentioned peculiarity of eroticism without possessiveness, without (in my case, as a rule) even physical possession.

The new Peter, Paul and Mary hit: "Don't Think Twice—It's All Right," a song of the sorrowfulness or anger of promiscuity, when it is sorrowful or angry (not always). I value it, it touches my heart. It has that trueness to life, even lowly, unlucky, disadvantaged, immature life or lives, which interest me in popular music. Plus, P., P. & M.'s lovely musicality.

OCTOBER 15

[Re the posthumous diary of Dag Hammarskjöld.]
The moral of Hammarskjöld is that it's not prohibitively difficult to keep from having a bad reputation. A reputation for mysteriousness (or for being a sort of saint or a sort of eunuch) arouses the suspicions only of peculiar persons like myself, freakishly speculative, interested in strange types of h. [homosexual] character, strange patterns of h. behavior, in the social context.

Homosexuality, the greatest of all conspiracies of silence.

OCTOBER 16

Aren't professors presumptuous? The one who has written a book about me [William H. Rueckert] arrives on Monday with not only his wife but, he now tells me, a four-year-old child and an eight-month-old baby and a dog named Burke. He has sent me his book on Kenneth Burke by first class mail, so that I'll be able to get it read before he arrives, in order to talk to him in a well-read way.

OCTOBER 23

At my dinner party, I wanted to tell stories about Cocteau et al, and to question Ned [Rorem], but Truman Capote shouted me down all evening, in his falsetto way, about various crimes and atrocities. As it happens, I have never been with him in all-male society before, and was astonished to find that the subject matter of sex doesn't interest him at all.

Keats' last words. Joseph Severn had never seen anyone die. It is thought that Keats knew this, and in the ultimate hour felt sorry for him.

"Severn, lift me up. I am dying!"

Then, in the goodness of his heart, he added, "Don't be afraid."

OCTOBER 31

Said [Joseph] Addison, wittily, in his elderly manner, "We are always doing something for posterity, but I would fain see posterity do something for us."

What it does, if we give it any thought—difficult to do perhaps in this age of apocalyptic science—is to remind us to write in language most likely to endure, that is, to continue to go on meaning more or less what it means to us, not in the jargon arbitrarily developed by university professors for their specialized intramural publications, not in the improvisational humorous small talk of immigrants and other such autodidacts, not in frivolous slang.

Language has a heart, a core, a slow mainstream, which is sacred.

NOVEMBER 6

[Re delivering erotic Tchelitchev illustrations to the Kinsey Institute, Bloomington, Indiana.]

I feel foolish about this expedition—Pavlik [Tchelitchev] bewitched . . . There has been a hex, beginning at the airport where I caught a happy-go-lucky TWA boy misrouting my bag to Bloomington, Illinois. Fog over Indiana; cancellation of the Lake Central plane at the last minute. From Chicago on I have been circumstantially teamed up with two traveling salesmen and a physical fitness professor—and sure enough, they have been talking about sex, Playboy Club bunnies, whores in Panama, etc., before daybreak. Needless to say, I have been worried, profoundly worried about the drawings, with the shifting of the bag from one public carrier to another. I wasn't allowed to carry it in my hand.

NOVEMBER 7

[From the *New York Times*.]
"High Court in New Jersey Overturns A Ban on Homosexuals in Bars."

NOVEMBER 22

The Death of the President. For some time I have thought of the young president with profound compassion—certainly he must have felt bitterly frustrated, disappointed and discouraged on account of the failure of his government program due to public apathy, due to the necessities of the rebelliousness of the Negroes and concomitantly to the defiance of the Southern branch of his party—or to some insolent powerful dictatorship and shift of power in Europe.

And so pessimistic have I grown that my first or second thought upon the news of his death was, "Oh, he's well out of it!" Weak of me, certainly; and in fact I do believe that he might have been hopeful of a turn of the political tide and better luck in his second administration.

I cannot think of any death in history so pathetic. Keats for example, though he might have become a Shakespeare, had become a Keats.

One of the inner seeds of fascism: My unwillingness to believe that the man who killed Kennedy was the communist or ex-communist, pro-Castro lunatic whom the Dallas police apprehended, my longing to believe (so to speak) the opposite. If there is to be any uncertainty or long drawn-out investigation, I kept thinking, would it not be a good thing to blame or at least suspect some segregationist, some John Bircher, some Goldwaterite?

Certainly I do not trust the Dallas police. Is this because I am homosexual, and therefore an outlaw, and consequently a cop-hater?

I keep remembering the burning of the Reichstag, the trial of Martin van der Lubbe, et seq.

In this dear land of the (mostly) free, better about heterosexual morals than anything else, what would have happened if the assassin had been a jealous husband or honor-minded father or brother?

Mrs. Kennedy, arriving at the White House from Arlington Hospital with her husband's body—not until 3:30 a.m. (of course it took the morticians hours to "restore" his bullet-torn face, for the viewing by his family and high government officials)—still wore the bright-colored dress she had worn for the parade in Dallas, still blood-stained.

NOVEMBER 28

[To Janet Flanner with GW's review of Colette's *The Blue Lantern*.]

Somewhat new inspiration. Last year's book seems to have emancipated me from being expected to write great novels, a mug's game for so many years. (What a weak character!) The same people who used to bully me and scold me about my fiction writing now constantly demand book reviews. And I guess it's time to do something different from either fiction or criticism.

NOVEMBER 29

Foolishness of love in matters of public interest, citizenship, etc: I find myself resenting President Johnson for so promptly going to work glamorizing the moon project by re-naming Cape Canaveral Cape Kennedy, diverting my mind from the fact that it was President Kennedy's dear project in the first place.

Though I ardently disapproved when Kennedy first started it, and since, I took it for granted—because I loved him—that he had good reason for it. I seem not to give his distinguished successor the benefit of the doubt—because I do not love him.

DECEMBER

To shame or punish a book because it stimulates the sexual appetite is as silly as to forbid a tragedy to make you cry, a comedy to make you laugh, or a piece of music to make you dance. I believe in the physical responses that the arts may elicit, i.e., tears, laughter, exaltation of patriotism, sexual arousal—only not in disproportion or excess but in moderation and proportion, not sobbing sentimentality, not belly laughter, nor riot or assassination or rape.

DECEMBER 5

Note that a good many receptive anal fuckers clean their anuses before making love—just as women cleanse the vagina.

Note that oral-genital intercourse developed as a widespread technique in the U.S. because of the greater availability of running hot water and soap.

DECEMBER 8

Discipline is a god, though indeed sometimes a possessive, jealous, maddening god. By saving time it permits more time for work, pleasure, and rest. It instills self-esteem. It gives us courage.

DECEMBER 20

[Re declining a magazine editor's request for a piece on Cocteau.]

Cocteau was one of my oldest friends, and his death has saddened me, although I am glad that he got out of life while still in the midst of it, with work in hand, with friends in close contact. It would have been sad for him to lie bedridden with senses impaired.

Someday I hope to write something about him, in a book, with other remembrances.

DECEMBER 26

Sometimes I think it might be easier to write a bestseller—like [Mary] McCarthy or Nabokov or Mailer—than to inch along toward the grave as I have been doing with a series of little challenges, séances of the intellect, love-affairs of the pen, invisible chess games; a kind of poet without verse. The trouble is that I hate the very idea of writing what I wouldn't enjoy reading.

1964

JANUARY 21

Certainly, in my case, career and sexuality and economics and family relationships are all exceptional—but for the life of my mind, the range of my reading and my mediation and my scribbling, literary and epistolary, sometimes seem to me fantastic; perhaps increasingly so. Age is not a simplifying factor.

JANUARY 25

Earl and Walter and David: The simplest continuous single act of intercourse, four men as mutually engaged as ardently as any heterosexual coupling, about half an hour of continuous action, with one change of position, and my own oral-genital activity the same throughout. No sort of conscious indecency or self-conscious eroticism: friendliness and sense of beauty predominant over everything, everything except sexual sensation and arousal and, finally, orgasm.

JANUARY 27

Katherine Anne this morning reminded me of an amusing exchange between us years ago. She had spoken of her desire to make a great deal of money if and when she got *Ship of Fools* done. "But you're bound to be disappointed in that way," I said. "At least in this country, the best things in life are free."

To which she replied, "I have had all the things that money can't buy. Now I'd like to see what a little money can do for me."

Just before *Ship of Fools* appeared, Christopher Isherwood said to me, "I hope for her sake that it isn't too successful."

"But why?"

"She has made too many enemies in the literary life, but even they have treated her somewhat indulgently because of her loneliness and hardships and penury. If they find that on top of her glamour and glory and influence, she has money, real money, they will tear her to pieces."

FEBRUARY 8

[On translating.]

In the course of our Colette telecast (Katherine Anne Porter and Anita Loos and I on "Camera Three") the subject of translation came up. I said, as I always do, that no one ever takes enough trouble or devotes enough time to it. As a rule it is hack-work, and poorly paid. There is nothing impossible to translate, except for the most complex verse forms: rhyme and rhythm and meter in addition to meaning and feeling really do defeat us. When we care about literary work in a foreign language, we are likely to love and prize and take delight especially in passages that express not only the temperament, message and feeling of the subject matter but passages that uniquely illustrate the spirit of the language. In other words, the least translatable authors are prose writers who are most like poets. But, by the same token, if you understand the language you are translating from and master the language you are translating into, you will come upon compensatory passages, lucky breaks: some things lend themselves to a foreign language more easily than in their original form.

MARCH 2

My Tchelitchev painting *The Lion Boy*: He isn't erotic for me any more (except for instance, in conversation)—I sometimes wish he were. I only see the blue and the gold, and feel the dreaminess of the gaze of his sentimental face.

APRIL

The Apple of the Eye penciled ms. in notebooks: I like to show this manuscript because it is picturesque and because I am stubborn. It was my first prose publication—I was 23—and I still like it. Recently I took the stenographer's tablet out of an old box for the benefit of a university man who had undertaken a Ph.D. thesis about me, and saw the torn condition of the first tablet. It shocked me. Who had been at it? Why? Then it gave me goose-flesh of remembrance: in a hotel bedroom in Munich, in 1922, during a quarrel with my beloved Monroe, I myself had torn it and flung it on the floor.

APRIL 4—5

The young are, above all, self-seeking. What a good word that is, meaning something very different from self-centered or selfish. They want and need to discover themselves, to learn to know themselves. Sometimes we can see at a glance deep things and future things that will take them a long time and great fusses (painful to all concerned) to find out. No matter; *es muss sein*; they can't learn much from us; they have to experiment with themselves and with us.

APRIL 24

Marianne Moore made a public appearance with Auden, introducing him before one of his lectures. "I cannot be meritorious," she told him, "but I will be brief; only five minutes."

"Three minutes would be better," he firmly answered.

As it is well known that he always wants to do all the talking, we all laughed. Monroe sprang to defend him. "But, Marianne, he only wanted to make it easier for you." Sir Kenneth Clark exclaimed, "Monroe, what a diplomat you are! And quick as a flash!"

Marianne wasn't as well satisfied with Wystan, as usual: "Well, he was unrestrained, barroom-like!" She said afterward, "I wanted to say bawdy, but felt ashamed to. Barroom was a euphemism."

APRIL 30

Hemingway, I seem to remember, used to hold that a well-constructed sentence could be easily understood without commas, etc.; therefore he forbade himself to put any in until the last revision. Syntax as simple as that, I think, leads to a certain monotonousness, repetitiousness, as in his case indeed; sometimes hypnotic in effect, sometimes soporific.

Sometimes it seems to me that my very own, very personal punctuation is most important for the conveyance of the rhythm of what I write, the breath of life. Is that because I read aloud so much, perhaps too much?

Every magazine, every publisher, has its own rules and tries to maintain some uniformity. I yield to them but irritably, and sometimes with a bad conscious, aesthetically speaking.

MAY 3

Monroe's enthusiasm about the style of Hemingway's *A Moveable Feast*— a pang of jealousy. I mean to say, rivalry. He remarks that the spell of the subject matter of Paris in the twenties affected him so that he was able to revert to his way of writing at that time; better than the way he wrote in recent years.

MAY 4

Almost all afternoon with Monroe, driving up the Delaware River on the Pennsylvania side, and down the Delaware on the New Jersey side, which is his delight—as it were a kind of loving intercourse. Every shade and nuance of infant green everywhere, and the apple orchards and the various ornamental Japanese fruit trees or fruit shrubs all in blossom.

How desperate it is to think that one's springs are numbered!

MAY 5

A long, tiring day—correcting the galleys of my Maugham foreword; copying the list of Tchelitchevs in the gallery of Modern Art exhibition that I'd like to have photographed, and composing a persuasive letter to Carl Weinhardt about this; trotting down to Baba's and hastily putting up plastic-coated wire for her clematises to grow on (not a moment too soon, as they are shooting up, all self-entangled); driving to Trenton with Ethel, trying to work in the train, but dozing all the way to town; then shopping, and cooking dinner at John's for Adair and George Howard as well as ourselves; letting John tell me his troubles, which cheered him up and saddened me; falling into bed, dead-tired.

MAY 9

Last night at the opera, returning to her box after intermission, the First Lady Mrs. Johnson stood graciously gesturing in acknowledgement of the general applause, then sat down—and just there, where she chose to sit, there was no chair. No harm done.

Someone used to say that one could distinguish between born royalty and any *parvenu* by their way of sitting down. The Empress Euginie would swiftly, though dignifiedly, glance behind her; Queen Victoria always calmly lowered her little body as it might have been in thin air, never doubting that some courtier or servitor would instantly advance whatever she was to sit on or in. The Democratic First Lady landed on the floor but rose with a pleasant smile and, said the newscaster on WOR, with no lapse of dignity.

This reminds me of an even less formal state of American manners. Baba's Aunt Harriet, Mrs. Charles B. Alexander, who was a Crocker (the robber-baron's daughter) came to lunch in Rambouillet in 1931. She was in her eighties and the Rambouillet dining room floor was highly waxed. She took my arm, from the vast living room floor across the hall, into the dining room. Just as I was about to put up her chair, she turned and gave me a piercing glance. "Now don't you pull that chair out from under me," she said earnestly. Perhaps in 1849 very old ladies were sometimes subjected to practical jokes by 30-year-old friends of the family.

MAY 16

The verbal culture, oratory, sermons, lectures, was so much more important than the forms of literature in early nineteenth century America. Van Wyck Brooks quotes Harriet Beecher Stowe (from her novel *Dred*): "If ever a woman feels proud of her lover, it is when she sees him as a successful public speaker."

MAY 21

Guggenheim Museum. Ladies at the Tchelitchev exhibition: one lady to another, "See, this same boy's picture over and over. Must have been a relative." Referring to Charles Henri Ford of course.

MAY 23

Samoan fire-dancers in a church in San Francisco set fire to themselves and their audience—half a dozen in their audience incinerated, a hundred injured.

Helena Rubenstein, confronted in the night by three masked thieves with knives, snapped, "I am an old woman, ready to die if you wish to kill me. But I will not let you rob me." They tied her to a chair, but found nothing and left without injury and without any loot.

JUNE 14

All morning and for a while in the afternoon I helped ghost-write Monroe's biographical outline of Bonnard. In the afternoon John drove me to Delatush's Holly Nursery in Robbins and helped me plant two good-sized Maryland Dwarf Hollies. Dinner on the north lawn under the black walnut tree for Monroe and John and Lloyd and Baba: casserole-roasted veal in the Dutch oven—marinated in white wine, one half cup of wine, one half cup of water, one quarter cup of peanut oil, with a tablespoon of finely cut-up rosemary. Mashed potatoes, green beans vinaigrette, Lambertville bread, strawberries with powdered sugar.

JUNE 23

Surprise party for Lloyd's eight years of service as President of the State Board of Control: Governor Hughes said that Lloyd might very properly be called the first citizen of New Jersey. The Commissioner thanked Barbara on behalf of the unfortunates in the state institutions, the officers and staff of the department, and the citizenry at large, for cheerfully, nobly sacrificing so much of his companionship pro bono publicum. Nobly, yes, but not very cheerfully.

JULY 2

In the breezeless heat, a bonfire, like hair standing on end; hair of gold.

JULY 3

I wish that the Fourth of July weekend was over and done with. I am about to be descended upon by two friends from the Southern provinces . . . I hope they don't talk Goldwater-ish to my brother. We Wescotts, having sent our grandfather and four great-uncles to the War

Between the States, have always had a hankering to pitch in again and finish it up.

JULY 10

What in the world is the Society for Indecency to Naked Animals, 507 Fifth Avenue, New York, NY? It caught my eye in the telephone book. There is a Society for Aesthetic Realism, 67 Jane Street; also mystifying.

Careless use of language conducive to error and/or dishonesty, on the radio just now. A news broadcaster, summarizing the most recent U.S. programs for Southeast Asia: "Beefing up our support of the Vietnamese government pacification effort."

Extraordinary, anonymous lowly persons to be glimpsed in history: The pickpocket in one of the crowds around L.B.J., the campaigning president, intending merely to ply his felonious skill, had his hand shaken by the smiling, indefatigable, fearless great man. Also, the young champion swimmer who always accompanied F.D.R. when he flew abroad, whose assignment was to keep him afloat in the event of a ditching.

JULY 29

[On writing.]

Experience certainly is the main literary matter; more interesting as a rule than invention, more heartwarming than tradition.

To a fifteen-year-old writer:

Begin on a small scale: an episode, an observation, a dialogue, a description. Make your own bricks first, before you begin to blueprint your architecture according to someone's ideas of what constitutes an essay or a story or a play, or according to your notion of what may be publishable. All that comes later. First, be personal!

AUGUST 12

Michael Miksche with whom I was intimate some years ago killed himself last weekend. My first thought was, "Fancy his not having taken someone with him!" He went mad in 1962 and at one point escaped from the mad-house and telephoned me very alarmingly, with the terrible mad prolixity alternating love and hatred. Released, divorced, doing well at his job, he couldn't bear what remained of his life.

AUGUST 25

[To Raymond Mortimer.]

Monroe has had a bad year, but it seems to have taken a turn for the better. A sort of menopause of spirit, with vague dark ideas and fitful emotions. No wonder. The unsuccessfulness of his exhausting lecture tour shook him. The prospect of his forced retirement at 65, with his helpless but viable parents using up his small savings, dumbfounded him; and having to evade that issue since last February 13—he was a party to the establishment of the museum regulation about it, years ago—put him to shame. He has begun to think of selling his pictures, which he will hate. So will I; we're old-fashioned. To much of the art-loving world now, the buying and selling are perhaps more fun than anything.

This improved prospect, as revealed a few weeks ago: the Rockefellers et al have decided to start another fundraising campaign at once, toward building another wing (fun for Philip Johnson); and therefore to keep all the top brass on for three years, regardless of their elderliness.

His Bonnard exhibition will be glorious, and his little biographical essay is just right, I think. I had to help him with it as time pressed, but he told me everything that he wanted to include in it more specifically than ever before, and he didn't let me make any final revisions.

AUGUST 31

I have a deep-seated stubbornness about when and how and, above all, where I write when a piece of my work is going well, on its last lap. I have tried to break myself of the habit of working in the kitchen. What is the matter with my admirable new study adjacent it? What is wrong with the expensively rebuilt upstairs—just an attic ever since the eighteenth century—even that now has air-conditioning. Yesterday the thermometer stood in the 90s, with smoldering humidity. The kitchen was suffocating, a sort of fiery furnace, but I kept on working there, drudging away until dinner time.

After dinner, to my astonishment and amusement, I noticed that the electric oven had been set to bake, at 350 degrees, all day long. I had used it to heat up a breakfast sweet roll, and forgotten to turn it off.

SEPTEMBER I

About a month ago one of the brown thrushes who have nested in my syringe bush for three successive years, and who have been daily visitors to my bird feeder at the back door, appeared minus his tail. I haven't seen him or his mate since and feared that one of the predators got them. I hoped that, having had a good scare, they started their migration south a month earlier this year.

This morning, behold, here he was on the great ash stump, tail all complete. He flew arrow-straight to the syringe bush. Has he been hiding in the spinney, shrinking and sulking while a new plumage developed?

SEPTEMBER IO

Auden: Of course he is a great poet, but a little like Verlaine or the old Wordsworth; one doesn't esteem him as much as one would like to. One disadvantage of his dread and detestation of confessional texts is that it has frightened him off the subject-matter of the private life, even in his poetry.

SEPTEMBER 22

Small children. My bus to Trenton was half an hour late—a flat tire— and I sat on the white cement doorstep in the sun, and went on writing a day long letter to Robert Phelps about my so-called sketch books and vast letter file. The school bus arrived and deposited near me a pretty little girl aged about eight and a pretty small boy aged five or six. They came close and gazed at me and the little girl asked, "What are you doing?"

"I am writing a letter."

"Who to? What for?" My simple factual answers to these questions did not interest her. "You have a big bag," she observed. "What's in it?"

"All sorts of things. Books. Peaches."

"Who are the peaches for?"

None of this interested the six-year-old boy. "I wish I had a bicycle," he said.

"Don't you like to walk? I'd rather walk than ride a bicycle."

"Why?"

"When I was about your age I fell off a bicycle and hurt my knee." I kept from mentioning the fact that the scar on my knee can still be seen. They'd ask to see it.

"Why don't you like to ride a bicycle?"

"Because I'm afraid I guess."

He grimaced contemptuously. He was a beautiful little creature.

OCTOBER 6

Anaïs Nin: A famous but not successful, very prolific authoress—best known, I guess, for work not yet published. For many years—perhaps thirty years—she has been keeping a total-recall, shameless, amorous and mystical journal. She is a well-born Cuban American; glamorously good looking in an old fashioned way; ice wouldn't melt in her mouth, you might think. And yet she is, or has been, a great immoralist. When I first knew her, in Paris, in circa 1930, she was the mistress of Henry Miller! Unimaginable, as in those days he was a sort of disorderly, disheveled, raffish, penniless fellow; one might almost have said, a bum—at any rate, a pre-beatnik. She also, at one time, played a great role in the life of Edmund Wilson, and figures in *Memoirs of Hecate County* as, if I remember correctly, "the princess with the golden hair." In the last two or three years she has had a great problem as to which she has consulted me a great deal: how to have her journal preserved for future publication, and at the same time, to make sure that her good husband shall never be allowed to see it.

OCTOBER 15

Will it never end? Yesterday one of the president's high-ranking aides, Walter Jenkins, had to resign, having been arrested for indecent behavior

in the men's room of the notorious Washington YMCA. He was arrested
for a similar offense years ago. He is the father of six children. Will foolish homosexual or ambi-sexual men never cease to involve themselves in
public service careers? I suppose the danger of the risks they run excites
them—just as the men's room surreptitiousness, the voyeurism, the exhi-
bitionism, intensifies their desire. Of course, his good reputation and
peace of mind as the father of six children and White House employee
depended on his channeling his homosexual appetite. If he pursued his
homosexual contacts in safe circumstances in h. cocktail parties, it would
have made scandal. Will this misfortune make the president more tolerant of homosexuals or less tolerant? Was the police officer who made the
arrest possibly a Goldwater-ite, or did the Republican National Committee pay him to pursue this quarry?

OCTOBER 23

John Knowles in the street, friendly, almost clinging; unshaven, un-
tidy, as though he had spent the night or indeed several nights in some
beatnik's pad in Greenwich Village.

NOVEMBER 4

Nelson Lansdale [*New York Times* obituary]: When we first met, I was
38 and he was 24.

The Pilgrim Hawk is dedicated to him. I shall never again want pleasure enough—or be sufficiently capable of pleasure—to pay the price of
mortification, insincerity, or boredom that I paid then. It is a marvel: one
outlives aspects of oneself.

NOVEMBER 10

A Visit to Priapus, or "Priapus in Maine," 1938 [unpublished in GW's
lifetime]: I remember that Paul Cadmus delighted in it. Monroe didn't;
I didn't expect him to—it was too unpublishable, and in its scandalous
aspect, foreign to him. George [Platt Lynes] didn't either, come to think
of it, he never liked anything I wrote about sex, which discouraged me.
I discourage easily.

In re the gradual planning of a volume of some portion of my sketch-books and commonplace books, regarding this Maine text as a failure, although I can't remember when I last read it, thinking that I could easily break it up and enrich the early sketchbook with the bits and pieces, I handed it over to Robert Phelps to read and consider.

On Sunday he telephoned in almost hysterical admiration—he thinks that it is my most original work, as good or almost as good as *The Pilgrim Hawk*. He rages against the cultural pressures and the general literacy situation (I should say the general *moral* situation) which have kept me striving and straining to write novels, failing to write a good many—when I have this other unique or at least strange power, form, all my own; subject matter that I understand better than anyone.

NOVEMBER 19

Georgia O'Keeffe says that I have come to resemble Carl Van Vechten, now that I have white hair. Do I like that?

DECEMBER 11

Election to the Academy, from the Institute of Arts and Letters: It reminds me sorrowfully of the dear great men and women whose passing brought about the vacuums that we four, Calder and Cowley and Tate and Wescott, have been elected to fill.

It reminds me of my age, not a great matter in itself, but bad enough, with respect to the work that I have done, the work that I have not yet done. I seem to have been chronically subject to a foolish juvenile feeling, as though I had plenty of time to fulfill my promise. There is no such thing as plenty of time.

DECEMBER 17

Not only do we often talk nonsense about what has influenced us at an early age, mirroring our elders in peering back at it as if it were a crystal ball—when in fact all we have in mind is but looking glass. But a good deal of the time it isn't calculation or self-flattery, it is forgetfulness.

My hypothesis: Readers of fiction sometimes read for reasons of the intellect, for the message, the uplift, the historical or sociological message—but that soon fades.

Two things last: education, because it is enforced, self-perpetuating. And the pleasure of reading in imagination, reading as a pastime—excitement, dream-reality, laughter, eroticism, vicarious sentiment.

The fiction writer's pleasure as a rule is the feeling that he is giving pleasure to the reader.

.

Monroe Wheeler notes: "Glenway before I met him."

Wescott as one of the emerging Chicago poets at nineteen, in 1920.

From poet to novelist with publication of *The Apple of the Eye*, 1924.

Wescott publicity photo, c. 1925, Paris.

At the height of expatriate celebrity, Wescott as author of the 1927
bestselling novel, *The Grandmothers.* (© Estate of George Platt Lynes.)

The Left Bank, Paris, 1930. GW: "my sweet-sour expression, spoiled but virtuous, voluptuous but tough, heartbroken but happy." (© Estate of George Platt Lynes)

Wescott exploring brother Lloyd and Barbara's farm in western New Jersey.

Wescott in French sailor shirt at Stone-blossom.

Coney Island: Wescott, George Platt Lynes, Monroe Wheeler, and Katherine Anne Porter.

During a visit to Fire Island, with playful friends George Platt Lynes (standing) and Paul Cadmus.

Monroe Wheeler and mother Josephine Wescott at Stone-blossom

A happy memory of Stone-blossom, Wescott and mother Josephine.

1965–1969

THE MID-SIXTIES ARE A TIME of strength for Wescott, personally and as a public figure. Several of his books are reprinted in paperback, and *The Pilgrim Hawk*, already in the Dell mass market paperback *Six Great Modern Short Novels*, is re-released in hardcover by Harper & Brothers. This leads to a respectful review in the *New Yorker* by Howard Moss that means a great deal to Glenway personally. Still, three new books that could have happened, all in this five-year period, slip away.

Regarding the often-delayed, reorganized "A Windfall," on December 14, 1965, the renowned editor Cass Canfield writes impatiently, "Please let me know whether there's anything we can do from the Harper end to facilitate things." The only major holdup is the long story "The Stallions," which Wescott needs to expand and finish. Though his fragmentary drafts are beautiful, he struggles with this last serious attempt at fiction. He could substitute something else, but won't give up. Even years after "A Windfall" is abandoned, he attempts to revive "The Stallions" draft, a hopeless perfectionist. Likewise, his *Life* magazine piece on Maugham leads to a book contract for the tentatively titled "The Old Party: An American Reminiscence of Somerset Maugham." He has plenty of material already written and plenty more in mind, but he loses interest in the work and it slips away, even as he sees inferior Maugham memoirs published. Finally, Katherine Anne Porter at the height of her fame suggests he organize a volume of letters, the years of correspondence between Porter and friends Wescott, Wheeler, and Barbara Harrison Wescott. It's a difficult editing chore but, even so, another contracted book is delayed from one deadline to another until Porter's editor Seymour Lawrence kills the project. Glenway could have used—rather than a highbrow editor like Canfield and his staff or a highly literary one like Robert Phelps—a ruthless shirt-sleeves editor (like Russell Lynes of *Harper's Magazine*) to help with these works.

On the other hand, "The Valley Submerged" (*Southern Review*, Summer 1965) reveals the aging Wescott at his best in a new form—not literary anecdotes and criticism, but the personal essay; storytelling in spellbinding lyrical prose. The essay about the state's flooding of Stone-blossom and the surrounding valley is filled with meaning deeper than the waters of Spruce Run Reservoir, and points to fine work up ahead. When Katherine Anne Porter first read a draft of the essay, she wrote, "Your 'The Valley Submerged' is in your best vein; I read it fast and then went back and read it slow, and wanted more."

Wescott's service at the Academy-Institute of Arts and Letters continues and includes important work for the federal copyright law revisions of 1966. Wheeler avoids mandatory retirement at the Museum of Modern Art by working for the board of trustees in fundraising and foreign travel for exhibits. Monroe's elderly parents pass away within a two week period. Lloyd survives a serious illness, but he and Glenway lose their sister Marjorie in California. Glenway's younger companion John Connolly changes his career from secretary to William Inge to lighting engineer for CBS television. In 1967 Connolly takes a partner, British Merchant Marine captain Ivan Ashby, who becomes part of the extended family.

The new Lincoln Center, especially the New York City Ballet, becomes an important part of Wescott and Wheeler's world. Their social lives remain rich, from celebrity dinner parties at Wheeler's apartment to Truman Capote's Black and White Ball at the Plaza, to the Rolling Stones at Madison Square Garden. Then at long last Wescott returns to Europe, with trips centered around visits to the Rothschilds for the winter holidays of 1966/67, 1968/69, and the early seventies. Glenway gives his future readers an inside view of the world of Baron Philippe and Baroness Pauline at Mouton Rothschild.

1965

JANUARY 2

Phallus worship. Am I what is called a size queen? Not really. Natural causes of this predilection due to (A) boyhood comparison, and (B) to tumescence itself. Why are straight men less subject to it? Because they are more self-loving, self-centered; also less preoccupied with symbols of sex, fetishes, and more concerned with sexual gratification, sensation and release.

Note that most of those I have desired most were genitally largely endowed—Jacques, Bernard, Samuel, Will, etc.—and most that I have loved were not—M.W., Mark, John, Earl.

JANUARY 3

Someday I'd like to take issue with the matter of whether or not I write for "posterity" more than I should. It was the first insult I ever had to suffer from a fellow-writer, namely Hemingway.

JANUARY 5

Raymond Mortimer, as he said good night to Monroe, and to a pair of friends with whom they had spent the day in Antigua, said, "Now that I'm old I experience the same ecstasy getting into bed by myself that I used to feel getting into bed with someone else."

JANUARY 16

Cold wind and snow. At daybreak my darling mourning doves took refuge on my back porch. When I went out with a replenishment of birdseed, away they flew with the built-in whistle of their wings.

JANUARY 29

One thing that can be said about me at this time of my life: I am not a dried up old boy. Even writing a note to X.—politely vague so that it

shan't make a scandal if read by roommates, friends, et al—I experienced
a rosy glow in my center and a notable pre-coital secretion. No fool like
an old fool, no wise man like an old wise man.

A cocktail party story at Anaïs Nin's: Mrs. Luce bought a Rouault at
auction, a head of Christ, in bright stained-glass colors, with a pious
expression. When one of the experts informed her that it was not by
the master, she said, "No matter. It pleases me because it is such a good
likeness."

FEBRUARY 7

My sister Elizabeth is torn with maternal pity and anxiety about
nephew Bruce [Hotchkiss] as well as his wife Dorothy. The latter knows
the fatal nature of her illness, but has illusions about how long she may
cling to life, and doesn't want to be put in a nursing home. Bruce sleeps
on a mattress on the floor near her bed, and she wakes him every little
while. He is a shadow of himself; even Dr. Goger is worried about him.
She thinks that people don't know. Isn't it strange how human beings can
adjust to agony, but almost never learn to let life go!

FEBRUARY 12

In the page margin of an old rough translation of Valery, words of my
own: "bright, energetic fountains."

Thus one might begin to write poetry all over again—poetry already
written is always the chief inspiration and matrix of poetry to come.

FEBRUARY 13

Astounding continuity and confoundedness of my life!—weighing
now downward toward my death by glorious contents of memory; everything simultaneous with the present moment. This indeed is the near
impossibility of my doing important work in the time I have left—too
much comes to mind constantly: fountain, flood, avalanche, torment of
leaves, wind in the waste-paper! Little assignments, such as book reviews,
keep me in check, but if I open my mind to the large forms of literature,
hell breaks loose; and even pages of my journal get unmanageable.

FEBRUARY 15

I am tired, tired, tired—not angry, not sorry for myself; but solemn. It is so hard to strike a balance between a healthy maintenance of the (so to speak) youthful aspect of one's life and the inevitable downgrade, the gradual, continual reduction and privation.

MARCH 18

[Re GW's *Life* magazine article on W. Somerset Maugham.]

I could not have let *Life* magazine's proposition go by, could I—their four million readers, *if* they all read; their one thousand bucks, perhaps payable on delivery of text, enabling me to pay Monroe some rent money that I promised, and to catch up on my pledge to Lloyd's hospital, and to buy a new dinner jacket. But now back to work—the Edith Sitwell review will take all the remaining time, deadline April 1; also I must revise "The Valley Submerged" for the anniversary issue of *The Southern Review* as promised—and keep the Maugham book ["The Old Party," planned but not completed] going. Whew!

MARCH 26

The Wasp Spared: At 5:10 a.m. in the kitchen, the first wasp of the year, large, silkily black, palpitant. I did not kill him; I took him in my handkerchief and loosed him at the back door in the dark soft rain.

APRIL 11

My birthdays henceforth will be days of mourning; never forgetting that they must be too few. I intend to distract myself from their universal grievance by my fortunate means: by writing, writing, writing, and by enjoyment of those I love.

APRIL 25

Re "The Stallions": Yesterday, a pair of teenage lovers, their romance crossed by disapproving parents, indicted suicide notes ("I want to be buried with Jack," etc.), set fire to a small thicket, lay down amid the flames, and perished, tightly clasped in each other's arms.

Suicide notes notwithstanding, one of the local policemen says that they have been trying to ascertain "whether it was a case of mutual suicide or just a tragic accident."

Trying to buckle down to "The Stallions," I have kept wondering whether I can make plausible and convincing the love-death of my teenagers, stark-naked in a parked car, asphyxiated by carbon monoxide gas while having intercourse. Inhibiting neurotic skepticism on the part of both law enforcement officer and would-be fiction writer.

In the pecking order at my back door only the purple grackles outrank the brown threshers. The mourning doves and the blue jays do not, though they too are heavy.

But the chief grackle, whose relations with my beloved couple of threshers I have been observing, is a fool as well as a bully. I have placed food for them in four places; having chased them from one place, he keeps following them to the next place: far sunflower seeds are the blackest, plumpest.

APRIL 26

I must go to Washington this week for a day, to cajole some senators about copyright reform, an important new bill, long worked on, coming to the vote—and, at the same time, to try to sweet-talk Katherine Anne Porter into not having me as her literary executor.

MAY 12

Back from Union College [in Schenectady, N.Y.], tired. Very little to report about my two days work except that all went well. I stayed in a large Philistine house, circa 1910, with all its ugly furniture, rugs, pictures and books intact; and there was not a single, practicable place at which I could have worked except the kitchen table. I worked hard at it; from 4:30 a.m. to 10 on Tuesday; from 6 a.m. to noon and 1 p.m. to 3 on Wednesday. "Memories of the Twenties" at 11 a.m. on Tuesday and a quizzing by creative students for two hours that afternoon. "Hemingway" at 4 p.m. on Wednesday, with a long, strenuous question period afterward. Lively, well-read courteous boys. Several serious youngish professors.

JUNE 5, 5:00 A.M.

Horror, horror! Our current astronauts in their fateful gyration have observed, the WABC newscaster announces, some "space junk," vestiges (already) of previous flights.

I asked John whether he had read Balanchine's credo in last week's *Life*. He admitted that he had, and gave me his scowl of extreme indignation.

"Did its anti-homosexual prejudice vex you?"

"Yes, of course. Naturally."

I then came back at him with an affectionate, mischievous, perhaps mysterious observation. "I suppose I am more tolerant of heterosexuality than you are."

JUNE 22

[To Katherine Anne Porter.]

I was really tormented by the [Thomas] Wolfe lampoon in the *Herald Tribune* magazine section, and twice took pen in hand to protest. I angrily put pen down because I regard it as a reprehensible publishing trick. Impecunious or meanly money-grubbing publications send out the rat Controversy on purpose; we chase it back to its hole; and, lo and behold, they have procured contributions from expensive authors, gratis.

I am the type of pantheist who believes that, generally speaking, even stones are alive. But some stones are dead, and deadly. All day long I have felt the fear of my sister Elizabeth's illnesses, one thing after another, as in the case of Job, on my mind and in my heart like a dead stone.

JULY 4

This morning an adolescent jack rabbit has visited our lawn for the first time; offspring of one of the couples that my brother bought and released last spring.

His tall ears catch the horizontal eastern light, gleaming snow-white.
He sits rather small and round, but in motion unfolds.

AUGUST 23

I am going out to the Fair tomorrow with Ned Rorem, to lunch with
Lou Ames, and to be taped for the latter's archives of creative personalities
for future NBC use. My thought was to tape and eat and run back to New
York, but it now turns out that Ned has never been to the Fair, and Lou
means to arrange a few key visits for us via the V.I.P. lounges, etc. Damn!

AUGUST 27–30

Three days and a half at David's with Walt. God's plenty; eight separate bouts of lovemaking.

Thrilling contrast of their bodies from hand to foot: Walt rosy-blond
and burly and exceedingly muscular though youthful looking, like a child
of giants, or infant Hercules. David darkly sunburned and lean; the
small of his back extraordinarily flexible. This is one of the secrets of his
virility at 40.

Corresponding thrilling contrast of their penises; both somehow
larger-looking than they are in fact, Walt's thicker, David's longer, Walt's
curved upward, David's almost straight out, the head somewhat weighing
down the shaft.

Thrilling to one's lips and tongue and throat when gorged by them,
the phalanges very sculptural, and the inner sinews very pronounced.

Which is nobler-looking: a race horse just past his prime, still at the
peak of his powers, or a young draft-horse still just in first possession
of his strength?

SEPTEMBER 16

[To Katherine Anne Porter.]

My brother is ill, or to put it more exactly, some sort of illness has
appeared in the x-rays of his lungs; tuberculosis perhaps. Baba and I are
trying not to panic or to be sorry for ourselves. I kept it from Monroe
as he flew abroad, in order not to worry him about us.

The other night Monroe's flight was delayed for an hour and a half, so we observed his fellow-travelers: about a hundred balmy, daffy, dotty provincial women calling themselves the "Fate Psychic Group," their bosoms all so labeled.

I shared a taxi back with two pleasant Chicago businessmen who quizzed me about what business I am in—I never dare to lie—and when I told them the truth one of them asked if I had ever heard of a writer with whom he had gone to school: namely, John Horne Burns. *Was* it true he committed suicide, he wanted to know. They were thrilled to hear that *The Gallery* was dedicated to my sister.

SEPTEMBER 17

[To Monroe.]

They sent Lloyd to a famous Doctor Wylie at Presbyterian Hospital, who has a full schedule for a month ahead but will operate just as soon as he can fit him in. Of course we have been thinking of it as cancer but speaking of it as tuberculosis. Last night Lloyd and Baba dined here and he spoke frankly. It may be a kind of tuberculosis that is operable, and they are already giving him the wonder-medication for that; and that is what Lloyd thinks it is or feels it is. The moving thing is to observe that despite his talk this long while, about not wanting to grow old, he now suddenly realized that he wants above all to live forever—like me!— not counting the cost, mustering up every ounce of his strength, every flicker of his spirit, to fight to the death.

SEPTEMBER 22

[To Monroe.]

In a sense all our lives are a unity. We shall all die a little in one another's deaths. Each of us will survive in the other's life and mind.

SEPTEMBER 30

At the Trenton railroad station, in the large, respectable though un-tidy men's room, at the far end of the urinals—I was urinating at the near end—a well-dressed, pleasant-looking youngish man, perhaps a businessman, stood brandishing his large semi-erect cock, half-turned to me, manipulating it in my direction. I only allowed myself one good look at this as I re-zipped my trousers and departed, up the stairs and out to my Lambertville bus. There was only one other person in the men's room at the time: a skinny young soldier repacking his suitcase, not within sight of the Priapic youngish businessman. Could the latter possibly have preferred elderly me to the young serviceman? Or was I expected to be a catalyst between them, triangularly?

What a comfort it is, in the autumn of life, to not be overstimulated by trivial eroticisms of this kind, the little everyday pornographics of the American way of life.

OCTOBER

Baba told me last night that there would be a great comet in the sky this morning, between moonset and sunrise—now the moon has gone down and the sun is imminent, and I haven't been able to discover any such thing. Come to think of it, I am always rather blind to things in the sky. Day before yesterday, Baba saw a hundred geese, low and very loud.

No comet but gold in the sky, silver mist all over the fields—and a passing, non-resident mocking bird, pianissimo.

The world is so beautiful, and I am such a fool, and I shall always be inconsolable because we all have to die.

OCTOBER 4

I took Will Chandlee and Bernard Perlin to the ballet last week with supper afterward. The latter in great looks, excessively lean and vulturine, like one of T. E. Lawrence's awful Arab band in *Seven Pillars of Wisdom*; but how heavy drinking, how punitive toward everyone, how conscience-stricken, how sorrowful—I am worried about him. But he reports that his nudes are going forward now apace. It is almost intolerable for an artist to be unfashionable during a boom, the one Jew on whom no manna falls. Will on the other hand at his best: his weight reduced, his pinkness more childlike, his eyes more sparkling, his entire attitude now affectionate. Due, I dare say, to his co-residence with the Persian gentleman.

Though he feels caged, nevertheless he gets more pleasure with less roaring around town, more sleep, less drink.

OCTOBER 5

Zachary Scott has died in Texas. John tells me that he had a brain tumor operation in mid-summer. It won't suit Ruth [Ford] to be a widow.

A long, pathetic and rather daffy talk on the telephone with Porter—she called me. She hadn't taken in most of the information in my last two letters, and lamented, "Oh, dear, I am afraid that I am losing my memory, I have been so ill, I have so many terrible problems, interruptions and interferences." Her latest ailments are psoriasis and arthritis. Nevertheless she seemed all set to deliver her lecture at the Library of Congress, and to attend the ensuing reception. I advised her to sit down at a table, or at least to have both table and lectern equipped with microphones, but she said, "Don't you know, darling, I have emphysema and I can catch my breath better when I am standing up." Once more, she says that this is to be her very last lecture. Once more she will wear her long white dress and cloud-like blue silk cloak. They are paying her a thousand dollars. She has turned down sixteen other engagements at that fee in the course of the year.

She concluded with ten or fifteen minutes of violent paranoidal plaintiveness about never having had any prizes or honors, never having been recognized by any of the literary organizations, "not even by that ragbag of yours, what's it called, that we are now bugging Eleanor Clark into, by main force."

OCTOBER 6

A beautiful little boy named Hank Young who mows my poor lawn has a bow and arrow and goes hunting with the Polish neighbor boys; the bow-and-arrow season has begun. I hope they don't kill or half-kill the doe who kisses my hand. The human species is unique, I suppose, in that it is both predatory and the opposite.

I felt positively honored to have Balanchine dance his Don Q for us, once more! How I envy him: an old creative man, in love once more, enacting his age and his passion himself, with the beloved in person in that garish popular theatre full of grand-bourgeoisie.

It is what I long to be doing now that I too am old (older than Balanchine, am I not?), and there is a tradition and precedent for it in literature, of course—but not for homosexuals; we have no applicable myths, and our up-to-date plots are dangerous, even to innocent bystanders.

Truman [Capote] says that his "new" form, more or less new—the non-fictitious novel—will serve for a great variety of subject matter. I wonder if he is thinking of homosexuality, probably not. In any event, all our shameless, hard-hitting fiction is about our submerged classes: hustling in Bryant Park or Times Square, kicking prostitutes to death, murder mysteries in Kansas—they are fair prey; they can only fight each other, they can't fight back at us.

OCTOBER 15

Lloyd's operation: When they finally wheeled Lloyd down the corridor we still had to wait outside his door until the nurses and the orderly got him settled, with the saline solution in his arm and the little tubes of plumbing under the bed. And then I let Baba go in by herself, but as I stood there, suddenly found myself unintentionally seeing their two faces through the crack in the door; eternal voyeur! I hadn't moved, the crack just happened. I heard his hoarse croak, asking what Dr. Wylie had removed. "It was a tumor," she answered, and he made a great grimace, with downward lips, like our mother.

They had to remove the lower lobe of one lung with the malignant tumor. Baba doesn't want the six letter word used for the moment, until Lloyd has heard it himself. The surgeon said that he regarded the operation as very successful. The prognosis is good.

OCTOBER 24

Did Stendhal really say and/or write, "Beauty is the promise of happiness." The master of one of the finest, fastest styles in the vast assortment of French literature, surely in some ways he was an ass.

NOVEMBER 3

Reply to a fan letter on the reprinting of *The Grandmothers:* Thank you for your letter. As you may know, an author doesn't often hear from any reader of an old book, even when it has been republished. To this day I do not understand why I haven't as many readers as some other writers, or, on the other hand, what makes my own true readers so responsive, so faithful. A mystery, not a complaint.

I have had the most privileged literary life; in some ways I am happier in it now than I have been in many years, and I have a deep and particular feeling about the unknown persons I write for.

NOVEMBER 6

To a student: I think *The Pilgrim Hawk* is my most original. Perhaps *The Grandmothers* is more important, and *Apartment in Athens* more skillful.

NOVEMBER 23

[Re Truman Capote dinner and *In Cold Blood.*]

How often writers, perhaps especially American writers, seem less intelligent than what they have written. On the other hand, Truman's account of *how* he did it was superb: problems and technicalities of the research particularly, releases from everyone for example, in order not to face libel suits when the movie is made, releases in *his* name, so that Columbia Pictures will have to mind him to the end.

Anita Loos telephoned me just now, exuberantly grateful for the evening. "That little man is a giant," she said. (I agree; he is original, decisive, indefatigable, brave as a lion.) "You are my only connection with the worthwhile world. For the most part I spend my life with trashy people, as indeed Truman does also."

DECEMBER 22

I shall be glad to see the last of 1965, a year of knocking myself out and losing ground.

1966

JANUARY 4

"A Book in a New Form Earns $2 Million for Truman Capote" (*New York Times*, December 31, 1965): A pleasant reminder of Thornton Wilder's advice to me—vide p. 255 of *Images of Truth*—about getting on the news pages, not just the book pages. But this is the first time that anyone ever got a headline in the *Times* about a literary *form*. Of course money, nowadays, is the news-worthiest matter; the jackpot that may come about if and when one has played at publicity well enough, long enough. Could he have done it without *The New Yorker*? He now claims that he could have. Could he have done it without Broadway and Hollywood?

For my part, the only thing that I am going to be able to pride myself on is having written in such a way as to *disqualify* myself from the big money. It isn't a merit; only a distinction, a characteristic.

JANUARY 7

My only important complaint of *In Cold Blood* is his excess of objectivity at the end, his not having the courage to bring himself on stage, witnessing the hangings, conquering the environing society, doing the work, made not only an anticlimax but a blur. A masterwork, nevertheless.

JANUARY 8

Beginning to pick up a great number of misplaced or unplaced books around the house, I reread and was charmed by Harold Nicolson's *Tennyson*. Late in life, that awful man of genius said, "The first poetry that moved me was my own at five years old."

JANUARY 11

[To Monroe.]

Janet Flanner asked if you were basically, subterraneously, responsible for the revived interest in Turner, in England as elsewhere—and ditto in Bonnard before that, and in Matisse hereafter. I shouldn't put it like that; it is a matter of the zeitgeist—you are the one, perhaps the only one, who knows what is going on in the minds of art lovers, and how that relates to what went on in the minds of artists themselves.

FEBRUARY 7

Amid the dazzling snow at the back door where I have placed trays of seed and an orange and two tomatoes, approximately four and twenty starlings, and in their midst, one burningly beautiful cardinal.

FEBRUARY 13

After television appearance: Eric Goldman asked Janet Flanner to explain the political divisiveness of the French, the plurality of their political parties. Said Janet: "Yes, France reminds you of an orange, segments enclosed in a skin. There is nothing apple-like about it." When I complimented her later, she asked, "Who said that? It's very good!"

"You did."

"I did. When?"

Most talkers listen to themselves.

FEBRUARY 19

Foxes mate at the end of January. Purple grackles arrive from the South at the end of February. Indians call February the Hunger Moon.

FEBRUARY 20

Thoreau was some sort of prude. Having visited Whitman, he wrote his opinion of *Leaves of Grass*: "It does not celebrate love at all. It is as if the beasts spoke. I think that men have not been ashamed of themselves without reason."

Is Marshall McLuhan of the University of Toronto to be taken as seriously as a writer, or is he just a university journalist, experimenting professorial paradox in non-English, so as to impress youngsters?

MARCH 23

In memory of Stone-blossom, an image out of Graves' *The Greek Myths*. One year we had a blizzard in April. The springtime followed it immediately, with remains of snow still lying on the hilltops like a vast, pale, dead body—over which three vultures kept slowly circling, spiraling.

MARCH 28

The way Jesus Christ taught, by means of disjointed sentences or very brief paragraphs, arresting, memorable, sometimes mysterious, was well established in Eastern tradition. It is sometimes called gnomic—the Greek word "gnome" means "a wise saying." A great deal of our secular, aphoristic literature derives from this. The word oracular—"uttered or delivered as if divinely inspired or infallible; sententious"—is also relevant, but that way folly and religiosity and other darkness lie.

I love aphorisms as other men love poetry. For my desert island, even in a minimum book bag, Logan Pearsall Smith's *Treasury*.

APRIL 11

This is my sixty-fifth birthday—the onset of old age recognized by law. "Retirement is the dirtiest word in the language," as Hemingway told Hotchner. For those of us to whom it doesn't apply, such as writers, there is a special pang, dread and (sometimes) self-commiseration. No one disqualifies us, no one except ourselves.

APRIL 13

Another ill-started morning; let it be a lesson to me, but it is an old refrain in my life and in my mind. Knowledge, including self-knowledge, is only a part of any education process; the other part, which is often decisive, is discipline, practice.

APRIL 17

Last night, New York: At the end, three-way orgasm, come to think of it. I lost track of Lou just at the close, and he came a minute or two too soon but stayed in our boy, banging him with all his strong maleness, and sexual kindness—female-trained. I didn't realize that he had come until afterward, concentrating on my own weary body and watching Don.

After that, I staggered to my feet and went to the bathroom and came back with a wet warm towel. They hadn't moved—Lou pressed in all the way and holding tight, blissful, without a sound, not even panting, his eyes bright, full of light; and Don hoarsely whispering something, purring, growling, and indeed they reminded me of my black backdoor cats at Haymeadows.

APRIL 20

NYC Ballet: Tchaikovsky-Hayden's *Meditation*, Suzanne Farrell and Jacques D'Amboise. This last adagio is one of the greatest experiences of dancing in my lifetime—one of Balanchine's absolute masterpieces. Thus, in the lyric, amorous expression—beyond the capacities of poetry or any other art—ballet's uniqueness. Just before dancing it, D'Amboise was invited to say what it meant to him: The Russian sadness, and the fact that Russians take pleasure in feeling sad. Balanchine quickly, quietly contradicted: "That is not so, no pleasure, no enjoyment at all." I should say the opposite of both: No sadness at all, except that in the rapture of the senses, the double tenderness, two-in-one, there is a kind of heavy-heartedness in the partaking of something eternal. Naturally one wants to be eternal and the heart knows that one cannot. In this sense, the maximum of delight and the maximum of regret, and in great measure one arising from the other.

APRIL 23

Dostoyevsky upon his first visit to Italy spent a week in Florence but never once visited the Uffizi; he stayed in his hotel room and read the four volumes of *Les Misérables*.

JUNE 2

The Academy-Institute of Arts and Letters vis-à-vis the National Council on the Arts: We have chosen to be the tail wagged by the federal dog; partly because we haven't the strength to do our own wagging. Many of us are weary, for one thing, having to moonlight our whole lives.

We are like a rich heiress (culturally rich) who was in love with Kennedy, fancied herself his fiancée, though he hadn't exactly popped the question, and is now under pressure to marry a great parvenu.

JUNE 11–12

The best kind of happiness is that which can lift one up over a sadness, happiness like wings.

JUNE 23

An evening of the kind of sociability that in the course of our lifetime Monroe and I have developed: perfect. Marianne Moore, P. Lal, the Punjabi teacher and poet, Emilienne Dermit [the sister of Cocteau's companion Edouard], Robert Phelps, and Isaac and Alma Bashevis Singer.

JULY 30

At Kinsey Institute for Sex Research, Bloomington, Indiana. Lonesome. Because I came here on short notice there was no room for me on the campus. I am in a luxury room in a motor hotel, awake at 5:30 a.m., no breakfast until seven. I am hungry, hungry in more ways than one. Sex at the Institute for Sex Research, at this late date—I first came here in 1949—isn't very personal or enervating or exalting. I am now a kind of visiting professor, an "authority," not a guinea pig. But it points me in the amorous direction, like a weather vane, and it is wind, not rain. The tired intellect gets lonesome for the body.

AUGUST

An early impression of Cocteau, in my letter to Bernadine Szold, October 6, 1925, Villefranche: "Cocteau is here: cool and subtle fireworks, serious, indolent, and sound. He has the tiniest boat in the harbor, and in billowy pajama pants of waxed black silk, which once belonged to Yvonne George, rows across the sleepy water with a handsome, sturdy boyfriend."

.

AUGUST 25

Science is tripartile: exploratory, explanatory, experimental. For example, respectively, zoology (including sex research), sociology, nuclear physics.

SEPTEMBER 1

Someone has calculated that today we left behind two-thirds of our century, enter into the last third.

SEPTEMBER 11

Often we are not able to evaluate the literature and art of our time as posterity will. Keep an open mind, if you can.

I seem to remember that Poe admired Tennyson, but Felicia Hemans also touched him to the heart. Van Gogh ranked Millet with Rembrandt.

Enmity makes mistakes; so does friendship. Naturally Sainte-Beuve abhorred Victor Hugo, whose wife he wanted, but he was no less scornful of Balzac and Baudelaire. Flaubert overrated George Sand; Edith Wharton underrated Henry James.

SEPTEMBER 18

Monroe was given the Legion of Honor by French President Vincent Auriel on his presidential visit to this country in the spring of 1951. Virgil [Thomson] and Mina [Kirstein Curtiss] also have received it. I envy it and in a way (my way) have deserved it. Too late now.

For a Frenchman the honor is not great; Tom, Dick and Harry have it. Foreign recipients constitute an elite, interestingly assorted.

SEPTEMBER 29

Travel, as I conceive it, desire it, not for sociability—which would take too long and rouse loose floods of unmanageable, unchanneled memory (as in 1952)—but to see things, especially paintings.

E.g., the *Danaë* and the *Prodigal Son* in Leningrad, the *Conspiracy* in Stockholm.

OCTOBER 4

I seem to have lost my M.M. [Marianne Moore] diary.

Horror! A sort of horror that is apt to be more and more frequent in the great ebb tide of age, but it can be greatly alleviated by using my intellect, devising little devices and disciplines.

OCTOBER 7

I learn that there is a fish in Florida, the belted sandfish, which in ten seconds is able to change from male to female—the male striped, the female unstriped—then in ten seconds change back from female to male, according to the circumstances and mood of its lovemaking.

OCTOBER 20

[To Janet Flanner.]

Truman Capote's Black and White Ball: When I dined alone with Truman last week, he discoursed to me for an hour about what the ball means to him: the dream, the technique, the powerfulness, the expense, and finally, the troubles and quarrels. It is costing him $35,000. A number of his favorite great ladies have been making a terrible issue of being allowed to bring friends or relatives of theirs who are going to have nervous breakdowns if they are left out. He can't allow them to do so, because it isn't just a party, it is a creation with its standards and inherent rules, and one of the rules is that no one, no one, was to be included whom he personally did not know and like, and felt liked by. Furthermore, he can have *only* (sic) five hundred people, because the ballroom at the Plaza has room for only so many tables. To hear him on the subject, one might think it another sort of nonfiction novel, just as fantastically documented as the tragedy of the Clutters; non-written, consisting of flesh and blood and money, and of orchestras black and white, and jet planes from everywhere, and black and/or white ball-dresses, with masks, some of them custom-made, against an all-red background—a vast mosaic of all the components of our civilization, government, finance, the mass media, the arts, international luxury, etc. Every name on his list, he assured me, would signify something to me, even to me, an elderly country mouse—except those who were just pretty girls and their husbands and/or lovers. "I realized that you couldn't give a ball without a lot of youth and beauty," Truman said, "and I made a kind of collection of that, little by little."

He really isn't a snob, as I define it, or if he is, it works both ways; he confers, while being conferred upon.

OCTOBER 23

The last dream of the old scientist in Ingmar Bergman's *Wild Strawberries*: "I stood by the water and shouted toward the bay, but the warm summer breeze carried away my cries, and they did not reach their destination. Yet I was not sorry about that; I felt on the contrary, rather light-headed." Does this not somewhat allude to the immortal echo of Isaac Newton, the greatest scientist of all?

As I remember that excellent film referred to the frustrations and shortcomings of his character in old age—alienated from everyone dear to him, of two minds about everything, extremely rational on the one hand, subject to eruptions of black humor and cruelty on the other hand—not a matter of limitations of his life work.

But it seems to serve as an image of my literary art, with its peaceful sense of the infinite, its strong self-assertion of my rather classical style of writing. The slightness of my success—against the hurly burly of popularity in this our somewhat vulgar era—allows a certain pleasure in the end result, a strange satisfaction and compensatory effect.

OCTOBER 30

[Re writers block with "The Old Party."]

Sunrise—delayed for an hour, the annual putting back of the clock— a flamboyant sunrise, orange and blue, pink and purple, auguring rain, and I stood staring at it, sick of my Maugham book, disheartened and not really capable.

"Can they unburn me?" said Joan of Arc (Shaw's Joan?) appearing to her king in a dream.

In the glorious, risky enterprise of literature, one makes a distinction between art and craft, between inspiration and skill. But be not misled—both are essential, neither amounts to anything without the other.

NOVEMBER 1

Educators, please note (posterity, please note): the vulgarity of a great part of our cultural explosion. Advertisement: "He was generous . . . timid . . . stubborn . . . lonely . . . impassioned . . . bitter . . . and blessed with the most splendid talent of his age. Will you invite Michelangelo into your home for 10 days—while Time Life Books pays his expenses?"

NOVEMBER 10

To Marjorie (Wescott) Barrows in San Francisco: "My beloved sister, Lloyd says that you desire to have letters from me, not being capable of much occupation or distracting during your ordeal of illness. It shook me to learn that you now have shingles in and/or around your eyes; horrible herpes zoster! Monroe was affected by it in that same way, years ago. I can't remember when; he was still at 410 Park Avenue. His doctor said to him: 'I must warn you of two dangers particular to this disease, because of the demoralizing pain: (a) drug addiction and (b) suicide.' Sometimes he would dash out of his apartment, down to the avenue, and up and down; and I would run after him, for fear of his stumbling in front of a car. And yet he recovered from it, in a couple of months. I hope that your doctors are kind, as to the relief of the pain. What's wrong with a little drug addiction?"

Going to the opera tonight with Beulah—but how painful our feeling about our dying sister will be!

NOVEMBER 13

The crazy boy in Arizona, crazy à la mode, who shot seven women all at the same time in a beauty parlor, killed five of them and was arrested, laughing. Premeditated. One of the two survivors played dead, fooled him. Of course she learned that by reading about the mass murder of the nurses in Chicago. That was probably his point of departure also. He explained that he wanted to make himself known. The worst cliché of the age: identity.

The oddest thing about the Supremes: three very different girls, with contrasting voices, yet always expressing an intensely individual emotion, or narrating a very personal event: "Get out of *my* life / And let *me* sleep at night."

DECEMBER 4

My beautiful niece has just divorced the father of her beautiful little girls and married a man who by all accounts and to all appearances is cruel and dangerous. The divorced one, in a vengeful spirit, with the excuse of extreme anxiety about the babes, is thinking of kidnapping them or otherwise exacting his emotions, one mischief leading to another. I must write him a letter that may have a deterring, calming effect.

Katherine Anne Porter, with a new team of professional advisers around her sick bed, seems inclined to blow up the project of a volume of our lifelong correspondence, on which I have done some work.

The Institute of Sex Research [Kinsey's successors] is about to begin a consequential study of homosexuality, with government financing, and, under the influence of two new youngish, inexperienced, university sociologists whom I know, is about to make certain mistakes, which I have been asked to counteract.

I am a ridiculous old fellow because, for a writer of my particular talent, the life I lead is ridiculous—or vice versa!

DECEMBER 7

I have, at last, consented to Monroe's plan, Pauline's plan, of my going to Mouton [Rothschild] for Christmas week; and therefore I must reduce my life to nothing but Maugham and (if and if and if) love, sex, which helps. Dinner parties and art exhibitions and cocktail parties, and meetings of the Institute and the Academy and the Authors' Guild and Authors' League, and sex research, and letter writing, all to be foresworn, bypassed—beginning tomorrow—or day after tomorrow.

DECEMBER 22

The weakness of evil men—and sometimes (it seems) our only defense against them—is that they go too far.

DECEMBER 23

Arriving in London. To Mouton Rothschild tomorrow. This is my first European trip since 1952.

1967

JANUARY 4

Paris, after December 24–January 4 visit to Mouton. Awake at six, in a cold room at the Hotel Vendome. Not having written a simple letter since I left home, not one, I got up for that purpose and made some instant coffee with lukewarm tap water and sat in my overcoat, desultorily reading, then trying to write, but found my talent ruined by the incessant conversation morning, noon and night at Mouton. Just halfway through my obligatory holiday I am homesick, but let me not repine, in order to enjoy the museum-going, Poussins and Rembrandts I have dreamed of seeing.

JANUARY 7

En route by train to meet Pauline de Rothschild in the Hague and Rotterdam. Holland is snow-clad, every twig an inch thick, and wrapped in bright white fog—bright enough, I hope to see Proust's Vermeer and my Rembrandt (*Saul and David*).

Monroe looks out the train window, impatient—this is a slow train— then laughs. At what? Sheep thatched with snow.

Paris was unbelievable. The Louvre broke my heart. I went to tea at Marie-Louise Bousquet, who narrated a visit last spring by Brother Pascal, my bygone unavailing Jean Bourgoint. We had drinks with Jacques Guérin, who narrated seventeen years of involvement with Violette Leduc in half a dozen well-practiced anecdotes.

The wonderful thing about traveling with Monroe is that he schedules more than he can endure to do, in fact, more than I would consent to, and then does it; and he conceives it so well that I enjoy it. For example, after the big Picasso show on our last afternoon—he didn't hesitate to schedule it for the last afternoon—he induced me to visit the Rue de Beaux-Arts, up one side of the street and down the other, when we should have been at the Hotel Vendome getting our bags together, paying our bill.

JANUARY 15

At Haymeadows. My European excursion was partly paid for by Pauline de Rothschild, ten days at their great vineyard, Mouton, and partly by Monroe, recklessly loving and generous. I scarcely wanted to go, as I am in the midst of my Maugham memoir, tired of it and afraid of not getting it done; but they wouldn't take no for an answer, and it was fantastically worthwhile. My first visit to Paris since 1952, my first journey with Monroe since 1938!

JANUARY 17

Morning after an evening of efficacious love-making (Lou and Larry and Sam)—the first such evening in a month—while putting the apartment in order, while washing the dishes, not only do I desire to record some of the singularities and humors and beauties of the event, but I am inspired to write to Pauline and Katherine Anne, dutifully, and to Clara Svennson (*Images of Truth*, 161–62) and to Bernard. Would that I could write with several limbs, as Siva dances!

JANUARY 19

Monroe back from Nuremberg; dinner at the Gold Coin—this in a fortune cookie: "Counsel after action is like rain after harvest," which, with reference to our relations with our youngsters, made us laugh.

JANUARY 22

As David and I were preparing for bed—with warm affection and voluptuousness but no spark to light our sense—the doorbell rang.

There, unannounced, a recent playmate of his and Walter's, not knowing Walter had gone to Rio, wanting pleasure, surprised to find me. Windfall and manna from the heavens.

FEBRUARY 4

My early morning euphoric, brainy talk is Monroe's delight. But it is an anguish to him if I begin it too soon before he gets his mind in focus, while he is reading his *Times*.

On the telephone to Robert Phelps, who returned from Paris night before last, I said, "How are you? You must be careful not to fall ill as a result of coming back to the U.S. Inverse patriotism is a kind of pneumonia."

"Oh," said Robert, "I'm almost recovered from that." Note the difference between forty and sixty. It took me three weeks to recover.

Bishop Sheen has on sale in subway stations a good-sized paperback titled *Guide to Contentment*. I remember that, one Christmas eve during World War II, he began a broadcast by saying, "Almost two thousand years ago tonight, Eternity established its beachhead in Bethlehem." I mockingly complained of this to Anne McCormick and Padraic Colum, not stopping to think that they were both pious Catholics. Padraic laughed aloud: "Oh, what a vulgar man! I can remember how he first made himself a reputation during World War I. He called the Virgin Mary, 'the first Gold Star mother in history.'"

FEBRUARY 11

[To Barbara and Lloyd in Mexico City.]

Marianne Moore has had another slight stroke and her guardian angels have provided her with a pretty nurse who sleeps in. We went to see her last week and will do so again this afternoon. We are lunching with Josephine Crane and Padraic Column on Sunday. Our world grows old.

FEBRUARY 24

Velasquez. One of the artists at the court of Philip IV, an academic mannerist of Italian extraction named Vincente Larducho, was especially jealous and disapproving of Velasquez, alluding to him as a "monster of dexterity and naturalness."

One day the fond king said to Velasquez, "They claim that heads are the only thing you know how to paint." The young master replied, "This does me great honor, Sire, for to this day I have never seen a head well painted."

MARCH 11

Due to longevity and intimate communications between the old and the young, the mind sometimes has illusions of striding through time. My father's grandfather was born in 1800, and in 1902 held me in his arms. Padraic Colum had his first play produced in Dublin the year I was born. Oscar Wilde died in Paris while I was in my mother's womb.

MARCH 16

Vermeer and Velasquez: Van Gogh, who loved Vermeer, "this strange artist," speaks of him as characterized by a color scheme of lemon yellow, light blue, and pear grey, plus black and white, whereas Velasquez, for the most part, delighted in black, white and pinkish grey.

Some fool of a collector once upon a time disliked the great pearl in the ear of Vermeer's Lady with a Lute (now in the Metropolitan) and had a more elaborate earring painted over it.

MARCH 28

[Re the Maugham project.]

I note as I go along that I keep including a good deal of landscape, weather, flora and fauna, and various country still life, which a more formal author would cut out (Maugham himself surely). But just as sensual pleasure is a relief from one's intellect and will power, nature worship offers a surcease to preoccupation with human nature. Also, in the great wild light of outdoors one can suggest emotion and premonition and mysticism that can scarcely be stated in so many words.

MARCH 31

At Mouton Rothschild we drank seventy wines in ten days, three with lunch, four with dinner, not counting pre-prandial and post-prandial champagne—followed by Paris and Amsterdam and London, three days each. It was a bad idea, with respect to my work. My life, as often before, out of context—but let me not knock it.

APRIL 11

[To Pauline.]

My birthday. On April 11, 1926, I was in Vienna with Monroe—it was very hot, humid, Guardi-looking—and he was ill. I was afraid of his dying then and there. In fact he had a perforated appendix. We got to Vienna just in time.

APRIL 15

One of the few things I really enjoy about being my own housekeeper (*bonne à tout faire*, to be exact) is putting away washed dishes and utensils, because I am somewhat ambidextrous. Picking up two objects at a time, placing them on the right-hand shelf and the left-hand shelf, whichever is handiest, gives me a pleasant sensation in the pit of my stomach.

APRIL 28

[To Katherine Anne Porter.]

While I was in town, word came that Monroe's beautiful, ancient, distracted, paralyzed mother had died. So, having got back here with Baba after midnight, I am about to go back, by bus and train, to fly out with Monroe. His saintly, ancient, almost deaf, almost blind father will be deeply stricken.

MAY 8

Lloyd's erotic curiosity about the sculpture of a multi-armed god and clinging goddess in the Brundage collection in San Francisco—were they actually joined in intercourse or in pre-coital or post-coital embrace? Several times he crouched quickly to glance up under their minimal vestments, but the sound of footsteps of an approaching guard or other museum visitor prevented this. At last he succeeded—they were in coitus, maleness and femaleness, thrust and vessel, were rendered in detail.

MAY 22

The worst aspect of family life for me is a kind of bad manners. I am hot-tempered, and violently intellectual, unintentionally arrogant. Monroe is cold and hypercritical and dictatorial. To put it very simply, I am hot-tempered and he is cold. Baba is in a phase of seething, masochistic irritability, more self-centered than I have ever known her to be. I can understand why; understanding never helps. Better manners, even on my part alone, might help.

MAY 24

[Presenting the Gold Medal for Fiction to Katherine Anne Porter.]

She has never projected herself upon her fictitious characters in the way of hero-worship or villain-hatred; but she had found their characteristics for the most part in the depths of her introspection, on frontiers of personal experience. Someone once asked Flaubert, "Who was Madam Bovary?" "I was!" he answered. "Moi!" Likewise, surely in *Ship of Fools*, Miss Porter was the fierce girl trying to be in love, the condesa pursued by furies, even the wild children, the Gemini, Ric and Rack, the folk sculptor whittling his miniature animals, for whose burial at sea the spiritual-looking whales passed along the horizon, even, as she herself once said in jest, even the seasick white bulldog.

MAY 26

The gold wig worn by Nijinski in *L'Apres-midi d'un Faune* is to be sold at Sotheby's on June 13.

That performance shocked its early audiences. Not only did Diaghilev's dear dancer electrify the audience by unmistakable pelvic thrusts upon the garment of the nymph, he outfit himself (I remember Cocteau saying) with a conspicuous false penis inside his tight leotards.

I remember during the late thirties a bookseller named Gabriel Wells offered for sale the penis of Napoleon pickled in alcohol (with authenticity documents). It was small. The other day I heard someone refer to its present whereabouts and ownership, but I let the information go in one ear and out the other.

JUNE 2

I have been acting as a go-between in the process of getting Pauline [de Rothschild]'s Russian journal published . . . unbelievable talks on the telephone, Venice to New York, Haymeadows to the Avenue d'Iéna.

JUNE 29

In newspaper: The manager of a sado-masochistic establishment in New Jersey. Does she not look like Hugh Walpole? A. C. Kinsey one told me that the cruelest sadist he ever discovered was a woman. He made contact with her through an advertisement in *The Saturday Review*.

JULY 15–16

Grand Adagio: Three matchless performances of sexual love, Saturday afternoon, Saturday night, Sunday afternoon. The beauty of their contrasted complexions—B's sun-darkened Eastern Mediterranean tawnyness, D's young face, unique in expression, still simple despite his sophistication, his violently sensual life. Continuous desire on all three parts with scarcely any suspense, with no impatience. Two overwhelmingly profound orgasms in my case, in the doorway just out of sight, or almost out of sight.

JULY 29

A good many of my odd pieces of reminiscent prose reveal the fact that in my later life I have become what is called a voyeur. Vicariousness as well as spectatorship. Many a time the facial beauty of one of my dear ones in increasing blissfulness has so seized my imagination that I have missed the exact erotic action. My excitement is apt to be aesthetic, affectionate, psychological; not altogether sexual. My imagination can adopt, borrow and wield the phallus of my friend.

Last night teenagers rioting in the Bedford-Stuyvesant area of Brooklyn shouted at Negro policemen: "Take off your black mask. Show us your white face."

AUGUST 4

George Washington in his will specified that all disputes were to be resolved by three arbitrators who were not to consult any lawyers.

AUGUST 20

[From GW's presentation of the MacDowell Medal to Marianne Moore.]

In both prose and verse, sincerity is surely one of her key characteristics. Sometimes it is indistinguishable from her spontaneity. Sometimes spontaneity takes the lead and brings about inner circumstances in which to be sincere is the only honorable, indeed the only reasonable attitude the mind can take. Spontaneity dives, sincerity then has to swim.

E. MacKnight Kauffer complained that his wife had never liked Baudelaire, to which Marianne replied, "Well, Edward, neither do I. I put up with him because I have to," and added, a moment later, perhaps in explanation, "I always need to be helped upward into a more optimistic atmosphere."

SEPTEMBER 3–4

A very large weekend, though so brief. L. [Larry] and M. [Martin] arrived by bus at noon. I went with Ethel to meet them. After lunch we visited the barns, they swam, I cooked. Baba dined with us and we went to the country fair. After that we sat up very late, talking, talking. Next morning, after I brought them breakfast in bed, they shamelessly began to make love, gladly calling my attention to each other's beauty and sexual power of intercourse. It was thrilling. It thrilled me.

We dined at Barbara's and went to the movies.

At about midnight we made love: that is, to be precise, M. fucked L. to climax (L. expressed a desire for the reverse of their roles but Martin insisted), then when he had come, held Larry in his arms while I sucked him to climax. It was wonderful, a ravishing experience, perfect for me, except that it went too fast. No matter. I shall relive it and relive it.

SEPTEMBER 8

Long ago I came upon the fact or fancy that young temple prostitutes in India learn to leap out of bed after intercourse and by a particular vigorous belly dance to prevent conception. Sometimes I am afraid that my muse is like that.

SEPTEMBER 16

To Marjorie Wescott: Think how many novels I have aborted; packages of scribble that took years to write, waste of time! *The Pilgrim Hawk* took less than four months. Now here I sit, flogging myself through "The Old Party," because by chance, I got to be the absolute authority on the subject matter of it (William Maugham), and because it seems likely to make a packet of money which, despite Baba's wonderful generosity, I need. But I am inclined to think that, in the end, I shall be known not for that, not for *The Grandmothers* or *Apartment in Athens*, but for my so-called journal, marginal pages or half-pages about this or that, some of them only half written.

SEPTEMBER 20

Early influences—in reply to a New York City high school principal: On the family farm in Wisconsin books were few and had great impact. Someone gave us the first three of L. Frank Baum's *Oz* books; after which my sisters and I wanted more of that dream-world, and at age nine or ten I pretended to revisit it in my sleep, and every few days narrated to them what happened there. That must have been the first stirring of a talent for fiction.

An aunt in Milwaukee sent us back issues of one of the Hearst magazines in which the popular problem novels of Hall Caine were serialized: *The Woman Thou Gavest Me, The Christian.* At age 12 it thrilled me to read about moral temptations and religious scruples and other controversial themes.

At age 16, Walt Whitman was revealed to me, great literature at last, and I composed a series of love letters in the style of his "Song of Myself" and "Calamus."

Then I read all or almost all of the novels of Henry James; another dream-world, devoted to profuse and subtle talkativeness and hot house emotions.

D. H. Lawrence's *Sons and Lovers*, which reminded me of my mother's charm and superiority, and of the maladjustments between my farmer father and myself, influenced the novel that I began as a freshman at the University of Chicago, age 18, and finally finished and published six years later.

OCTOBER 11

To Philippe de Rothschild: I am in Washington, spending 24 hours with Katherine Anne Porter, who is in declining health. I had to telephone her twice yesterday, mid-morning, to make sure that she felt well enough to be visited, and mid-afternoon, because my train was an hour late. She was asleep both times, and by the time I arrived, at six, she had dropped off again. I had to shout under her bedroom window; her servant didn't stay the night. But then instantly we had a bottle of champagne and ate wonderfully well. I wish that I could steal away without broaching, what she and her publishers have asked me to broach: the volume of our letters to be edited by me, for remuneration, some of which I have already received and spent. I do not believe it will get done in her lifetime. She lately talked about her revolutionary youth in Mexico to a Mexican journalist who took it down on tape, and (it appears) he has now put words in her mouth, anti-gringo, pro-Villa, pro-Castro; lawsuits or worse are pending.

NOVEMBER 5

[From the *Sunday Times* of London.]

Cyril Connolly: "We must never let ourselves be ruled by non-enjoyers; the greater their efficiency, the smaller our freedom."

NOVEMBER 9

WOR radio in a commercial about one of its newer interview programs, Joe Franklin: "the Marcel Proust of the entertainment world!" Do
they know whereof they speak? It would be amusing to alert them in an
anonymous letter. Some poor queen with a swelled head and a compulsive sense of humor might find himself in hot water. Not necessarily.

Is not J. Edgar Hoover suspect? Alfred Kinsey, apropos of the
McCarthy syndrome, by means of his taking sexual histories in and
around Washington, knew of homosexuality in high places, which of
course he kept mum about.

In England especially for many years sexual morality has been a class
distinction; scandal has consisted of revealing things to the vast world
of one's social inferiors. Twice in the lifetime of some persons still living
an aristocratic breach of the peace about homosexuality had brought
about revolutionary change. We all owe what liberty we have to Wilde,
that vain, histrionic, self-destructive, exhibitionistic playwright. The somewhat similar folly of that ass, Lord Montague of Beaulieu, led directly
to the Wolfenden Report and the recent blessed legislation.

NOVEMBER 15

[From the *New York Times*.]
"Marianne Moore, the poet, is 80 years old today and she's going to
have the sort of birthday party she likes. Monroe Wheeler, a counse-
lor to the trustees of the Museum of Modern Art, will take her out
with Glenway Wescott, the novelist, and with her brother, Captain John
Warner Moore, U.S.N., retired, and his wife."

Monroe's party at the Coffee House Club, with W. H. Auden. Meat
and vegetables, ice cream with fresh raspberry sauce and a Royal cake
with candles. A bottle of Cos d'Estocarnel, most of which Wystan
drank avidly. He scolded me for drinking water. Warner Moore told long
unhilarious anecdotes about admirals. Wystan boasted of having outdis-
tanced T. S. Eliot in one particular: he preached in Westminster Abbey

last year, which Eliot never managed. Dear senescent Marianne looked pretty, whittled thin by fatigue, and brightly flushed.

NOVEMBER 25

At 5:30 a.m., a portion of the moon shown down from a circular iridescence like an art nouveau plate, with a piercing star close by. At six I telephoned Monroe to wish him a good flight to Madison, but as I had been worrying about John, which I do almost incessantly, I dialed his number instead of Monroe's. His muffled, small voice, like that of a little child not letting itself cry, saddened me more than I shall ever be able to tell.

Erotic imagery in pop rock songs: "Light My Fire," which is the title of The Doors' smash single.

DECEMBER 5

Another great sunrise. Stripes of sallow and seemingly stagnant brightness in the winter woods; soft long lavender clouds in the east, and gold in the south. At seven o'clock on the other side of the house, the entire fifty acres of dormant hay and corn stubble, last week's snow having melted away, is pink.

The color schemes of Gauguin and Bonnard were found, not invented. Nature worshippers, they waited and watched and seized upon the sublime moments and chance effects, then conveyed the emotions of what they had seen.

DECEMBER 12

At 6:30 a.m., homeward bound (via Penn Station and Trenton and the bus to Stockton), in East 55th Street, in a cold but not freezing rain, I met a beautiful boxer dog, with no master anywhere in sight, presumably abandoned or lost. He turned and lifted his fine black-muzzled, white-starred face to me, hopefully. I am not a dog lover but his face in the icy dark downpour moved me.

In the mid-30s I had to live with a boxer dog and learned to feel some affection for him; but my emotion concerning this dog did not derive from those old circumstances. It was pity for those who love me and need me now, whom I can scarcely help, and it was self-pity, colder and darker than I have known in many years.

DECEMBER 13

A Pacific island which sank beneath the waves some years ago re-appeared yesterday, while a sea captain witnessed its rebirth.

Ivan [Ashby] said about my tentative Christmas plans: "After all, it is your house."

I must say that I don't often think of it as mine. No such luck—no such good luck, no such bad luck either.

DECEMBER 30

The Verifax [print copier, a Christmas gift from Barbara] demonstra-tor arrived and put me through my paces for an hour and a half. "Don't read the instructions! They'll only confuse you." Upon which, in a mem-orized voice, with slangier jargon, he confused me to the point of pain. As I learn by reading rather than hearing, I'll have to compose instruc-tions of my own, in simple literary English, to be thumb-tacked over the machine for a while. How much abler our inventors are than our design-ers of mechanism!

1968

JANUARY 3

In several places off the coast of Brittany, the fishermen point to this or that location of the fabulous city of Is, and tell strange tales of it. On very stormy days, they assure you, the tops of its church steeples are seen to appear in the troughs of the waves; and on calm days there rises from the abyss the chiming of its bells, spelling out the appointed hymn of that day.

It often seems to me that I have at the bottom of my own heart a city of Is in which obstinate bells keep summoning to the holy office of the faith a congregation now deaf to them. Sometimes I pause and bend an ear to these tremendous vibrations, which seem to arise from infinite depths, like voices of another world. Especially at the approach of old age, I took pleasure, during the repose of summer, to harken to these far-away sounds of a vanished Atlantis.

JANUARY 8

I am too perverse, too contrary, to hold myself to specific resolutions, but I can now say no to myself. Now I must learn how to say it to other people.

JANUARY 21

I went to bed last night exhausted and woke up exhausted, not early. No lovemaking, because the sweet sound of John's singing in the bathroom while getting ready for bed made Ivan cry, uncontrollably though softly; therefore I left them alone. This is his last weekend here before being returned against his will to his native England.

FEBRUARY

Glimpses of my father, ever-lovely in my mind and heart. As a part-time taxidermist, supplementing the livelihood of a very poor piece of farmland in the winter months, one winter he undertook to preserve someone's valuable and beloved horse. Assembling and wiring and erecting, inserting beautiful glass eyes and painting the nostrils and muzzle, he took no cognizance of the size of the creature as a life-like mummy— it wouldn't go through the door! A section of the outer wall had to be removed, then replaced, which wasted a good part of the poor proud taxidermist's fee.

FEBRUARY 4

The fifth anniversary of Jean Cocteau's death has provoked me to read *Opium*, the brave book he published in 1930. Although he was writing about an addictive drug, much of what he says could equally apply to marijuana which is generally agreed to be non-addictive:

"Alcohol provokes fits of madness. Opium provokes fits of wisdom."

"After smoking, the body thinks. The smoker has a bird's eye vide of himself."

"Opium lightens the mind. It never makes me witty. It spreads the mind out. It does not gather it up into a point."

Cocteau must never be dismissed as camp. Such diamond-precision of utterance has seldom been combined with so wide an aesthetic range. "The only possible style," he once declared, "is the thought made flesh."

I delight in little far-flung facts, the poetical content of newspapers and magazines. For example, Keats was only five feet and three-quarters of an inch tall; two and one-quarter inches shorter than Truman Capote.

FEBRUARY 6

The life dedicated and devoted to literature is fraught with a strange predestination.

FEBRUARY 13

In the train, en route to Bernard's. This is Monie's 69th birthday. Inadvertently I woke him up an hour earlier than he wanted. While I packed my bag we talked for half an hour, mostly about my editing of Porter's letters, because he is going to see her in Washington this afternoon. I telephoned him from the station in extreme uneasiness, to warn him not to undermine my editorial plans and tactics at this point. And I forgot to say, "Happy Birthday." Rough, hurt, and hurtful stoic that he is now, he will tell me that he'd rather have his anniversaries ignored by one and all. In fact, he is constantly preoccupied with his increasing elderliness, and thinking of it ages him.

FEBRUARY 20

En route to Washington, D.C. Yesterday morning I awoke with a sensation of having aged by ten or fifteen years in my sleep. Presumably

I had dreamed some extreme aggravation of the facts of my life. No wildness of grief; no tears, not even a lump in my throat; nothing that could have been relieved by talking to Monroe when he woke up. I was philosophical about it, but desolate. I kept thinking: too late now, too late for pleasures of love, too late to write anything more, just time to put my affairs in order. It was like recovering from the anesthesia after a castration; almost worse than that would be at age 67—indeed, I may have had my share of pleasure, but I am still committed to great love, both old and new, and I have things to write, small things perhaps, but fine.

FEBRUARY 25

The great hourly daily impediment to my finishing the book that I have promised is not my housekeeping or my family life or my sex life or lack of sex life, or my neurotic habits of mind, resentments and depressions—it is my always having something else to write.

FEBRUARY 27

Farmhand Ethel: While waiting for the bus this morning Ethel told me that someone has just made her a present of all the newspaper clippings of her trial for homicide; thrilling for her, especially the photographs of all concerned. She is going to put them in an album, in sleeves of acetate. She has never once told me, or even implied, that she was innocent; but on the other hand, she never shows the least feeling of guilt. In her psychology, there has been atonement; she has "paid her debt to society," as she herself would express it; the sin has been remitted.

MARCH 5

On the worst afternoon of the crash of the stock exchange in 1929, Lady Mendl [Elsie de Wolfe], who had never been beautiful and was then in her seventies, said to a group of friends who had come in for cocktails: "Well, my broker tells me that I lost a million dollars this afternoon. It troubled me at first, but as I have my youth and beauty, it doesn't matter much, does it?"

MARCH 16

One afternoon at the Institute, in my distress about the Vietnam War—I think it was in the spring of 1966—I asked George Kennan, "Can you read the *New York Times* these days and sit down immediately afterward and write history?"

"I try to put off reading anything until I have done the day's work." He thinned his lips together for a second, then added, "I am afraid that the president of the United States has declared war on history."

MARCH 21

Elizabeth came to dinner at Barbara's and brought a packet of photographs that I delight in. We look so much alike, all in a row. But sister Marjorie's not being in the row makes a shocking effect, like a smile minus of a tooth. I look a little drunk in two pictures, and a little like William Buckley—that will keep me from vanity.

MARCH 22

There is a time for everything, except youth.

APRIL 2

The Emperor Justinian passed laws repressive of homosexuality because he believed, directly or indirectly, it caused earthquakes.

APRIL 11

Upon my 67th birthday, left on my pillow in 51st Street: "Dearest of all—Happy Birthday! I can't believe this is our 49th year together—with so much loving devotion still to come. I adore you—Monie."

APRIL 19

"Frank and explicit; that is the right line to take when you wish to conceal your own mind and to confuse the minds of others." Said by Disraeli, a number of whose sayings have seemed to me cleverer and truer than Wilde's.

MAY 3

In Portland, with John Yeon. I have never in my life seen anything more gloriously beautiful than the succession of great pointed volcanic mountains of the Cascades: Adams, Rainer, St. Helena's, Hood, Jefferson—soaring up separately out of dark blueness; snow so pure that the small clouds floating alongside in the sunshine looked gray.

I could have gone to Brazil with Monroe; I could have visited Pauline and Philippe in their rented Dutch-Renaissance castle—and Rembrandt's *Night Watch* is as beautiful as the Cascade Mountains. But in the fiery Indian Summer of my waning life as it has been of late, over-stimulated by what may be last love, I was incapable of going anywhere unless I could envisage a possibility of sexual pleasure; not a probability . . . an acknowledgement both of my weakness and my strength.

MAY 21

At the end of the hard day of the invasion of Barbara's house and Haymeadows by six hundred symphony-supporting ladies. Lloyd and Baba fed me at Lorenzo's in Trenton and deposited me at the station, asleep on my feet. I slept in the train, and could scarcely keep awake until Monroe arrived from Rio via Brasilia and Trinidad. He is manifestly happy about the success of his show in the Argentines, publicized like Ringling Brothers' Circus; happier still to be back with me; girding his loins for his return to Chile, with perhaps a two-weeks' vacation in Brazil, land of young beauties. He can't bear, now, to travel for pleasure without a companion, but kindly refrains from pressuring me to go with him this time. How rapidly he had aged all this year—but with improvement in health and strength the while (it has seemed to me). In which antithesis I discern a kind of philosophy, happy for the most part.

JUNE 6

After the assassination of Senator Robert F. Kennedy: This dark historic day, I find myself more afraid than sorrowful. It sets a terrible example to evil politicians to see a candidate for the highest office shot down just when the popular vote has gone in his favor. Monroe's friend

Mrs. Parkinson talked with close friends of the Kennedy family yesterday; the doctors had already warned them that, at very best, he would be helplessly crippled, blind, and perhaps worse.

I didn't like him, but recognized his bright intellect and good intentions. I hoped that, if Gene McCarthy fell by the wayside, he could wrest the nomination from Humphrey; my brother did not agree.

A good-looking old wizened black man who shines my shoes at the barbershop said this morning, "This Ay-rab's been here since he was twelve but he didn't care nothing about this country; only the Ay-rab troubles, like against the Jews. His whole family weren't even citizens, just permanent residents; why did this country let them come here like that?" Then he lifted his head from my shoes, with an evangelical smile. "Kennedy was the only one who was for the poor people, all the poor people, not just blacks; and the poor people were for him."

JUNE 7

Fear yesterday, disgust today, brought on by the headlines in the *Times*. For example, our new Roman Catholic archbishop, appointed by President Johnson to a commission to investigate the causes of our assassinations and to recommend remedies, along with Eric Hoffer, our dear old authoritarian longshoreman aphoristic-writer, and ex-President Eisenhower's brother—more spankings for boys and girls by their fathers and mothers I suppose—the archbishop says this morning that "we must shun va-lence" (that's the way President Johnson pronounces it).

Of course fools are always quicker to express themselves in the heat of historic events than those of talent and good sense.

JUNE 13

On Monday I slipped over the edge of an asphalt walk on a turkey farm and fractured the base of the fifth metatarsal bone in my left foot. I have a plaster cast from the bottom of my foot up almost to my knee and am, and shall be for another fortnight, on crutches, which I do not manage well. But I must fly up to Schenectady day after tomorrow, to be given an honorary degree by Union College the following morning.

JUNE 17

Before luncheon at the college president's house, I stood on one foot for half an hour. After luncheon I had to talk non-stop with good young Frank Gado . . . a true teacher, impassioned about literature; my literature a specialty of his.

After dinner, back to the Albany County Airport. Robert Phelps with his obstreperous kindness met me at LaGuardia, with wheelchair.

JUNE 30

I helped Barbara give a grand al fresco dinner for sixty neighboring grandees in support of her Trenton museum; co-host and floor show: elderly juvenile disabled literary brother-in-law on his pogo stick from table to table in the green-striped tent. Come to think of it, my entire family is indomitable, and how!

JULY 4

A good deal of the time lawyers' language is intentionally confusing, so as to require the services of fellow lawyers to interpret and apply it. But sometimes it goes to the other extreme: bulldozing expressiveness, glaringly unmistakable. The prosecuting attorney representing New York City in preventing Bertrand Russell's professorship at City College declared that his lifelong work was, "lecherous, libidinous, lustful, venomous, narrow-minded, untruthful, and bereft of moral fiber."

JULY 11

Fears are strange and complex, and (I suppose) idiosyncratic more often than not—courage ditto—mingling the physiological and the mnemonic and the imaginary. My fear of heights seems to be bodily; I don't think of it, but suddenly a pain punches up in my testicles, even on John's familiar and beautiful balcony. My fear of the air has to do with our human insolence in being there at all, as though we were gods; the Greeks called this hubris. My fear of the sea is awe; it is the oblivion out of which we are brought to birth, into which we die duly, no exceptions, which is religious, isn't it? Religious imaginativeness conditioned by childhood memory. My poor father, whom I resented and distrusted, tried to teach me to swim by main force; I used to vomit in anticipation and never learned. Then, too, I have never forgotten my horror of the sinking of the *Titanic*; I went down across the lawn to the post box, and read the headline in the newspaper, read it in a loud voice to my grandmother standing on the porch; she spread her arms and clapped her hands and cried, "O merciful God!"

Did you ever hear one of our Negro ballads entitled "Go Down, Titanic"? The world champion boxer, Jack Johnson, a sensational man with a white wife, intended to return to the U.S. on that maiden voyage; at the last moment his passage was cancelled for the obvious reason of segregation. The song expressed that perhaps merciful God had lost patience on that occasion.

Young Americans not only pass a large part of their life with rock and roll songs in their ears but make a cult of it. Do they understand the words of hit-parade songs all the way through, or is it a matter of vague mysterious catchy phrase chanted over and over, which is the case for me—as it were, liturgical music.

JULY 22

As Monroe and I sat on the terrace, eating cheese and crackers and salad and red raspberries, the bright-colored doe wandered out to the south meadow, at peace except for her white tail rapidly fighting the flies. Then out of the spinney came her twin fawns who caught sight of her afar, ran to her, slowed up around her circularly. A little later, an extra fawn, smaller than the others, still spotted, raced out of the spinney, between us and the barn, calling for help at the top of its voice, half bleat, half bark, and disappeared into the corn field. Why? I have never seen an infant ruminant so alarmed. It returned after a while, silent, but still unhappy. I sat there, ashamed of my recent emotions; my life so fortunate, whatever its crises.

[Re the journal of Denton Welch:]

He was an exquisitely gifted youngster whom a violent motorist crushed when he was riding a bicycle, who then devoted his remaining few years, bed-ridden and anguished, to an account of the joy of living, self-expressive sensuousness and malicious humor. That also shamed me, with a lesson more applicable than the panic of the small wild animal minus its mother.

JULY 27

I went to town to dine with Monroe and with Marianne Moore, night before last. We never see her now, without the thought that it may be the last time. She is fantastically frail, although also fantastically unreduced in mind and charm. Monroe took us to the Plaza, the vast old-English room looking out on Central Park—a perfect place for the occasion . . . She has just finished a poem but hasn't sold it yet; her poetry editor at the *New Yorker* is vacationing on Fire Island. She has been commissioned to write a text about Central Park to accompany beautiful color photographs; she will be paid one thousand dollars. Fancy working to the day of one's death like that—glorious!

JULY 31

Oh, perfectionism and the sin of pride! I haven't been greatly tormented by these weaknesses in my life and human relations, but art is a great folly—especially when one has had more opportunity than talent, more esteem than success.

AUGUST 2

I dined alone with Lloyd and Barbara. We took a walk to look at the new Holsteins; Lloyd is beginning to love them. I often wonder if I would be a more productive author if I had a simple or simplifying mind like his; perhaps a contradiction in terms. It is all a kind of Garden of Eden, with a bit of snake in each of us, where (I suppose) it belongs.

AUGUST 6

The Republican Convention: A shocking spectacle, ballyhoo and carnival—it is an American tradition, like letting the children play while their parents are in the kitchen quarreling and cooking. But it seems worse now that it is all put-on and a show for the great mass media, directed by professionals at vast expense. Rockefeller is attractive and honest, and in his way a humanist, but so much less gifted than Nixon as a politician, one might even say less intelligent, and with amateurish advisors. Nixon does not wish to be reactionary, not any more, but his mind is so commonplace, his frequentations for years have been so low-level, that he will slip back into reaction, almost be forced back.

AUGUST 10

We are having our worst hot weather, steaming and enfeebling. As soon as Monroe got back from Venezuela, dead tired, his Museum asked him to go to Australia. The new National Gallery of Victoria in Melbourne, almost a decade in the making, is to open its doors with exceeding sociabilities and formalities. Monroe hates the assignment, too tired and too hurried, but is proud of it in a way, and thinks of it, in principle, as incumbent upon the emeritus man, in self-defense against the take-over generation.

AUGUST 13

(L., J., D.)—A small orgy of familiar friends, four of us who haven't been together for more than a year since last summer. Pot and a dildo, humor and affection, courtesy and respect for one another, mutual criticisms, all sorts of differences notwithstanding, confidence and orgasms.

AUGUST 23

Homeward bound from Washington, D.C. Very mixed feelings about my visit. Katherine Anne has lost weight and seemed stronger than in May . . . We "worked" assiduously, and I felt pleased, given the bitter stupidity I had fallen into about the entire project . . . She declared that as the volume of letters was my conception in the beginning and has only gone forward by my effort, if there is to be a renegotiation of the contract it is to be upward, in my favor; not downward. This I shall take with a grain of salt until the very day.

SEPTEMBER 1

What a luxury: my relationship with the commonplace of nature. My doe with one of her twin fawns and the extra fawn were softly grazing in the north meadow. Where was the other twin? The extra one kept its tail up while grazing. I went toward them when all their backs were turned, but they seemed able to hear my footsteps. Then six almost mature hen pheasants flew up with a great whir.

SEPTEMBER 12–13

I often think of two immortal youngsters who didn't even have lasting art; they were dancers. A Greek boy whose gravestone was found near Antibes, on the Riviera where I lived. "Septentrion"—and I think they're not sure whether that first word meant "one who came from the North" or whether it was his name—"Septentrion, aged twelve, danced and gave pleasure." An Egyptian girl, who lies or used to lie in the Musée Guimet in Paris, a teenage mummy with a good-sized bouquet of ancient brown roses still in her arms. Anatole France was inspired to write the novel *Thaïs*, which Massenet took for the libretto of his opera of the same name. Which novel and opera prompted Maugham to write his story on Sadie Thompson, "Rain."

SEPTEMBER 24

To Anita Loos: My cocktail party for Robin Maugham: The noble lord arrived tight, in a nice, funny way *until* the end of the evening. But Monroe disliked it, and that made me nervous and perhaps ineffective in my role of host or half-host. The strangest thing: Robin Maugham is animated, indeed possessed, by nothing in the world but ruthless revenge and pecuniary aspiration by means of it. Hell hath no fury like a nephew scorned! What a plot—better than anything that I shall be able to bring into my little memoir, romance of the literary art; and perhaps, no doubt, that is the "controversial" scenario he is preparing for Embassy Pictures.

SEPTEMBER 25

A journalist asked Jean Cocteau, "If your house were on fire and you could only take one thing, what would it be?" He answered, "I'd take the fire."

OCTOBER 3

Funny: Margot Hentoff, a *Village Voice* writer, reviewing Tom Wolfe's two recent books scathingly, remarks that his fatuously tough hard-bitten style is often reminiscent of Dorothy Parker's "Big Blonde."

OCTOBER 6

[From the GW interview with the *Trenton Times*.]

"It's absurd, isn't it? In a country where there is so much security for the distinguished professors of the other learned professions, science, medicine—there are thousands of full professors who have permanent tenure, who are supported in such a way that they cannot be in want in their old age. On the other hand we've writers, composers, architects, painters and sculptors, some of whom are world famous and absolutely impoverished in their old age. They outlive their earning capacity and it's not only pathetic but I think it's a disgrace to a great art loving, literature loving, education loving plutocracy, you know, that art is just not a first-rate career. Families could say, 'Don't go into that; you'll end up in the street.' A lot of them do."

OCTOBER 12

I saw myself on television the other evening, and was amazed. I look quite old and fat, but (I felt, amazingly) pleasant; a matter of peaceful, subtle, humorous, affectionate expressions—physique of a sea lion, but with a dolphin's intelligence.

OCTOBER 13

Marvelous ability of some writers, especially French writers, to belittle and besmirch our human plight. Lèautaud says, for example, "I haven't seen anything very great in life except its cruelty and stupidity." If that was the truth of the life he knew from start to finish, not just a final disillusionment, what did he live for and how could he endure his impoverished lonely fate?

Last night's lecture was a sort of failure. Despite the pleasant telecast, and two full interviews in the Trenton papers, there were only about seventy-five people in an auditorium that seats four or five hundred. To console me, Ethel tells me that "Satch-mo," Louis Armstrong, also found Trenton cold.

OCTOBER 18

In the Penn Station, three little white boys were tinkering with a candy dispenser, at 7 a.m.! Were they criminals, trying to loosen the coins out of it, or had the mechanism itself wickedly taken their nickels and dimes? A baldish young man, not handsome but respectable-looking, stood at one of the new urinals, brandishing an erection, at 7 a.m.! The men's room in the old station was, as you might say, virtuous, with high partitions; whereas the new installations have maximum exposure, facilitating improprieties—one wonders whose design that was, and why.

OCTOBER 25

Pauline and Philippe de Rothschild have to be answered; nothing could be more difficult or emotionally disturbing. They want me to spend about half of each year, for perhaps five years, at Mouton and in Holland and Norway. They truly believe that my work would go better if I were living their life than it has gone in the situation that I have gradually committed myself to in New Jersey. I cannot simply say no; I must explain myself and my life in some measure, in gratitude and for reference in the years to come. Meanwhile, Monroe has determined that I am to deliver the volume of Porter letters to her and to her publishers before I go abroad at the end of December. It will scarcely be possible, but I must knock myself out in the attempt.

OCTOBER 28

In yesterday's *New York Times Magazine*: a profile of B. B. King, the so-called King of the Blues, sorrowful and humorous both in his life and in his repertory, and an important interview with Herbert Marcuse, an elderly professor of German origin now in vogue as the chief dissident of the intellectual establishment.

A strange truth: the homosexual minority is closer to the Negro minority in the U.S. than it is to the Jewish minority. I am closer to, let us say, B. B. King than to Norman Mailer. Norman Mailer is closer to Marcuse than I am. This has nothing to do with lifework or aesthetics. B. B. King and I have been repressed and frustrated. Marcuse is revolutionary, but is a successful, highly paid establishment figure.

NOVEMBER 3

Auden on J. R. R. Tolkien's *The Lord of the Rings*. "Better than your wildest dreams." How good is that? One of the elements of discomfort in one's admiration of this high-ranking poet: he is insincere as well as hypocritical. He says things just for effect. In a tone of strong conviction he indulges in rhetorical devices.

Worse than one's wildest dreams. . . .

NOVEMBER 5

I have never finished any book that I have been contracted to write—I remember Cass Canfield's shocked look when I told him this, in response to his inquiry about "The Old Party," when it first began to be behind schedule—as soon as I sit down at my writing table I am apt to be seized by some inspiration having nothing to do with the book supposedly in progress, sometimes by several inspirations at once. Let me just jot something down, an aide-memoir I say to myself; and away I go—with that mingling of the reminiscent and the visionary and the verbal which is my talent.

NOVEMBER 6

The election has made me as nervous as a cat, as anxious as a crystal gazer. [Hubert] Humphrey, if he surprises everyone and gets elected, will not make a very strong or very original president. Nixon, on the other hand, will do his best, beginning with perhaps a better cabinet than H.H.H. could muster. But his cleverness and discipline in the daily routines of politicians have gone to his head; he terribly lacks judgment; in two minutes flat he will make the most dangerous mistakes, already has done so.

NOVEMBER 14

Shameful selfish cry: I want a record changer, I want all the recordings: Schubert, Strauss, Fauré, Poulenc.

NOVEMBER 23

My grandmother Wescott, large, plain, profound woman, would go outdoors to greet every new moon, walking up and down along the fence west of the house, looking up at it. "I always think of all my loved ones looking up at it at the same time, wherever they are; even those who are dead," she would say.

NOVEMBER 25

One of the odd details of literary history: it was the authoress of *Uncle Tom's Cabin* who first published the tale of Byron's incest, which was what the French call a *secret de polichinelle*, 18 years after the beloved sister Augusta's death, nine years after the horrified wife Lady Byron's. It was the last mentioned who told Harriet Beecher Stowe about it.

NOVEMBER 30

Said Mark Twain: "Truth is stranger than fiction—because fiction is obliged to stick to possibilities; truth isn't."

Tolstoy's last words: "The truth . . . very much . . . I love truth."

DECEMBER

Aphorism: "I speak Spanish to God, Italian to women, French to men, and German to my horse."—Emperor Charles V.

DECEMBER 27

In Madrid with Monroe. We had bad luck here, in that the Prado wasn't open at all on the 24th and 25th, compensated for by warmly diffused sunlight all day long on the 26th. It was worth the entire *aller et retour* for just the six hours we spent there yesterday, dancing around the great rooms, talking the praises of Velasquez and Goya and the glorious rest: what Titians, what Rubens. Especially joyous for me, preferring the northern Baroque painters to almost all else. My youthful indifference to much of Italian Renaissance has begun to recur.

1969

JANUARY 1

Mouton Rothschild, Pauillac, France: Yesterday was Pauline's birthday, so that last night's maximum dinner party had a dual purpose, indeed triple, if you take into account the fact that in France adults exchange *gifts áu jour de l'an*, not on Christmas Day. On the whole, it seems to me, the great occasion, the week as a whole, has bogged down in its tradition and management somewhat since I was here last. But now Pauline's housekeeping has gone off a bit—all things are relative—perhaps because she has been, is, ill. And having written her Russian journal has opened a Pandora's box for her; she is ready for change. Her great long-term invitation to me meant that, among other things: instincts and calculations.

JANUARY 2

Mouton: A world apart, no matter how many friends our hosts, with characteristic willfulness and munificence and cheer, draw here from far and wide. The great salon with its 16th century mantelpiece, expansive floor of pink and white and blue, and large dispersed noble furniture, occupies about a fourth of the second floor of Grand Mouton, and is a hundred feet long. Petite Mouton thrusts its rooftops out of tall trees, a fairy-tale castle. My room overlooks the far right hand corner of the courtyard where the doves are fed, about a hundred; their monotonous Paphian wooing music goes on all day and part of the night.

There has been a natural rivalry and no great liking between Mouton and Lafitte, the chateau and acreage to the north, belonging to Philippe's cousins; but now (I gather) Mouton has won and in both fact and feeling. The young Baron Eric, after dinner last night, charmed Monroe, who asked of him, "What is your intention in life, your special interest?" "Wine," he answered, "I want to do for Lafitte what Philippe and Pauline have done for Mouton."

Last night at about 1:15 a.m., Monroe and Balanchine and I went for a walk in wondrous moonlight; in a very small geometric pool amid the vines the white ducks quacked in an undertone, kept awake by the brightness. The cultivated soil of the vineyards, full of small rounded stones, refracted like magic. Balanchine, who is almost primitively Russian, that is, Georgian, thrust his forefinger straight up and said oracularly, "Snow, snow!" He was right. Before daybreak, I heard my dear doves in some agitation on the window-sill and as I found when I drew the heavy curtains, one had tried to come in and left a foot-track and a soiled tail feather.

Monroe will spend the weekend in Wimborne with Raymond Mortimer and Messrs. [George H. W.] Rylands, [Dennis Christopher] Shawe-Taylor and [Patrick] Trevor Roper. I shall stay here until next Thursday, spend the following weekend in Paris with little or no sociability in prospect—I shall concentrate on pictures: Poussin, Courbet, Monet, Bonnard—then London, return to New York and Haymeadows on the 15th.

JANUARY 6

Last night I heard an owl at about nine o'clock, while I was dressing for dinner—we dine late, like Spaniards—the little flexible flute, quivering down the scale. And it had quivered down only three times when Philippe called me on the telephone, from his bedroom. "Are you listening to the *chouette*? Didn't I tell you that we had one? Doesn't it make a pleasant little screech?"

I noticed that his voice was sad, almost as sad as the *chouette*'s. But he refrained from telling me, until after dinner, that Pauline's temperature had gone up again, that he was worried and alarmed.

JANUARY 7

Mouton: The timing and scheduling of everything is uncomfortable for me: dinner at 9:30, and nearer 10:30 sometimes, when Pauline is not confined to bed and makes us wait . . . Yesterday I got up at 3:15 a.m. and kept scribbling till 9:30. Nothing to eat until then—the servant didn't get to bed until after midnight either . . . Of course I eat too much but haven't put on much weight. Two long walks a day with Philippe—the laborious routine of the country-dwelling leisure classes. We don't sit down to lunch until 2:30, and usually set out upon the far-flung vineyard pathways as soon as lunch is over.

Only one houseguest left now besides myself, and Pauline's doctor who came down from Paris late last night. Monroe and Raymond went to London on Friday, which our hostess minded very much, in fact bitterly resented. She has been ill almost all summer, viral pneumonia, on a basis of perhaps irremediable heart trouble; and she shouldn't have had the house party, certainly not on the scale it developed. On Saturday morning she had a relapse: congestion of her lungs, high fever. I wanted to leave as soon as this happened—but it would have broken her heart and frightened her. Instead I have given up the four days in Paris I had planned. Philippe thinks that it will do her good to talk to me—long anticipated talks—whereas I am afraid that it will be over-stimulating and over-emotional for her. If the doctor agrees with me, I may depart on Friday, via Madrid.

JANUARY 15

Earliest Wescott in *Dictionary of National Biography*: Captain George Westcott, 1745–1798, captain in Navy, started life as a seaman and fought in the Battle of the Nile—killed by a musket-ball to the throat—monument to him at public expense erected in St. Paul.

Earliest Wheeler: Sir Francis Wheler, 1656–1694, sent by Britain from the Barbados to take Guadeloupe and Martinique away from the French—failed with great losses. Ditto Quebec—another failure—neither was his fault, said the authorities in England, and he was knighted.

JANUARY 23

A hurried dinner at Brooke Astor's with pleasant guests of some consequence to see a Pinteresque play of psychological obfuscation, moral ambivalence: *The Man in the Glass Booth*, coarsely performed by a well-known actor, Donald Pleasence—praised by almost all our critics. Our hostess, Monroe, Alfred Lunt and Lynn Fontanne, Mrs. Katherine Graham, Jack Heintz, Arthur Schlesinger, and a superior Englishwoman named Mrs. Daly were all bored by it.

On my way to town, Hella drove me to Trenton where we attended Ethel's father's funeral. None of us had ever seen Ethel in skirts until this day.

FEBRUARY 1

I remember one of Monroe's stories of Edith Sitwell. At the time of her first mortal illness, when she was in a nun's hospital and resented the routine of waking her up early, for breakfast and bath and medicine, customary in hospitals everywhere. Also, Edith complained, every day there followed promptly a young priest, to hear her confession. "Father, what can I possibly find to confess?" she wanted to know; "an old woman confined to bed surrounded by nuns."

"Your thoughts, Dame Edith," he answered. And she answered back, "My thoughts are savage, but they are pure."

FEBRUARY 5

The best ballets are those that are closest to music, and least explainable in words. Years ago, after the first performance of a ballet of Tudors (was it called "Interplay"?), Balanchine came to our apartment and someone asked him what he thought of it. "Well, ballet is particular art," he said, in his terse but polite way. "Can portray some things well— like, for example, lovers, and mother and son, and friends, and brother and sister—but cousins! No! Very difficult, very impossible."

FEBRUARY 17

[Re a *New York Times* clipping: "Padraic Colum at 87."]
Compassion toward Padraic, upon whose face, this spring, the shadow of death has appeared for the first time. I believe that, like myself, come what may, he desires to live forever; chiefly for literature's sake.

Yeats: "Think where man's glory begins and ends, and say my glory was I had such friends."

FEBRUARY 25

Montaigne: "A wise man sees as much as he ought, not as much as he can."

Magical taste: a ripe apple seed, perhaps especially the seed of a yellow apple.

MARCH 18

Turgenev, sick at heart and conscious-stricken at the guillotining of a murderer: "The horses harnessed to the vans and calmly chewing their oats in their nosebags seemed to me at that moment to be the only innocent creatures among us." The uninventible detail! What joy to come upon it in a review of Raymond Mortimer's at 4:20 in the morning.

I do not dispute the greatness of Dostoyevsky, when in my moments of thanksgiving for the reading matter of my life I prefer Turgenev, who seems to me nobler. Likewise I prefer Forster to Henry James, Dinesen to Faulkner, etc.

First principal of the art of fiction: It seems to me that every kind of imaginative narrative must pretend to be true—even fairy tales, within the confines of the given text—and with no desire to fool or mislead anyone—but mainly for perspective and norm and life-likeness. The factual reality is the only point of reference to measure plausibility. If you disregard it, there really is nothing to curb your extravagance. If your characters are eight feet tall, why not twenty? If your weather is always perfect, presently you can have no seasons.

APRIL 18

Telephone call from Michael Lifrieri in Chicago—Bill Cockerell having been strangled to death by someone unknown.

MAY 28

Rockefeller Cultural Mission to Latin America on behalf of President Nixon. Governor Rockefeller, with Monroe in his train, has been rioted against in Columbia, my kitchen radio keeps telling me. Oddly enough, I feel no serious premonition.

JUNE 10

The Verrazano-Narrows Bridge. On the evening of April 1, returning from Miami, we were stacked up for an hour; circled around and around over New York and New Jersey and Long Island—the rivers and bridges and islands from different angles of flight, so that I often felt lost; gradual magic of electricity flowering in the dusk. And then I happened to see the bridge, lights turned on, diamonds on pearly air.

～

A mystery man—a practitioner of power for power's sake (Lloyd thinks)—possibly a future political leader: Ralph Nader.

JUNE 14

Monroe, on his purchase of a drawing by a local artist: "It looks like a Chagall. Every amateur painter, one day, paints a good picture—like Richard Pride, and like my father."

JUNE 15

I am like a banyan tree: What seeds? What fruit? What use?—except to amaze tourists.

[From the *Sunday Times* of London.]
"There is one thing there are no professionals at, and that is dying."

JUNE 16

John Connolly's new television lighting work: John worked a double shift yesterday, and of course it will be double or even triple today. He expected to be paid by David Frost and Company yesterday, for the first time—the lighting engineer who came to work without an invitation! The satisfaction in his voice as he told me this was like fantastic music. John wants me to watch the Apollo launching but I haven't time or spirit, alas.

9:30 a.m.: I turned on the radio just a little late—the launching sounded like a great drum.

JUNE 18

Last night at dusk, I noted an agitation of rabbits in the shrubby corner of the lawn, and approached them from the back door with binoculars: the mating dance! The bigger of the two sat still until the smaller charged head on, fast—upon which the bigger leapt straight into the air, quite high, and the smaller darted under the leap; again and again, as in a ballet. They both got tired; the bigger lay down on his side, showing his whitish belly, under the low branches of the ilex opaca [holly]; the smaller crouched on the grass, turning her back, and the rays of sunlight gilded her.

JUNE 26

Hermann Hesse translated Thomas Wolfe.

Modesty, humility, almost humiliation: I feel like Victor Hugo—but I work like, let us say, Emily Dickinson, or Emily Brontë.

JUNE 28

Monroe has to attend a State Department briefing this afternoon, and probably dine with one of Governor Rockefeller's twenty-three other advisors. They leave at 6:45 tomorrow morning, a little timid this time, I gather. The Argentine government isn't as efficient as the Brazilian dictatorship, and those who set off time-bombs in fourteen supermarkets the other day were certainly professionals.

JULY 1

[After a neighbor's house fire.]

It happened to Aldous Huxley, toward the end of his life. His California house, like our houses, was full of works of art and literature and letter files and contracts and documents. He was there and stood gazing at the conflagration with his myopic eyes, wringing his hands. Some time later Natasha Spender met him and expressed her sympathy. She reported to me what he said: "At the time I thought I had lost my past. Now I realize that it was my future." By that time he was in the grip of cancer.

JULY 3

Superstition: Grandmother, the Witch, in Bergman's *The Magician*, mumbles this invocation on the way to bed: "He calls you down, he calls you out, beyond the dead, the living, and the living dead, beyond the raised hands."

JULY 4

A bad bit of symbolism. Not surprisingly, the astronauts intend to plant our flag on the moon. But there is no breeze up there to make it fly. Therefore our government, not counting the cost, has had a special cloth woven with fine wire as well as silk or cotton thread, so as to give the impression of a stiff wind blowing.

My father's mother, the principal character in my half-fictitious book [*The Grandmothers*], was a Ross. According to tradition in the family, she was descended from the more or less fictitious flag-seamstress, Betsy.

JULY 13

But how impenetrable is human nature; in its sorrows even stranger than in its felicities, especially in the transitions of age, the seven rivers it has to cross! At some point between insomnias my dream must have whispered words of wisdom—in hypochondriacal and Cassandrine sadness, how come I listened?—one of my lovers, or two, or three, held me tight and kept out my self-criticism. Whatever happened in the subconscious, I am in better spirits than I was yesterday.

JULY 18

En route to Pawling, New York. A hot country, in July and August . . . Wisconsin was like this; I still quail at the memory of the violence of my father's fields; I often thought I was going to die. Was it fear of my father and as I awoke into boyhood, resentment of his having intimidated me?

At Stone-blossom, my old mother, observing me in the iris beds, or lugging furniture from room to room, and boxes up and down the attic stairs, would marvel at my strength: "When I think what a delicate, easily exhausted, daydreaming boy you were!"

JULY 28

To Katherine Anne Porter: Poor international Monroe, like a fish on shore, taking a rest before setting out on his next world-itinerary; meanwhile plagued with job offers from all sides; nobody seems to have any thought of paying him for any of it. That's what retirement means in his walk of life.

AUGUST 7

With Katherine Anne Porter, College Park. She has sent to Switzerland for an expensive target pistol, to be smuggled in. She declares that it is to be used in self-defense if some hoodlum ever breaks into her house. But she is apt to mention it just after she expresses fear of the final chapter of senile deterioration, nightmarish boredom and uselessness. In her renegade way, she is a pious Catholic, conditioned against suicide. But she thinks of it; any violence better than none, in the last impasse.

AUGUST 12

When Lloyd drove me home, rejoicing in the fact that the hybrid corn on the left, which the cloudburst brought to its knees, had straightened itself up, to ripen and be harvested, he said, "We did inherit our love of corn from out father. It was his favorite crop; the dearest thing in nature." Which made me shiver, with my strangely mixed filial emotions, bereavement no longer painful.

Tonight a simple but evidently skillful locksmith came from Flemington, and as his little wife has lately had a stroke, and is sad and frightened, he brought her along; and she turned out to be an enthusiastic reader of *The Grandmothers* and *Apartment in Athens*. We talked while he tinkered. Baba boasted to her of my having portrayed her and her French house in *The Pilgrim Hawk*, which thrilled the locksmith's wife.

AUGUST 21

Memory itself dreams, sometimes lies. Language itself, in all the poetical past, is invention. The question in the shaping of a story is how to apply imagination, when to loose it.

AUGUST 24

Males have to lie to females quite frequently, I find. Even if we tell them our truths, they are deaf to them, or they mis-listen; and as between men of good will and women of any consequence, our untruths are better than their own, better for them as for us.

LATE SEPTEMBER

[Glenway accompanies Barbara Wescott to London, Paris, and Amsterdam, where the Rijksmuseum was celebrating the three hundredth anniversary of Rembrandt's death with an exhibit of his paintings and drawings.]

Monroe was very jealous of my going on the Rembrandt pilgrimage with Barbara, while he is in the Mediterranean with Raymond Mortimer and Brooke Astor. He set out before me and I went to Kennedy Airport with him, and in farewell I said, "I shall miss you at the Rembrandt exhibition." He answered almost solemnly: "It is always a waste now when we do not look at pictures together."

SEPTEMBER 26

Paris, with Barbara: Despite the shopping and art-dealing, telephoning and telegraphing, we did get to the Louvre and saw its Rembrandt self-portrait and the Claude Lorrain and the Poussins in a better light.

OCTOBER

[After the London, Paris, and Amsterdam museum trip with Barbara.] Monroe has fallen in love with Italy, whereas I, in consequence of having traveled with Barbara, want to go to Berlin, Dresden and Leningrad.

OCTOBER 10

Oh the sad lunatics in our country. In the Trenton railway station this morning a young woman, not without physical distinction but starved-looking, wearing a black cardigan, an improvised skirt of unhemmed white cotton, and broken white sneakers, pacing up and down, hugging herself tight with her thin arms, singing softly, tunelessly.

OCTOBER 26

A journal is really the best of the literary forms for this day and age, for those of us who cannot or will not fabricate pastime-reading-matter for the trade. I feel like old Moses looking down in the Promised Land, with Aaron/Robert Phelps holding me up for my vicarious look.

It was cold last night. We turned the clocks back but my inner clock followed its summer habits. I went outdoors and stood between the morning star and the full moon; fantastic brightness. The barns and the outbuildings stood around me like palaces. I thought of taking a walk, but felt afraid to do so alone. Afraid of what? Of the beauty, imagining that it might lure me to my death—*nunc dimmetus*—or at least over-awe and benumb and downgrade my poor creative faculty. Perhaps when confronted with really great subject matter, it is best just to dip one's mind in it—and then to recall it with pen in hand.

OCTOBER 30

Norman Mailer: Certain critics have now declared him to be the highest-ranking American author; no one else, it must be admitted, has his facility. By insinuating intelligence, which is a better trick than his applause-getting figures of speech, he must be influential—if only people really read him. Do they? He isn't easy to read.

NOVEMBER 28

Amplified Music—The Rolling Stones: Nine seats in the front row of Madison Square Garden, African drumming, the kids three or four tiers over us, the crowd noise like the sound of the sea, the tidal wave of dancers down the center aisle . . . the beauty of Jagger.

DECEMBER 5

Tea with [artist] Clement Hurd, a good respected friend with whom I had a brief episode of love in 1935.

DECEMBER 13

[To Philippe de Rothschild.]
I had to hasten to town to hear Borges the blind prose-poet, at the Poetry Center, because I have proposed our inviting him to give the Blashfield address at the Academy and must be certain that he can be heard and understood by my old confreres. Borges said, "All literature is one book, all authors are one author."

DECEMBER 26

Mouton Rothschild, Pauillac. We are in the so-called Italian apartment on the ground floor, under the staircase, with portes-fenetres opening out into the great vineyard, now just visible in veiled moonlight. But only for one night, Pauline has decreed, although my favorite maid Olga had already unpacked and put away all my belongings. Why? To remind me of my joyous first visit, I guess. Her caprices are, as a rule, well thought out. Back in the green room with Chinese furniture and green wallpaper and green orchids, with music of the extremely amorous white doves above and below the windows.

Our dear hostess's heart condition has worsened; at last the French doctors have passed the buck back to our American specialists, where surely it belongs. She is going to the Leahey Clinic in Boston [after the holidays], for all the tests and presumably for surgery. She doesn't want Philippe to go along, he tells me; they are too emotional together, I dare say. I impulsively offered to escort her, but I don't think she will want that either. As is often the case for women, a great deal of her courage and strength is keeping up appearances.

I was more anxious last year, when I thought she was afraid to know the truth and might settle for a shortened life.

DECEMBER 31

[Mouton Rothschild, a gift inscription to Monroe.]

To my nearest and dearest, this volume (an anthology of poetry, Pound's latest), now that our life together has got to be a sort of poem in itself.

At this time of my life I despair of facts; for my part, in terms of my own endeavors and potential, I believe only in language.

∽

"A Heaven of Words." This is my presumptive title for the final volume of my journals: the time of my life when I hope to enjoy writing more than ever before.

1970–1974

D URING THE 1960S WESCOTT still had some periods of public celebrity—on the television, on the radio, and in mainstream publications. By the 1970s he is beyond that, though he sometimes appears in gossip columnist Liz Smith's society page, or in a *New York Times* photo of a literary event. Nevertheless, throughout the entire decade Wescott is still one of the most brilliant and spellbinding public speakers anywhere. He is a frequent speaker at the Academy-Institute of Arts and Letters and at many other literary and social events. As always, it is a special experience to hear him read, whether other writers' work or his own.

Meanwhile, Wheeler continues his worldwide travel for MoMA. Their exchange of letters continues, with Glenway at Haymeadows and Monroe in Europe, the Far East, and Latin America. At Monroe's New York City apartment they keep up their tradition of dinner parties for their famous friends. While it's a shame that Wescott didn't experience European travel in his middle years (except for a short trip in 1952), now their winter holiday trips to Mouton Rothschild allow for side trips to Paris, London, the Netherlands, and elsewhere, to see the great museums as well as friends. Perhaps conscious of their place in the art world and as a storied couple, they seldom fly on the same plane, so that there would be a survivor in the event of a tragedy.

In the final phase of his writing career, Wescott's interest is clear: personal essays and journals. Time is too precious for literary reviews, or for the tar baby of fiction. The very last time he attempts fiction, trying to revive the unfinished "The Stallions," he frustrates and upsets himself. But fortunately, Wescott is contacted by a man named Coburn Britton, a poet with a city apartment and a country home near Haymeadows. The publisher of a handsome quarterly called *Prose*, Britton offers Wescott a thousand dollars for any piece he chooses to write. Three beautiful essays follow. "The Odor of Rosemary" is Wescott at his lyrical best, as he recalls his 1935 ocean voyage to Spain. Leaving honeymooning Lloyd and Barbara alone, he befriends a tragic young man. The essay ends on a note of compassion as a breeze carries the scent of rosemary from the coast of Spain out to sea. "The Emperor Concerto" recalls his relationship with Wheeler in 1928, 1933, and up to the present day. "Memories and Opinions" recalls the 1920s in London and Paris. Another piece, a humorous self-portrait called "The Breath of Bulls," appears in the anthology *Works in Progress, Number 6*. The idea of a book of essays with the title "The Odor of Rosemary" comes to him—and Harpers is interested— but he lets it go.

As for journals, once Robert Phelps secures a contract with Farrar, Straus, and Giroux in 1972 Wescott really begins to see his journals and his career retrospectively. He produces less material for current journals and devotes more time to organizing papers, photocopying old manuscripts, tape recording interviews, and reading Phelps's selections for private gatherings. (He comments on this endless task in his last entry of 1972.) The rest of his time is absorbed by family, the Academy-Institute, and social events.

When their friend E. M. Forster dies, Wescott and Christopher Isherwood see to the publication of his long-suppressed novel *Maurice*, written in 1913–14, with proceeds going to writers' awards. Another great loss is Marianne Moore at eighty-four. Elderly Janet Flanner is now living in New York and Glenway visits her at Natalia Danesi Murray's city apartment and Fire Island house. Pauline de Rothschild's frail health and visits to Boston hospitals become an issue. Glenway himself begins to have circulatory problems in 1973, but his health remains fair to good for another decade.

Aside from literary politics, Wescott despises the politics of Richard Nixon, the tragedy of Vietnam, and police suppression of gay rights. He is still in communication with the Kinsey Institute. Privately, he enjoys the new era of gay erotic films at Manhattan theaters like the David, Adonis, and the Jewel. He especially enjoys the sentimental, romantic films of Toby Ross.

He turns a page in his private life in late August 1974 when friend Earl Butler brings along John Stevenson for a weekend at Haymeadows. A success in advertising in his twenties and a serious photographer, Stevenson immediately finds a soul mate in Glenway. John Connolly is still Wescott's longtime companion—aside from Monroe—but most of Connolly's time is devoted to his television studio work and to his life with Ivan Ashby at their city apartment. With Monroe usually in New York or traveling, loneliness can often be sensed in these journals, along with short bouts of depression. In Stevenson, Glenway has the joy of a handsome, bright, and charming escort for the ballet, concerts, dinners, and some weekends, and a welcome phone call in the night. Likewise, Monroe, nearly three years earlier, met Anatole Pohorilenko from Philadelphia, a sophisticated young art student and teacher who proves an invaluable support. Over the decades, Glenway and Monroe had a succession of younger companions who later remained friends. Now they both find younger partners for their late years.

1970

JANUARY 4

Mouton. I did not get around to New Year's resolutions on New Year's Eve which is also Pauline's birthday and in French tradition the equivalent of Christmas, with great fond commotion, gift-giving and extra eating and drinking, even extra kissing! At midnight, the solemn sound of a melodious, dark-toned gong. I managed not to kiss anyone unappealing. Philippine ordered the young Alain Chastagnal, one of her pulchritudinous protégés, to be kissed by me. I did it in the French way, very slowly twice, that is twice doubly, first on the right, then on the left, and very slowly, in order to taste his skin and to distinguish between his body odor and his expensive scent.

I talked about Isadora Duncan which somehow disappointed them. Someone prompted me by asking for more stories of the Hotel Welcome and Cocteau, Jeannot and Jeanne, and Jean Desbordes, which enchanted the youngsters. In the end they called me "Uncle Glenway."

Paris. In the bourdon of Notre-Dame, the "flawless" exquisite F-sharp bell is named Emmanuèle. When it was cast or re-cast in the seventeenth century, Parisian women contributed gold and silver ornaments and jewels "to gladden and perfect his timbre."

JANUARY 20

Poetry moves the heart and the senses; fiction leads the imagination on a merry chase, or on a stations of the cross.

A factor in our campus disorders that we are apt to forget: the underlying pessimism, no wonder! Said a Harvard student leader named Samuel Bonder: "Youth today must decide how to face the end of the world."

Said Ghandi (quoted by Malraux): "It is better to fight than to be afraid."

JANUARY 27

I observe this about my aging, shrinking mind: whereas I seem not to have been put off by ideas when I was young, now I don't like to be made to think about things that are (for me) untrue or odious. No more Sade, no more Dostoyevsky, no more Faulkner. Although I quibble. I bracket Proust with Balzac and Tolstoy. Now our youngsters read Hesse—a million dollar business for Farrar, Straus. This weekend I had a weird conversation with Yale graduates, one of Baba's nephews and a couple of friends, and they said that Hesse was "relevant"—they used the word!—and Proust wasn't.

[To Raymond Mortimer.]

Pauline entered the hospital in Boston on Sunday, and had test after test all week. They had found what was feared: a serious leakiness of the mitral valve. Now for a fortnight of treatments in preparation for surgery.

FEBRUARY 3

Boston, Logan Airport. A great pity: Philippe hurt Pauline's feelings before dinner last night, and she fought him in two or three long telephone sessions before he went to bed and again this morning. Some of it I discount as a kind of exhaustion and danger, disguising her fear as drama. I have been tempted to tell the great cardiologist to curtail her visiting hours and to ration her long-distance telephoning. This last would serve a double purpose; Philippe's comment on her hundred dollar phone chat with Elsa in Paris was the point of departure for last night's unhappiness. She is a great wife, but in her defiant extravagances often behaves like one of the great courtesans, Lora Pearl or Lena Casaliers. He loves her profoundly and who knows which of them spoils the other the more thoughtlessly. Perhaps he is richer than he admits; in any event, sometimes he rebels against her inability to add or subtract. Upon which she reproaches him for overworking her with his translations, and not leaving her time or peace of mind enough to write the books she has her heart set on writing before she dies.

While waiting for the bus I telephoned him and heard his pitiful report of all this. Eurodice about to descend into the netherworld, trying to make Orpheus promise her a different life, first this, second that, and then the other thing; threatening not to come back to life unless he can guarantee these essential changes.

FEBRUARY 7

Secretary of State Dean Acheson quotes General Marshall as having said, "There are two kinds of men: those who deal with action and those who deal with disruption." Isn't there a third kind: those whose thoughts and utterances are prophetic somehow? This further question: haven't we had disastrous secretaries of state as far back as I can remember, some too weak, one or two too strong, sometimes inflexible, sometimes change-able? (Hill, Marshall himself, Dulles, Acheson himself, Rusk.)

MARCH 13

This is Friday-thirteenth, traditionally unlucky; not so in the tradi-tions of my life. My oldest, closest friend, who rescued me from poverty and illness and ignorance, and more important still, from having to keep everything about myself secret from everyone, and from not having the slightest idea of a lifework or a livelihood, was born on a Friday-thirteenth. It was one of the first things he told me about himself.

That was in Chicago, in the early spring of 1919. I was ill most of that year, at home in Wisconsin; and then I went to New Mexico where he visited me in the summer of 1920. That in itself was a kind of rescue, as I was in trouble, in a slight scandal, with all the people I knew out there quarreling with me or about me. Back in Chicago in the autumn of 1920, Monroe took me to live with him and his parents, which his mother dis-approved; and our intimacy began. . . .

Poor Monroe! On Sunday at Haymeadows he got up awkwardly out of his folding chair at the back door and hurt his arthritic back; and now he is suffering from sciatica, just able to walk—but of course walking, business and pleasure as usual. His stoicism and exceeding strength of character naturally make him willful and proud. He is the most generous man in the world, and the most flattering, but with sometimes a streak of unkindness. He was unkind to me yesterday, and I shed tears, which was perhaps harder on him than me.

A propos of Monroe's threatening to retire to a nursing home be-cause, in my concern for his health, I try to exercise authority over him—which made him weep bitterly—I remember something he said to me in the railway station in Nice in the early summer of 1928. His relationship with George [Platt Lynes] was well under way, and he had asked him to spend the summer with us. But relations between George and me were then tense, though with good will on both our parts. Monroe got tired of this, and decided to travel back to New York and Evanston, leaving old love and new love to work things out and to make peace. That day on the platform in Nice, reproving me for my hot temper and bad tongue, he said, "I'd rather earn my living in a brothel in Constantinople than live with you when you behave so badly."

Strange as it may seem now, I was the breadwinner in those several years.

MARCH 14

Two new hit songs: one by the Beatles . . . one by Simon and Garfunkle. The first absurd in its specific Roman Catholicism, with an excellent melody: "Let It Be." The second, written by Simon, sung by his halo-headed blond Garfunkle: "Bridge Over Troubled Waters." Both of them in a new fashion, accompanied by the piano, with Brahms-like chords.

MARCH 18

The body of a teenage youth was found this morning in the branches of a tree in mid-Manhattan.

MARCH 21

Said Juan Ramón Jiménez in his letter of acceptance of the Nobel Prize: "My wife Zenobia is the true winner of this prize. Her companionship, her help, her inspiration, made my work possible for 40 years. Today, without her, I am desolate and helpless."

For very old people love is ineluctably tragic, even when the beloved has gone before.

MARCH 24

I have never loved Haymeadows as ardently as I did Stone-blossom. Perhaps because I am older, more preoccupied with my own shortcomings, shifting the onus upon realities around me.

There are compensations. For instance, when the wind blows at a certain speed, from certain directions, especially the East or North, my end of the house, especially the kitchen, makes music: six or seven whole notes in a row, then silence, then almost the same strange melody, repeated and repeated; loudness and softness more variable than tunefulness—somehow not characteristically American, rather Japanese.

MARCH 30, 6:30 A.M.

Haymeadows. Beautiful winter; porcelain white with shadows of pale blue. The snowstorm had ceased after dinner; starlight when I went to bed. I saw the smallish moon low in the south at about 3:30. At 5:30 the small pre-auroral light seemed brightened by the crystalline surface of the earth, pale green and pale pink over the little sassafras trees, through the aging silver maple.

APRIL 20

This week's *New Yorker* in its lead editorial says that the war in Vietnam "has lost even the pretense of purpose, and has become *nothing more than a bloody playground for our idealism and our cruelty.*" Eloquent words underscored by me.

APRIL 28

Said Aristotle, approvingly quoted by Montaigne, "To be shamefaced is becoming to young people, but disgraceful in old age."

MAY 5

[Haymeadows.]

Last year for some reason the upper half of both my fields adjacent to the woodlots was changed from hay to corn; which acreage is now being re-plowed. The five-share plow and the three-share plow make an immense possessive sound, handling and turning and purring. The earth is in exquisite condition for this ritual or (I might say) sexual act, just moist enough, not too moist, opening like pages of a book. Blissful intimate earth-odor! Certain large clods in each furrow, polished by the steel, catch the afternoon sunlight.

Along the lane downhill, and in the fringes of the deepening hay, lie many dandelions like gold coins, some mustard like gold dust.

MAY 16

I am sick at heart about the crazy expansion of the war which to all intents and purposes we have lost; disastrous government; mortal and fateful clashes on the campuses and in the Southern cities.

JUNE 3

There is almost something bird-brained in the nature of my talent: brief and swift, with a long-distance eye, a flickering movement, then a soaring movement, and what might be called falcon-feeding, magpie taste. The journal-like but peculiar form of these pages has awakened these characteristics, set them in motion—whither?

I seem to have my heart set—my talent has its heart set—on a flight longer than my heart is apt to last.

Robert Phelps delights in my *Fear and Trembling*. Style is within my grasp, although perhaps I have devoted more time and energy to it than it is worth.

JUNE 19

Year after year in the 1920s I attempted Balzac and Dostoyevsky, a novel a year, finding faults, missing the point. Then, in each case, the virginity of the mind passed, the great gateways opened, and I read right through the collected works at the rate of about a volume a day (French paperbacks); astounded, bewitched. Shall I try Dickens again?

JULY 3

Hearing is believing. Monroe, at rest in the sun, called to me: "Do you hear a strange musical note, far away? Can it be a bird? Can it be a burglar alarm?"

Two or three notes, it seemed to me, deceleratedly tremulant. It might have been, I thought, a large new egg factory: tens of thousands of hens exercising out of doors, very far away.

Next day we learned that it was the tenth recorded major infestation
of the seventeen-year Cicada, in neighbor Allec's woodlot and up along
Federal Twist. "I can't hardly sleep these nights," said Walter Zdebski,
"they holler so."

Unique creature, native North American, in the last year of individual
life it lays its eggs in twigs of trees, harmlessly. The new generation,
when hatched, descends and takes up its abode underground where it
feeds on roots for sixteen years and eleven months. It has protruding
compound eyes; why? For country dwellers, even close to the big cities,
nature is, among other things, a principal amusement.

JULY 7

A useful truism by Alfred N. Whitehead: "The art of progress is to
preserve order amid change and to preserve change amid order."

JULY 11

Time [the June 29 issue], along with one of its sincere but soft little
essays, entitled "The Silent Generation"—Thornton Wilder's phrase—
has listed about fifty men and women in their 30s, people of consequence and/or celebrities. I found that I admired only six of them: Bill
Cosby, LeRoi Jones, Ralph Nader, John D. Rockefeller IV, Philip Roth,
John Updike.

AUGUST 7

Sorrow is by its very nature superstitious.

AUGUST 9

As a rule, painters' signatures are more beautiful than writers' handwriting. Bernard Perlin has found Miro's signature on the back of Baba's
picture and photographed it: calm, level, youthful.

AUGUST 10

Monroe always keeps a large bottle of Nembutal and Seconal mixed—
more than I think one should have on hand, of this suicidal drug, and age.

The wings of the mourning dove, flying up from the feeding pan, sound like creaking of the tiniest fairy windmill, turning swiftly in the smallest gust of wind.

AUGUST 12

Due to age and irremediable circumstances, sometimes I have to live out days on end like an actor on stage, playing the part of Glenway Wescott, a supporting role.

AUGUST 24

What we really know about Joyce is *The Dead* and Molly Bloom's soliloquy—what we understand or seem to understand. Wittgenstein tells us: "If a lion could speak, we would not understand him." He was a lion, he did speak, we have understood only his small talk.

In 1923, my first prose fiction was accepted by *The Dial*: a sort of brief life nouvelle, a long story of the biographical kind called "Bad Han," afterward incorporated in my first novel, influenced partly by Flaubert's *Un Coeur Simple*, heaven help me!—one of the crossroads of my entire life.

I spent an hour reading *The Apple of the Eye*—I don't suppose I have done so for twenty years. I felt proud of the descriptive passages, like mediaeval illuminations or Eastern enamel. I wish my young people talked with more sound of voice. The moralizing making a rather childish effort, but it does prefigure that belief in eroticism, or shall I say, belief in amorousness, in which I have persisted. Though I didn't read it all, I imagine the whole of this work is better than the parts.

AUGUST 29

"The only good thoughts are second thoughts."—Lloyd Bruce Wescott.

SEPTEMBER 17

I am in trouble with "The Stallions," as to what Coburn Britton [of *Prose*] expects on Monday—but I am not sorry. Even clarity is a two-edged sword: I conceive new material, culling one way; I sink into old hollows and dried-up path in the manuscript I began with, culling the other way.

SEPTEMBER 25

Spookiness in everyday life: In the hour before daylight, watering the nine houseplants in the living room, and as I come away from the room, I hear their gurgle as they express themselves behind me in plaintive, individual, very inhuman voices.

OCTOBER 2

The Republicans have a term for their nucleus of electoral strength—hawkish, pro-war, patriotic, militaristic, prudish and puritanical, philistine. The "Silent Majority" they call it, and they make great with the term.

Now in a plausible and right-minded though caustic editorial (NYT, Sept. 26), Gore Vidal reminds us that this combination of words was Homer's, and in that ancient and poetic use designated the dead.

Presumably some professional speech-writer found it in a dictionary of quotations.

AUTUMN

Mohonk Mountain House, near New Paltz, New York. Cass and Jane Canfield's two-day party—the opposite of a house party—with dinner-dance in between. With Monroe.

OCTOBER 3

Pauline is still unwell—perhaps always will be. During late June and early July she wrote me a wonderful long letter: half a page a day about convalescence; about pretending to be as good as new, to cheer one's friends and family, to flatter any physician.

OCTOBER 4

[To Monroe.]

On the telephone the other day I quoted myself to Bill Maxwell: "I am still subject matter more than I am a writer, or to be more precise, my life as subject matter is far superior to my capabilities as a writer." And what do you suppose he quoted back to me? Walter Scott's "One crowded hour of glorious life is worth an age without a name."

OCTOBER 10

Monroe spent a couple of days at Mouton last week, during the grape-harvesting. Pauline is as well as can be expected; attested by both the surgeon from New Zealand and the good diagnostician from Boston, who have been there. She is more eccentric than ever, with (I think) a sense of borrowed time. She stays awake almost all night, almost every night, reading and writing; wakes up at 2 p.m., and devotes the after-noon to running the house and to her bathroom and dressing table; first meets her guests at teatime in her bedroom—teatime at 7 p.m.—and dines at ten.

How I hate all this! But I understand; and perhaps no one else does.

OCTOBER 27

[To Lloyd.]

Dearest brother, Having you back on your feet, with an easier look on your face, is like the sun coming out, subsequent to frightening, destructive bad weather.

Now please reform a bit—live in a more elderly way, live longer, all of a piece.

Sometimes I think that there is just one moral principal above all others: moderation.

OCTOBER 30

Life goes on. The seasons come around, revolve and return. Once more a mocking bird is here this afternoon, eating ink-berries, and mak-ing up his mind whether or not this is a good winter resort. I must begin again putting out sunflower seeds and fat and hard boiled eggs with some regularity. The little birds will notice at once, and the mocking bird will follow their lead.

The gray squirrels, now that the red squirrel is dead, have moved around the house to the largest, oldest walnut tree. In my dead darling's day as in the long lifetime of his father, the gray squirrels weren't allowed to stay on the south side of the house.

When I am a bore, it bores me so that I seem to myself to be going mad. A problem of old age, up ahead: I shall not always have the energy it takes to enjoy dining with Baba, or to take part in the functioning of the Academy/Institute.

NOVEMBER 2, EARLY A.M.

All Soul's Day. The worst problem of age in my case evidently is going to be euphoria followed by exhaustion. The teenage septuagenarian! I have to overwork in order to concentrate, and of course the life around me is intensely de-concentrating.

NOVEMBER 3

One of the sublime anecdotes in literary history: the day that Balzac, having seen how he could organize what little good fiction he had written at that point with everything that he planned to write thereafter all in the *comedie humaine*, hastened across Paris to see his sister and announced to her, "Today I have become a genius!" I know my stature and for many years haven't wanted to be a giant, or at least haven't regretted not being one. My invoking the greatest novelist who ever lived isn't paranoid. It is what Monroe calls euphoria. Even in my small post-mature work I see visions of originality.

❧

When Boswell visited Rousseau, he asked, "Is it possible to live amongst other men and retain one's singularity?" Rousseau said, "Yes, I have done it."

"But to remain on good terms with them?" Boswell asked. "Oh, if you want to be a wolf," Rousseau admitted, "you must howl."

~

Jane Austen to her sister Cassandra: "I am still a cat if I see a mouse."

NOVEMBER 9

[To Georgia O'Keeffe.]

Two words about my reaction to your paintings: the thrill of a woman's paintings, so rare in the entire history of art; the joyous sorrow, the sorrowful delight, of nature worship in that great part of the world where you live, where I spent a year, aged 18–19.

NOVEMBER 15

I wrote a letter to William Maxwell sorting out in my mind the possibility of a book to be made around "The Odor of Rosemary" essay, which my editor at Harpers wants to see in this connection before I go abroad. I telephoned Robert Phelps, ditto, ditto. Some of this, I realize, was just boasting . . . I'll have the proofs of *Prose* magazine, half of it to be read at Wimbledon. It's a great life if I keep calm enough and get enough sleep. Now to grapple with my strange shipboard acquaintance off the coast of Spain—the breath of my title herb out of sight of land.

~

Re: "Odor of Rosemary" ms. One more miniature incident having to do with sense of smell. A friend of Monroe's, Robert Gathorne-Hardy, the poet, Logan Pearsall Smith's penultimate secretary, gardened somewhat energetically and took pride in some things that he was able to make flourish in Surray. One day to his considerable satisfaction Virginia Woolf visited his garden. He called her attention to a species of fritillary native to some distant clime and foreign soil, white-flowered, fragrant.

The beautiful woman of letters knelt close to the exotic plant and took deep breaths of its unfamiliar fragrance, then looked up at her host and exclaimed, "Oh, it smells like semen!" and blushed, and arose quickly and changed the subject. Robert G-H told Monroe this.

NOVEMBER 20

What a day Tuesday was! I began writing at 4:30 a.m. and continued until 6:15 p.m.—a couple of telephone calls, and food two or three times: a piece of cheese and a small pear. To be capable of that—and without inferiority of literary product—when pushing three score and ten, is remarkable; and for my years ahead, a good omen and a great blessing and reassurance.

I arrived in New York at midnight and kept myself awake until Monroe returned from his sociability toward one a.m. "Are you sleepy?" I demanded. "Not really," he answered. Whereupon I read the final section of the first half of "The Odor of Rosemary," twelve pages, and marked the typos and small mistakes and listened to Monroe's criticism of certain passages. Fatuous old pair that we are, we were thrilled.

NOVEMBER 23

[Re a photo of flamboyantly-dressed heavyweight boxing champion Joe Frazier with the newspaper caption "The Day After."]

Captions: the future role of writers (perhaps) in a picture-oriented world.

NOVEMBER 29

The new oil furnace will cost twelve or fifteen hundred dollars. Such are the disadvantages of living in a home instead of a rented apartment. My brother will have to finance it for me, at least for the time being. Such are the advantages *and* disadvantages of being a mandarin writer, with more genius than talent, and not enough of either; out of season and out of fashion.

DECEMBER 29

Mouton Rothschild. "Decorative Fabrics of Cecil Beaton." When I referred to this advertisement approvingly with humorous approbation—

a propos the hat, a version of which he wears at Mouton—he gave a manner of philosophical groan: "What a ghastly photograph! Oh!"

One of those laborious, self-enriched men who thinks of his way of successful life as having happened to him. I don't suppose that he is sorry for himself—no such comfort!—but he seems to have no notion that anyone might be envious of him.

DECEMBER 31

[A note card with "Dove of the Holy Spirit" detail from the painting *The Virgin of the Annunciation*, by Gerard David.]

For beloved Pauline upon her birthday, between one year and another—once more at Mouton—this bird of the holy ghost of good health, also of the holy ghost of literary inspiration—needing no symbol of our affection, as the years have made a habit of it, given proof of it.

1971

JANUARY 1

Mouton Rothschild. Year after year, at exactly 12 midnight—it marks the end of Pauline's birthday as well as the great change of date—the lights in the 80-foot room are reduced to only Renaissance fireplace light, and the men-servants enter, one bearing a bright candelabra, three with an immense gong with a bass voice, very solemn. Then Philippe and Pauline kiss with gentle formality. Then everyone kisses.

Finally I got through the crowd to Pauline. "I have left you to the last," I said to her.

"Let us walk down to the end of the room," she replied. We walked slowly, along the half-circle windows. She asked if I knew what it meant to her to have me work on a book in the chateau of which she is the chatelaine. And I said, "I cannot help equating my good fortune in writing another work with your returning from New Zealand in good health."

"Oh!" she replied; just the one syllable.

I did not try to express my uneasy self-consciousness in another of its aspects: the present slight flare-up of my talent may die down soon—how soon?—with ashes ahead.

JANUARY 21

Sunrise. When one can no longer keep from thinking of oneself as old, one's errors, failures and bad luck suddenly grow more oppressive, and more or less break one's heart. One wants another chance but there isn't time. Unable to buckle down to my morning's work, how long had I tried in vain without looking up? I did look up—and saw the sunrise. There was the pre-auroral palette—ethereal ravishing pale colors washed across the south east: steel blue, lemon yellow, lime green, bluish pink, mushroom. Nature is an immortality. Nature is a consolation.

JANUARY 25

The nineteenth anniversary of my first meeting with John [Connolly].

JANUARY 31

The great excitements of art in London, December 1970–January 1971. Upon these brief visits, one thing after another in swift succession, I suffer from the great miscellaneous museums. It isn't surfeit, it is confusion: chameleon on plaid.

My maximum enjoyment of art is with Monroe, although our attitudes differ. Intense momentary experiences are what he seeks, with a very great appetite and some thought of continuing to educate himself; taking refuge, in those consecutive admirations, from pain and disappointment and the fears of prospective old age.

My aesthetic responses at the same time are fewer and colder, with rarer enthusiasm and a ground-base of dislike. I find fault even with the work of the very great masters, when they somehow miss their mark, or when the painting has suffered damage and deterioration. Whole entire schools and periods vex me: i.e. late Hellenism, the peak of the Italian Renaissance, the Vatican, and Versailles especially. It seems that I am neither proud nor ashamed of these limitations of my mind and senses. Upon arrival in a museum what I like to do first is look for and concentrate my senses on a few masterworks comparable to my taste, to saturate my memory—for future reference and introspection and enjoyment, later in due course.

After lunch with Will [Chandlee] on Friday the 15th at Victoria and Albert Museum, "Warrior on Horseback" by Riccio (1470–1532, Padua) was my chosen masterpiece, my thrill. As it strikes me in this great image of the martial romanticism of the Renaissance: the excitement of the horse is so much more beautiful than the rider's pride and rage. Grimace as a form of rhetoric.

FEBRUARY

[Re a *Time* photo.]

A patrol of Cambodians returning (with two human heads) from a successful encounter with North Vietnamese military personnel, photograph by a West German named Dieter Ludwig. Perhaps the worst of this strange juncture in history is that it seems quite impossible to know what to think. Our governing class obviously talks irresponsible nonsense all the time, the anti-establishment hasn't even tried to be rational or historical, and most who have imagination and a realistic habit of mind feel so powerless between the upper and nether millstone that we escape into our private lives and aristocratic fine arts and philanthropics, more or less inarticulate about current needs.

FEBRUARY 12

Envy, need I remind my readers, is one of the seven deadly sins— ancient and slightly obscured by the passage of centuries since their first listing—still worth pondering, but in need of interpretation (sloth, for example) (lust, for example).

FEBRUARY 15

Our fields haven't been free from snow and ice since the weekend before Christmas; never very deep but never melted, often replenished— and the deer herd together and stalk to and fro day and night in nervous agitation of hunger. John saw about twenty-five yesterday.

FEBRUARY 18

A thrilling and haunting little movie: part of Brentwood's "Six-Pack." Brentwood is a Hollywood studio that has been producing hardcore films. Now six of them are showing at the Adonis and the Jewel. The first one is entitled "Right Away, Sir," and I want to see it again and again.

What a boring thing about pornographic publishing: the hit-and-run distribution—how and where can one get the paperbacks of last month or month before last? Someone has palmed one of my favorites, or perhaps my consort Monroe picked it up and hid it from me (and from himself). He thinks they will be rare books when Nixon gets done with us. "We ought to keep them for our old age," says he.

I am overcome with frivolity this morning. Euphoria goes before self-hatred; pride before a fall.

FEBRUARY 20

My genius-friend I. B. Singer, whose glory is mainly in English but who writes in Yiddish, was asked at the end of a lecture: "What would you say if you were to meet God face-to-face?"

His answer: "I would ask Him to collaborate with me on some translations."

I. B. Singer: "It is only a few days since my little parakeet died. I never thought such a little creature could go through such suffering, and for this I will never forgive the Almighty. For this, He can give me no explanations."

Very few writers have been able to write full-scale, full-length novels in an entirely controlled and poetical way. Flaubert did. Virginia Woolf exhausted herself in a series of vain attempts; but as a rule, life is too short. The spirit is willing, all too willing, but the pen or the typewriter or the Dictaphone is weak.

Camus' *The Stranger* is a sort of easel painting; whereas a real old-fashioned novel is like the Sistine Chapel.

Fiction is not the opposite of the truth. Fiction is the opposite of journalism and the opposite of history; a matter of form and function.

FEBRUARY 25

Threads of green are stretching upward in considerable areas of the worn and faded lawn. Day before yesterday, I still saw a patch of gray-white, vestige of snow bank; gone yesterday. Of course we still anticipate some storms, as usual. But this morning, behold, a dozen mourning doves picking at the new grass or at the thawed ground between blade and blade; up they went in their little whistled harmony.

At the present in the northeastern third of the United States (east of the Rockies and north of the Carolinas), there are 25 species of turtles, 16 lizards, and 57 snakes.

MARCH 1

Homeward bound, across town in a taxi cab, Monroe quoted Picasso as saying, "I'd like to be a poor man with a lot of money."

"How odd," I said, "what I want, I think, is to be a rich man with no money at all." Quick as a flash, Monroe said, "Then you must be well satisfied, for, surely, that is what you are."

MARCH 9

I am apt to blame the Congress even more than the chief executive for our reckless and unsuccessful war-making. For reasons of political expediency and economic advantage they have allowed the development of a vast armament industry, and an overpowering Pentagon, from which comes irresistible pressure on the president, who is more intent on running for office than anything else.

MARCH 15

A shadow at the back door—in and out of my peripheral vision—a ghost peering in. These are the days that lend themselves to premonition and irrationality, and self-indulgence of sadness.

MARCH 18

Baba now has two brilliantly polychromatic, vaporous, radiant Rothkos; three, if you count the little one that Monroe recommended to her in the first place, even if she fails to sell the Corat. Poor little creature, like the dog in Aesop with the bone in its mouth, seeing a second bone reflected in water!

As it seems to me, incessant publication of what Baba calls "the art scene" isn't good education. One ought to improve the general taste; to discourage the vulgarization and commercialization of the new in art; and to beautify all the settings and scenes of our lives.

MARCH 19

[From the *New York Times*, March 19.]

A few bits of one of Plato's dialogues, the *Parmenides*, on a piece of parchment three inches square, a chance purchase by a Duke University professor said to be a milestone in paleography. Parchment has lasted better than papyrus. There are a hundred thousand pieces of papyrus in museums and libraries here and abroad; only about 20 percent of them have been identified and deciphered. Only about three percent of ancient Greek literature has survived; only seven of Sophocles' 120 plays.

MARCH 21

Willa Cather, that violent, beautiful, not good woman—though a good writer—wrote, "Life began for me when I ceased to admire and began to remember." By "admire," did she not mean love?

MARCH 22

Homosexual marriage: The only small talk in the world that I enjoy is the 50-year-long colloquy of G.W.-M.W. It's one of the elements of my loneliness when he is away.

What's so good about it? He goes far out into the great world, sometimes very far out, and reports like a dream. I on the other hand keep thinking of things to tell him. But does he listen? He likes the sound of my voice; I delight in the steely colors of his thought, the warmth of his heart, despite the pain and weariness.

APRIL 2

A strange thing about the lapse of inspiration and talent and creative spirit: sudden depression and fatigue halfway through the day. My handwriting goes to pieces. At daybreak I still have the calligraphy script that I invented as a teenager, because I had been taught badly at the little red school house in Orchard Grove. My shame when I come across recent pages that I myself cannot decipher—though they might be recent—is like madness.

APRIL 11

My birthday—Monroe said, "Well, I'm sorry that you have to be 70 years old, but as it has to be, you must make the best of it; and that you surely do."

APRIL 12

Yesterday on my birthday an infant climbed out on the family windowsill and fell down nine stories, 90 feet, onto a soft cushion of bushes, and apparently was not harmed. An Easter miracle, said the radio newscaster. A birthday miracle, a good omen.

Emerson: "There are asking eyes, asserting eyes, prowling eyes, and eyes full of fate." Emerson is one of my guardian angels; our pint-sized Montaigne.

APRIL 16

Alone on the subway platform at 53rd Street and Third Avenue. A good-looking, unkempt, unshaven, lean, poorly dressed youngish man paced up and down, and circled around unsteadily in desperation, perhaps aggravated by drink, talking to himself loudly enough to he heard fifteen or twenty feet away. "I was out there in Vietnam in 1962, four years I was. I saw all that stuff and it was hell."

I would like to have stayed within sight of him and within earshot—watcher and listener that I am—but surely he would have ceased his self-revelation and changed to some contact with me, panhandling, aggression, politics, pathos. Not, as the youngsters say, my bag.

APRIL 25

It is difficult to envision the horrors of the past. For example, the poor in England by the end of the eighteenth century were held in check by insanely severe petty legislation; the statute books listed two hundred offenses punishable by death—e.g., "planting a tree in Downing Street" and "impersonating a Chelsea pensioner."

MAY 6

Off to Washington Tuesday noon to dine and stay overnight with K. A. Porter. Lunch with my Authors League colleague, Herman Wouk, and a meeting with Senator [Frank] Church on Wednesday.

～

Maugham's little attacks on people were exciting and worth pondering, but Rebecca West's humor was delectable, even giving pleasure when it mortified the butt of it. When George Davis' *The Opening of the Door,* his one and only novel, almost won the Harper Prize in 1931, she reviewed it as an example of my dubious influence on a number of writers of the late twenties: "Mr. Wescott had devised a new way of narrating the life of his native Wisconsin, and the formula is this: There once was a small boy who loved his grandmother so much that when he grew up he wrote and published a novel about a small boy who loved his grandmother so much that . . ."

Sometimes when lecturing on campus I found it pleasant to begin with this joke. The students seemed to admire me for having the nerve to give an opinion of myself so derogatory.

JULY 2

The small, simple admirable goods and chattels of our beloved immigrant [Ivan Ashby], mostly clothes and books, were delivered on

mid-afternoon Friday by two of the most attractive human beings I
ever encountered on earth: an erect, great, relaxed, rosy-cheeked, smiling
well-spoken young man named Mitchell and a husky eager boy with an
almost-healed injury of his nose. They called each other, respectfully,
Mitchell and Mitch. They were obviously lovers, unable to take their eyes
off each other. At one point, while addressing me about something, with
courteous enthusiasm, the elder caressed the younger, with a kind of
happy forcefulness, rather more like a brother than a father. He constantly taught and trained him. They were charmed by me, and blissful
to be in our luxurious countryside. They had with them a Doberman
Pinscher, also blissful.

Almost painfully, though not unhappily, I desired to see them again.

JULY 5

Early yesterday, when I heard Monroe's bath splash at the top of the
stairs and took his orange juice up to him, with several domestic questions, I found him reading Cavafy, and he called my attention to "He
Came to Read" in [John] Mavrocordato's [translation]. "For me," he
said, with a happy ardent note, "this is more erotic than all your indecent
books."

JULY 12

Glorious Yeats, tone-deaf, and color-blind!

JULY 13

I have borrowed this for a new start in life: "Henceforth I seek not
good fortune, I myself am good fortune."—Walt Whitman, "Song of
the Open Road."

JULY 16

Pauline last winter suggested I write five little volumes, one for each
of the senses. I couldn't do all five; furthermore there are more than
five.

JULY 18

Problems of my life, our lives. A group life—without entire group communications; with inner alliances; with secretiveness. For example, Lloyd versus Monroe. For example, Ivan versus Adair [John's friend].

JULY 30

Empathy: when weeks of dry summer have turned to rain, my feeling about the corn, for the corn, almost *as* corn.

JULY 31

Re: Monroe. Our fighting is dangerous now. Each of us has strengths and weaknesses, too well matched—the outcome might be just by chance. I so loathe myself for my raging and weeping, at the time and for days afterward, that it verges on self-destruction. I can't even bear to think of Monroe's weak position, with strange relentlessness and perhaps egotism pitted against my brutality.

Pace, pace. It is a familiar problem for me, tried in earlier crises—expected to be a good man rather than a vigorous man. Now I consent to whatever enfeeblement as a writer in the final ten years of my literary endeavor—*our* literary endeavor—may result from another repression of my desires and instincts as they come naturally to me.

Emerson: "Our moods do not believe in each other."

AUGUST

[Sculptor] Antonio Salemme, born in Gaeta 1892. In 1924 he attempted a small standing nude of me—he never finished it. We also lured each other to bed; that too was unsuccessful.

His beautiful wife Betty, who had a brief affair with Paul Robeson, informed Frances Robbins of my need of money to go abroad and write *The Grandmothers*, and gave a party which brought us together to wonderful effect.

AUGUST 6

[To Bernadine Szold, re her health.]

As to the martyrdom and perhaps peril of your respiratory condition, what can I say? At our age, as to matters of fact including physiology and psychopathology, destiny has us in its hands; and no one can escape dying. On the other hand, no one has to die more than once. Only we have to suffer.

Whereas the spirit, in its various aspects—goodness of heart and sunniness of disposition; literature and the arts; great causes, such as Lloyd's reformer's zeal about hospitals and medical schools, and Barbara's family philanthropy; stoicism, Monroe's for example, in re his arthritis; the bravery of the manic-depressive, myself for one, with great intelligence often wasted in emotion and self-concern—the spirit (I say) can rise above illness and ignore the passage of time, a good deal of the time.

Monroe has a new protégé [Anatole Pohorilenko]: a central European of golden good looks, speaking six languages, indefatigably studious and ambitious, a winner! His having a friend is a situation that has always immeasurably helped me—compensating for some of my inadequacies toward my dearest of all.

AUGUST 7

How weakness of character has haunted me—not so much disadvantageous as shaming—a thousand little submissivenesses that have seemed to me all right—but unworthy of the vocation of a man of letters, frittering away my self-respect. For example: *Apartment in Athens*—to think that I allowed my title to be altered by supposedly expert publishers.

AUGUST 17

"Katherine Anne Porter: confessional conversation: 'My own loose wanton self.'"

My dearest of all is a phrase lover. His notes too fragmentary: haiku of the landscape of the mind. But they are beautiful, worth keeping and pondering. I was compulsively sorting a box of clippings, slowly waking up to strains of Mozart, with the light of the day delayed by river fog, when I found the above note, and for various reasons it made my heart ache. How I wish that I could inspire him to put his journal notes in order! In the event of his dying before I do, they will tempt me terribly. Meanwhile I believe he would take both pleasure and pride in the task and the outcome. I must not, cannot, force him to do or not do anything. His strength hates my strength, and perhaps vice versa.

AUGUST 19

A. E. Housman. "On the idle hill of summer, / Sleepy with the flow of streams / Far I hear the steady drummer / Drumming like a noise in dreams. / Far and near and low and louder / On the roads of earth go by, / Dear to friends and food for powder, / Soldiers marching, all to die."

Housman's elegiac obsession may not have been all amorous. With a conservative temperament, wounded by his failure as a student at Oxford (no honors, not even a passing grade), in an exceedingly conformist society, he was a pacifist and a radical.

AUGUST 27

[Re a youthful photo of Marjorie Wescott.]

This small snapshot came to light and gave me a bad pang of old mortality. The most beautiful of my sisters, except for an anxious expression verging on a frown. To think of her in the last years of her life defaced and deformed by cancerous lymph glands, a martyr to optimistic, experimental medicine. The only child, grandchild, or great grandchild of our parents to have died, as of this date!

SEPTEMBER 2

Going to Fire Island for the wild Labor Day weekend with Janet Flanner and Natalia Murray—that is to say, not just for fun, certainly not for games. On October 25 I am giving a reading of Foster's posthumous homosexual love story *Maurice* at the 92nd Street Y in New York. I accepted that invitation without stopping to think that it may be landmark-like in my small personal case, as in the overall trend of moral-cultural events: Wilde's trial, Lawrence's floggings, Maugham's will, the Wolfenden legislation, the [Lytton] Strachey biography, the $135,000 advance to the Institute for *Maurice*. Wescott the great sheep in sheep's clothing.

SEPTEMBER 4

Fire Island, Labor Day Weekend. Writing at daybreak in an alcove window facing the bay—suddenly a huge black Persian cat passed across my window. Cherry Grove is full of almost-marriages, serious liaisons. One beautiful pair together seven years. The strange morale: a place dedicated to debauchery, characterized by sexual cohesiveness. Tensions, were it not for the meat-rack and the gang bangs. Byrne F. gave his account of having hustled himself to two or three businessmen: "Nothing is easier if you are a beauty, as I was, and I could always get an erection." Bodybuilders with hard boozy faces and bodies like Greek ephebes. And lower class teenage boys with little paunches. The extreme hedonism, booze and sexual debate, does not necessarily undermine community spirit. Neat, clean, well mannered. More dinner parties or cocktail parties than Newport or Palm Beach.

SEPTEMBER 9

To Paul Cadmus: I am busy (and overdue) with a miniature memoir of Forster for the *New York Times*, marginal to the homosexual novel, and your letter lifted me out of my inferiority complex about it, relieved my aches about it, and ennobled me a little.

∾

One must never forget the impact of the trial and imprisonment, and moral and economic ruination, of Oscar Wilde upon English writers of the next generation, Housman, Maugham, the Lawrences (both D. H. and T. E.), Strachey, and in a very different and almost saintly way— incapable of scandal and dishonesty—upon Forster.

∾

Three fourths of the literary remains of Blake were destroyed after his death—not for indecency but for blasphemy.

Certainly a great many individual human beings have an itch to destroy.

SEPTEMBER 12

On Thursday afternoon, walking along the north side of 51st Street between First and Second Avenues, suddenly, for the first time in my life, I was aware of no longer fearing my death. If I was thinking of anything in particular when this idea or sensation occurred, it was wiped clean from my mind. But as I looked back on it and reported it to Monroe, scarcely expecting to be taken seriously, he gave me a joyous smile and fond glance. "Oh, I'm so glad," he said. "You know, the fear of death is useless, no help to us." He is a more intense realist than I. The knowledge of the futility of certain emotions like that don't help either. When they fade from the mind it is, as people used to say, by the grace of God.

SEPTEMBER 20

To Isabel Bishop: Did I tell you that we [the Institute of Arts and Letters] got $135,000 in guaranteed royalties from the American book publication of *Maurice*, given to us by magnanimous Isherwood for an E. M. Forster award.

News item: Farrar, Straus & Giroux have bought my monster Journal, from 1937 on, and Robert Phelps is editing it for publication . . . the final transaction and decision took place yesterday. It gives me gooseflesh. Playing my ace in the hole.

SEPTEMBER 24

There will have to be a great many more books like *Maurice* before the homosexual life will cease to be a mystery, with its extreme friendliness, its great gamut of emotions, its erudition of sensualities.

Almost awe-inspiring calm of my becalmed sex life, leaving a routine of pornography and masturbation, not at all sorrowful or grief-stricken, not unhealthy, which sufficiently alleviates physical tensions. I remind myself of a predatory bird no longer able to swoop or eat.

What is left? A great sense of beauty, my imagination as voyeuristic as ever, the mind's eye of memory still keen, tenderness more or less paternal, admiration acute, and haunting anxiety, and a kind of prayerfulness verging almost on religion or love.

OCTOBER 6

[Notes on E. M. Forster's *Maurice*.]

There are three great themes in the work. 1. Chronology, with the maturing processes little by little almost scientifically observed, pecking order, arousal patterns, etc.; nuance by nuance, softly stepping, cat-footed from boyhood to the mid-twenties. 2. Intelligence on the increase, as Maurice's almost sterile, dry, hard temperament is dug into by plow or (rather) by spade and hoe and rake, moistened by the storms of sorrow; extreme conventionality giving way to an almost religious independence and eccentricity. 3. Style and form, animating and sharing the work according to these two developments: the language less and less chatty, more and more lyrical; the scenes as in a play, Maugham-like, giving way to scenes as in an oil painting, Bonnard-like, profoundly colorful and only half representational; post-coital communications between the protagonist, finally, a kind of telepathy.

OCTOBER 17

With Barbara to New Canaan for Philip Johnson's reception at the Glass House. A beautiful house with its three adjoining buildings: the windowless guest house, the underground picture gallery, and the new sculpture museum. Autumn reds and pinks, golden yellow and bronze.

OCTOBER 31

A sudden realization, 6:30 a.m., on All Soul's Day as I buckle down to a fortnight of onerous though proud drudgery, preparing the total text of my so-called Journal 1937–67 to be Xeroxed: I want to write a series of short stories, the same old series (A Santa Fe Scandal, Dear

German, The Lieder Singer, The Little Ocean Liner) but with all my new technique.

O Wescott, beware now, on your last lap, lest your imagined enterprises get to be a disastrous obstacle, as indeed they have been in the past.

Bill Maxwell's advice: "Never less than one complete sentence, every morning at about sunrise."

NOVEMBER 2

Yukio Mishima. Any sort of playacting is perilous. So many suicides, intended to manifest the tragic situation and state of mind of the suicidal one, to act out his suffering and bafflement, needing help, needing at least sympathy, not intended to go all the way to death—end fatally by some accident: ingestion of one barbiturate too many because one has previously imbibed one drink too many, etc. Likewise the demise of certain masochists.

Accidents happen inside the mind as well as in areas of circumstance and physical excess. Until almost the end, I think Mishima may have been showing off, promoting his literary production and dramatizing his political program (à la Hemingway, [Gabriele] D'Annunzio, Colonel Lawrence, Stefan George); then suddenly he went mad, with the last stage set, the sword in his hand, his four companions trained to play their supporting roles.

A man of astonishing abilities and energies; unattractive to me (in so far as I can judge him, sight unseen)—but liked, not just admired, by discriminating, dear friends of mine.

NOVEMBER 4

Five a.m. A surprising conclusion, perhaps a decision—great manuscript preserver that I am, the foe of the burners and ostrich-heads:

The chief legitimate function of university libraries is to keep our manuscripts and documents safe for future biographers and historians.

NOVEMBER 12

[A postcard to Bernadine Szold.]

Dear, very dear Bernadine, I have been reading the reminiscences that you sent Monroe: your gentle, enthusiastic, never intolerant breeze blowing upon my heaped-up autumn leaves. Robert Phelps, at work on my journals 1937–46, is obliging me to remember as much as possible—so much of my miscellaneous writing is around and around the fact or the event, leaving mystery, leaving ego.

NOVEMBER 15

Robert [Phelps] was still here when I arrived on Friday and we had another of our bouts of contentiousness. He frankly enjoys them, and baits me. For example, he wants a lot of illustrations, mainly of me— "Your beauty is an important part of the record!"

He took away 1937–1946 [the journal binders]; all that can be crammed into Volume 1, he thinks.

A happy weekend with John and Ivan. Lloyd and Baba were in New York for the Horney benefit dinner. We saw *Sunday Bloody Sunday*: very well done and clever. I wasn't convinced by the relationship between the woman and the boy.

I sent Marianne a telegram: "Happy Birthday ever dear friend and great poet whose every re-reading entrances Glenway and Monroe."

NOVEMBER 22

The eighth anniversary of the assassination of President Kennedy. I remember that I happened to be washing dishes, listening to rock and roll on my rasping little Japanese radio, so that I heard the first word of shouting in the street, the gunfire, the first announcement of the death! A few moments later, Earl Butler, on the phone weeping: "Not only have we killed our best president ever, we are providing the worst Texan there is."

DECEMBER, COPENHAGEN

[Re the aborted novel, *The Deadly Friend*.]

In 1932 or 1933 George Lynes had wanted to try to write a novel and couldn't think of a plot. I like a fool invented this implausible love imbroglio, the ugly lover disguised by facial surgery. George soon tired of it, but it caught me and wasted two or three years of my life. Every man his own octopus.

DECEMBER 5

Wide awake at 3 a.m., due to the battering of my psyche by the great power-mad librarian, Lola Szladits [curator for the Berg Collection, at the New York Public Library]. Now I am due at the Academy, having maneuvered the happy-natured, handsome, affectionate poet Richard Wilbur into the presidency thereof.

But it's not the right sort of life. Let's start all over again.

1972

FEBRUARY

Marianne [Moore]'s funeral. One of her mottoes was "Rejoice Evermore," two words extracted from a hymn: varied by her in a lifelong fugue. Let us now play parts in it, in honor of her.

FEBRUARY 7

Glimpses of the Past: Upon the day of Marianne's coffin lying lonesome in the Presbyterian chapel next door to her apartment:

Said Emerson, senile, at Longfellow's funeral, passing beside the open coffin, "That gentleman was a sweet, beautiful soul, but I have entirely forgotten his name."

FEBRUARY 15

Began Monroe's 73rd birthday [February 13] all over again; happier. I must be active somehow, with some bit of writing every day. His problem is going to be in town, and his cities and high society. He will get too tired and perhaps eat and drink too much, and out here at Haymeadows he will be bored. Every day that I spend with him I must think of something to do with him and/or for him.

MARCH 20

Half-asleep metaphor: I feel like an old but still promising race horse, taken out into the paddock with his peers, within sight of the track, sound of the crowd, smell of dirt and grass; but laden and bewitched by extra harness and heavy blanket and inexplicable bondage; no injury or pain; only the certain knowledge that he is not to run that day's race.

MARCH 26

Robert [Phelps] said yesterday: "Of course you shall have what you want. But first you must hear what *I* want. And I feel sure you will want *that.*" Masterful.

APRIL 8

A Persian proverb: "If at noon the king should say, 'The night is falling,' it is a wise man who answers, 'Behold the stars!'"

APRIL 14

Poets always go too far: I myself am both my good and bad fortune.

APRIL 30

Love-song of doves: Mourning doves, misnamed of course. Their obsessively loving discourse, though soft in texture, carries through the air like a knife: throbbing phrases at the base of the throat, with R's rolled not as Parisians roll them, but in the way of the Balzac country, where young diplomats go to perfect their French.

Not many creatures on earth fight their own species to death as humans do, as doves do. Beware of inordinate amorousness.

MAY 13

Everyone knows what a novel is, what biographies, autobiographies and memoirs are—but what is a journal? It is an immensity that is always (and has to be) fragmentary.

Handwriting—graphology. I had a common and low-class handwriting when I was a little boy—it was what I was least good at, and some gentle criticism of my mother's made me ashamed. I began to print and little by little I developed what might be called a calligraphy, affected in the twenties, very satisfactory after that, but slowly declining now.

∾

One of the great pitfalls in literature and indeed other arts is conceiving some piece of work in a matter of minutes or hours or days which in fact is going to take months or years to do.

∾

A good many writers of great consequence have been half hack, half amateur. The word genius must not be applied to us; neither can anyone entirely be ruled out of that category.

JUNE 4

To do Volume 1 of my so-called Journals what Giroux wants is to require me to use the better parts of "The Old Party" and the "Portrait Sketch" of Kinsey.

Re: Robert Giroux. When dealing with superior men one must resign oneself to not knowing what they are working toward, or whether they are acting on instinct.

JUNE 6

The theme of Harper's last bestseller, *Love Story:* "Love means never having to say you're sorry."

Surely, surely love means the opposite: always, always.

JUNE 10

East 51st Street. My tête-à-tête luncheon (with Lou) forcibly interrupted by two plumbers with equipment—the kitchen next door overflowing, had to be approached from under the sink. What a sad omen of my elderly sexual situation! What a comical bit of symbolism!

JULY 20

[To David H.]

Dear David, I love you fondly. I am grateful to you for pleasures and beauties. I'll never forget a day in New York. I'll never forget a night here . . . the first time I ever saw an orgasm expressed on your beautiful face, starting, peaking, subsiding—that wasn't very long ago. Tear this up if you like. Or perhaps better still, send it to me for the final volume of my journals and remembrances which is to be entitled *A Heaven of Words*.

SEPTEMBER 14

I think I can say truthfully that I have never begrudged Monroe anything, even when I happened to be burning in inner hell: never envied him.

Envy must be a sin of old age, in many if not all cases. It must also enter the artist's temperament in some measure, or vice versa, as it is a matter of imagination.

SEPTEMBER 22

Ethel came with the mail a little while ago, shouting in her rasping way about this and that; and just after her departure, she shouted louder than ever, almost frightening. As I ran out I heard sweeter shouts in a chorus over the barn, over the ash trees, and I made out Ethel's words: "Here they come, Glenway! Here they come! Listen to them!" Two dozen geese, loud and clear, black and white and glassy bright silver in the sunlight. Glory be to God.

SEPTEMBER 27

My father's German brother-in-law was a bank teller and embezzled a bit; relations had to put up a lot of money to keep him from going to jail—shocking to me at about ten years of age. Said bank teller was also the father of my 17- or 18-year-old cousin, the first person I ever desired, all night long in the same bed, two or three nights, the first person to hurt my feelings along that line. He set a clock back to get me to bed early, so that he could seduce mother's hired girl, unwatched.

Saying goodnight to John, having to pretend that I didn't know where and why he was going: Sobbing broke out in my mind and heart, but I forbade it; that is, I kept silent, dry, upright, and active around the house—having no right to any such waste of time.

OCTOBER 7

What Yeats said of our two greatest writers, Emerson and Whitman: "They are as great as writers can be without a vision of evil."

OCTOBER 9

The preliminaries of Monroe's hernia operation, by Dr. Salerno: "Monroe is nervous about this, perhaps because he has seemed to fail in health during the summer, or because his life has grown more pleasurable, so that he is afraid of its getting away from him. He puts his foot on it and growls."

OCTOBER 11

At dinner Baba was in one of her irritating states of mind. Intensely political these days, not letting me get a word in edgewise for sentence after sentence, with gestures, she pretends that I underestimate McGovern, or worse still, that I non-admire Nixon less vigorously than she does. With defects of the psyche so antithetical, isn't it a wonder that we have managed so well so close together for thirty years?

OCTOBER 13

The man I have loved most of all, for more than half a century, was born on a Friday the thirteenth of February. Lucky for me and (I dare say) lucky for him.

We have reached the time of life when we must begin to expect bad luck and to learn to put up with it, and not just on Friday. He has in prospect three surgical operations.

OCTOBER 20

The year that Monroe and I went abroad to write, 1925: In Dayton, a small town in Tennessee, a science teacher named Scopes taught evolution, which was against the law. The reactionary state of Tennessee sent for the most famous orator, William Jennings Bryan, to prosecute, and the great brilliant atheist, Clarence Darrow went at his own expense to head up the defense, and ferociously attacked the aging statesman. Five days after the trial, Bryan died—some said that Darrow's excoriation had destroyed him.

OCTOBER 31

First reading of my sheaf of memories of the 1920s in *Prose*. What whisks through my mind like the crack of a whip is the question: Do I not overindulge in commas?

NOVEMBER 3

My life has been a great book but, alas, I am weak as a man of letters; a small, slow writer, still too much involved in living to excel in literature, in fact more involved than ever.

NOVEMBER 15

My first cerebral-vascular accident, before the Institute dinner, after which I was to have read "Bill Benet's Death."

NOVEMBER 27

While Monroe prepared his café au lait I read to him my hundred-word citation of the new Poet Laureate for election to honorary membership of the Institute and Academy. His comment was in question form: "Haven't you used the word 'Everyman' too often recently?" I railed back at him but without drawing blood or shedding tears.

Monroe's recent hernia operation was like a miracle. In less than 24 hours he was walking up and down the corridor, in less than four days he was back at Haymeadows, unstitched, sleeping upstairs. All that week I had to fight to keep him from driving his cumbersome old Cadillac. We were wonderfully happy together.

≈

I feel that no man is so nearly "married" to another man as I am to Monroe, and that I could explain this feeling and testify to it in some factual way, so that it would be acceptable.

DECEMBER 2, 6:45 A.M.

Sensational sunrise filling four of my windows, east and south. In the great corner between east and south, plumes of burning flamingo on fire under a vast wing in neighbor Allee's woodlot and in the great branches of my twin black walnut trees, under a vast wingspread of purple. Due south, bright yellow on the horizon, with five shades of blue above it, interspersed with pink.

DECEMBER 22

Orly Airport, Paris, six hours wait. A pleasant flight, though I slept very little. Bedlam here, due not only to the holiday traffic but to a strike of baggage handlers. I lugged the suitcase around quite a lot but no harm in that, good exercise.

The aging process is an adventure, and ought to be a discipline.

DECEMBER 23

Mouton Rothschild. When we sat down to dinner here last night Philippe's first topic of conversation was Raymond Mortimer's *Times* portrait of Coco Chanel, with self-portraiture at the margins.

"Couldn't Raymond do an entire book of character studies like that, bringing himself into things now and then?" Philippe asked.

"Of course he could if he thought he could," I answered presumptively.

Having been indolent for about half a lifetime, it shames me now to beseech and reprove other writers. Raymond has had a laborious life and may not want to work so hard in years to come. For my own part, last summer when I realized what I had signed up for, volume after volume of scribble to be put in order, tidied up and abridged here, amplified there, oh, I sickened with self-pity.

1973

JANUARY 6

Mouton. The Disraeli Pillow: One evening, walking along Park Avenue past a shop, looking into its bright show window—I was in need of a bedspread—I saw a small deluxe pillow embroidered with these four words: "Never Complain Never Explain."

Had it been the precept of an angel whispered in my ear I should not have been more impressed. It gave me gooseflesh, but I seem not to have taken it to heart in the intervening years. Who's precept was it? I remember my curiosity. I mentioned it to someone, Lady Cunard, and was told, "Disraeli."

JANUARY 9

Lisbon, Hotel Mundial. Tomorrow we are going up into the wooded hills, where there are famous little castles, and out toward the open ocean. I scarcely care, having fallen in love with the city as such, almost at first sight. The last such romance in my life, perhaps; Amsterdam, Copenhagen, what else? I fell *out* of love with Brussels last year, except for Leon's black boulle and Rubens. Had I not promised Monroe all autumn to travel somewhere with him for a week or ten days, I'd have been ashamed to stop here, with my pen-hand itching to get at certain pages. Thank goodness I did, and thank goodness we opted for a cheap hotel. At Tagus level, with the Visigothic castle overhead, the Phoenician voices rising from the street to our large seventh-floor windows, as 'twere saws sawing, axes chopping . . . I kept getting up last night and looking down, until almost dawn, then slept; then was aroused by a small rooster, not very virile or strong rooster, but persistent. A voluble population, and they don't sleep much; they half-run most of the time, catty-corner across the largos and the pracas, and in and out of the side streets. Intently sexual scrutinizes from young men now and then.

JANUARY 16

"Where there is too much, something has been left out." A Jewish proverb expressing simplistically though perhaps profoundly one of my principles of the literary art.

JANUARY 24

One of my Monroe's bad habits is addressing envelopes to Pauline, Raymond, Anatole and others containing sometimes clippings, sometimes jottings, and leaving them unmailed. An analgesic for conscience-stricken affections; an aggravation of our Collyer-brothers-disease, packrat-ism.

FEBRUARY 13

Monroe's 74th birthday, the New York City Ballet.
In the taxi: "Happy Birthday."
"You are my birthday present; you and those dances. Can there every have been so ravishing a company?"

[Malcolm] Lowry is a one book author, everyone says, and the excellence of that book is accidental because he never learned how to write; he continually started and stopped, commenced and abandoned.

MARCH 1

[Re commemorative stamps of George Gershwin.]
Gershwin, a friendly acquaintance of my youth. In 1925, at a party at Nancy Cunard's apartment in the Ile St. Louis, he was a pleasant pianist and our almost weirdly beautiful hostess prevailed upon him to play for us. The Duchess de Gramont (Marie Raspoli) talked the while, which flustered the young celebrity. In a strong whisper someone informed her that he was the composer of "Rhapsody in Blue," not just a professional from a nightclub hired for the occasion. She whispered back contritely in her Italian way.
At another party, in 1927 or 1928, at Carl Van Vechten's in New York, instead of a duchess we had an opera singer, the contralto Marguerite

D'Alvarez, a lush looking giantess. With great curves and sighs and parted lips, she sat beside Gershwin on the piano stool. She would have liked him to accompany her in something from her repertory but, unmoved by her ego or her libido, he made her sing "The Man I Love" instead, first in a musical murmur at his elbow, then standing up, with might, like Delilah, like Carmen, like Orpheus. If I remember correctly, it had been written for *Funny Face* and not used until some later production.

He took notice of me that evening, and afterward we happened to meet in Fifth Avenue and walked along together, when he told me that he wanted to write an opera and needed a theme or a plot. If anything occurred to me, and appealed to him and his brother Ira, he thought, I might try my hand at a libretto.

APRIL 4

Jill Krementz is the type of female that my type of homosexual is enraged by. But she is the best portrait snapshotter in the country.

Kurt Vonnegut Jr.: Where there is satiric fire, there may be surrealistic smoke.

APRIL 14

James Stewart, the still-celebrated star, once said that "the great thing about movies is that you're giving people little pieces of time that they will never forget."

His is the only delectable and emotional, valid counter-tenor voice.

MAY 28

Monroe: Our love life has worked wonders and now another wonder is called for. And strong as each of us is independently, even when ill or in pain, we appear not to have the necessary mutual strength for the next step, the last lap.

JUNE 10

Death of William Inge. A hot, shining Haymeadows Sunday—John and Ivan and Adair here, Monroe joining us at noon. Then Lillian Hall heard the bad news on the radio, telephoned Ethel, who telephoned us. John's mixed emotions.

JULY 7

Harry Robbins Haldeman: The worst face in our present nightmare news: the glaring, imploring eyes; the heavily sculptured lips, sagging, taking some secret pleasure, the chin not in the middle, the overall look of headaches due to grinding his teeth.

AUGUST 8

To Thornton Wilder: Dear Thornton, Galley proofs of *Theophilus* reached me last weekend with a joyous note from Cass [Canfield] . . . In a depressive passage of my own work in progress (it *does* progress), I hid it in Monroe's room for several days, not to be seduced away from myself.

AUGUST 30

My attire in late teens and early manhood was unconventional due to vanity and penury in combination overlapping. I had brought back from New Mexico a cowboy hat, a fawn-colored corduroy suit, and painted boots with high heels. The cape came later. I remember acquiring it very cheap at an auction one summer afternoon in 1921 in or near West Cummington, Massachusetts, along with a red-flowered carpet bag. Upon my first visit to Munich the following summer in 1922, an aggressive porter seized the carpet bag and one or two of the larger suitcases, and when I tipped him he said, "*Danke schön, Herr Dichter.*" (Poet, writer.) I felt a pleasant glow of pride and then realized how obviously I was dressed the part.

SEPTEMBER 6, 8 A.M.

A fact ever recurrent in my existence and in my thoughts these days, which I hope to elucidate before it gets lost in the shadows of the passage of time: senescence is as interesting as adolescence.

OCTOBER 20

Nixon has compromised with Senators Irvin and Baker in the matter of the tapes. What a bore it has been to have been right about Nixon in re Watergate all this year (that is, to have felt my rightness), and to have been talked down not just by Lloyd and Ivan but by Baba, who regards herself as the only real Nixon-hater.

DECEMBER 3

The other day I went to the spooky, shameless, embarrassing little Jewel Theater in the East Village to re-see a film. It is more active than the other five all-male movie theaters, the young men really cruising, more aggressive, the older men really stubborn, unabashed, less hopeless.

DECEMBER 22

For present purposes of my lifework, last lifework: Sacrifice present experience and the record thereof to the great past, half written and the other half, until now kept secret, wasted.

[Re *Jimi Hendrix*, the movie.]

I hope that this will still be showing when I return from abroad. At the time of Hendrix's death, which was at the height of his cult popularity, one could buy a plastic replica of his erect cock, useable I was told.

DECEMBER 27

At Mouton, working on my Don Bachardy foreword, in a storm of creativity. Fascination and drama: what a triangle, Philippe and Pauline and I.

∼

Posing for Don Bachardy: I have known Don Bachardy since he began to be the closest friend of an important friend of mine [Christopher Isherwood]. He was a sprightly figure, fraught with friendly though uneasy smiles. I once saw an infant squirrel taking its first steps down a steep branch, clutching, eyeing the air on either side. In Don's early look, unlike the squirrel's, there was neither hunger nor fright, only something of a wild creature's concentration. He seemed to like every bit of life around him, above him, beneath him; and his own life was a venture, not just an adventure. Especially when his talent started; it challenged him. He drew me in 1964.

DECEMBER 28

Is it safe to say that I lack genius? That grand substantive noun, ambivalent down through the ages, is too great. Talent is too small.

The only important talent I have is memory.

1974

JANUARY 1

One thing that homophile men cannot understand is the fact that he-men and womanly women have the gall to pretend to understand our sex-lives and our way of thinking about love.

MARCH 15

Thomas Moore as a teenager in Edinburgh came upon Robert Burns sweeping the sidewalk in front of his poor dwelling place, and with precocious insolence and wit exclaimed to him with his power of improvisation: "You Scottish loon, / Lay down your broom / And let a man pass by."

To which Burns, an aging, indeed dying man, still famous but poverty stricken, retorted in even better form: "You Irish ass, / There's room to pass / Betwixt the all and I."

APRIL 29

I have talked to Pauline half an hour a day almost every day. Hard work, in terms of my emotions—so many spider webs, invitations and involvements to sidestep, and little cheering fictions kindly intended.

MAY 2

The present is the enemy of the past. In some cases, perhaps most, the reverse is true.

Even with Proust's remembered emotion, even in that first chapter, he has to keep uncovering it, reclaiming it, from a strange cloud of egocentricity, a befogging forgetfulness. It is what it says it is: a search for a time that was lost.

Glimpses of the past: Mozart's wife said he was an even better dancer than musician.

AUGUST 15

The Peeper at The David Cinema, West 55th Street, with Monroe, who praised the triangle, especially their post-coital hugs, silky dark heads viewed from the top. Also, he said, "I have never seen such beautiful kissing."

SEPTEMBER 7

I don't dream for a moment that I am to outlive Monroe, despite his agony of arthritis, and his lifelong habit of me—the restless, massive silence in which my voice for fifty years has rattled and rattled, gloated and complained. All my life I have believed in the unique excellence of his journal, mosaic-like—only glancing into it now and then, never reading it, except when it came to me from his faraway places in letter-form. And now he hasn't the courage or the energy or the virtue to put it in order or even to read it.

OCTOBER

[Re pressed red rose in clear cellophane folder.]

The rose that stood in a glass of water on John Stevenson's round table in Minetta Street Mews, the October 17, 1974 night he cooked hot and sour soup and cubed chicken with almost raw shallots for me, just before my weekend with Pauline at the Ritz, October 18–20.

~

To John Stevenson: Did I ever tell you how obstinately M.W. pretended not to know which of my principal John's I might be referring to? Robert Phelps wanted me to nickname you Jeannot, after Cocteau's most loveable beloved of the mid-twenties [Jean Bourgoint].

~

[Note card jottings: four examples of undated notes GW wrote on colored index cards during the 1970s, probably meaning to expand later.]

Anthony Butts: Seen from a taxi cab in a 1938 veil of rain crossing the Place de la Concorde. Great flashback all the way to 1923.

Witter Bynner, 1924 in his fifties, New Mexico, intimacy.

K. A. Porter: Until late in life she understated her age by four years; then shamelessly, unabashedly, happily informed *Who's Who* and all and sundry of having done so.

Charles Henri Ford, *The Young and Evil*, 1933: chapter seven, pp. 79–84, Theodosia = Djuna [Barnes].

Wescott in 1950s publicity photo.

Publication of *Images of Truth*. GW: "My notion of myself, fairly constant from year to year." (© Estate of George Platt Lynes)

Wescott's first days in the house at Haymeadows.

Across the century, the enduring relationship of Monroe Wheeler and Glenway Wescott.

Wescott friend Baroness Pauline de Rothschild, formerly American fashion
designer Pauline Potter.

Family matriarch Barbara Harrison Wescott at the New Jersey State Museum in Trenton.

Robert Phelps, devoted editor and generous friend. (with permission of Roger D. Phelps)

Wescott at Haymeadows, 1970s. (with permission of John Connolly)

GW: "A shadow at the back door—in and out of my peripheral vision—
a ghost peering in." (with permission of John Stevenson)

John Stevenson: "This gaze has always looked right through me to my ghost." (with permission of John Stevenson)

Outdoors at Haymeadows, Wescott, 1980s. (with permission of John
Stevenson)

Reflections of a lifetime, Glenway Wescott, 1901–1987. (with permission of John Stevenson)

1975–1979

THROUGHOUT THEIR MID- AND LATE SEVENTIES, Wescott and Wheeler continue the pattern of their lives, with some moderation naturally. Almost heroically, Monroe keeps up his foreign travel for museum exhibits and business, even as he requires strong drugs every day for painful arthritis. Glenway is relatively healthy—"I think of myself as young"—with occasional cardiac slumps that slow his activities and require medication. Late in the decade he sometimes wears a neck brace when a disc problem affects his circulation and balance.

Despite his worrying about Monroe, and their losing many of their famous friends (including Janet Flanner, Anaïs Nin, and Paul Robeson), Wescott still experiences real happiness in these years. He is proud of Monroe's stoic example, glad for the New York companionship of John Stevenson and a young crowd, as well as the country visits of John Connolly and Ivan Ashby. The hero of his journals project, Robert Phelps, continues to encourage him, interview him, and deal with the publisher. The journals have become an all-encompassing part of his life and legacy. Well over one hundred bankers boxes of material, many organized, some in disarray, make it all seem hopeless at times. But his reading aloud of Phelps's edited journal selections delights his friends and himself at Monroe's apartment and at the new East Village loft of John Stevenson. At one reading, Brooke Astor insists that there should also be a volume of the lifelong correspondence of Wescott and Wheeler. Glenway does believe the journals will bring balance and perspective to the highs and lows of his long career. However, in an August 1977 entry he says he will never live to see a book published to the satisfaction of himself, Robert Phelps, and the publisher.

While some of his books were reprinted fairly regularly over the decades, a surprise is the 1977 Leete's Island Press reissue of the humorous 1932 *A Calendar of Saints for Unbelievers* in its original form with Tchelitchev's illustrations of the zodiac. (There had been a 1933 Harpers edition that censored the artwork.)

Adding to the complex world of Haymeadows in these years is the fact that four tigers, later joined by two leopards, are kept in a one-acre, high-fenced compound near their house. Barbara and Lloyd Wescott's daughter Debo is in her second marriage, and husband Thane Clark enjoys these dangerous pets. Glenway humorously says he dreamed the newspaper headline, "Author Eaten by Tigers." Only after the marriage dissolves are the animals eventually (July 4, 1981) moved to a tiger farm in Florida.

The biggest losses in these years are the two great women in Wescott's life. Baroness Pauline de Rothschild finally loses her battle with health problems in March 1976 in Santa Barbara, California. Before she takes that last trip, Glenway spends "four magical days" with her at a Boston hospital. And Barbara Harrison Wescott, the matriarch of their extended family, who had supported Glenway for most of his life, succumbs to cancer in April 1977. In May, four hundred honor her as a great patron of the arts at the New Jersey State Museum, including the current and past governors, other politicians, and trustees.

The great partnership continues, however. Wanting Glenway to see Europe again, Monroe takes him on a whirlwind trip to the places of their youth and to their many friends overseas, including Baron Rothschild, filmmaker François Reichenbach, and the French lover of Glenway's Paris years, Jacques Guérin. In New York and at Haymeadows, they keep up the rich and colorful life they've shared.

1975

JANUARY 7

There is in Brussels a red-figured Greek bowl, portraying a boy with wreathed head, perhaps on his way home from a banquet, rapturously masturbating: his head back, shoulders straining like the wing-joints of a bird, phallus at full stretch; and the inscription is "I greet you—I want you."

JANUARY 22

Having a poor head for dates—indeed for whatever is mathematical or numerical—I like to recall things as contemporaneous or as coming before or after other things.

For example, Goethe was born before Mozart and outlived Byron. Mozart died the year the French Revolution started.

FEBRUARY 2

Once at the close of lovemaking I heard my tired, foolish voice saying, "The best! The best!" and my love replied, in a joyous but stern way, "The best so far!" with sweet laughter.

The moral is—the same in the case of literature as in the case of love—patience! But without wasting any time.

FEBRUARY 8

A blissful night and morning with John Stevenson last Saturday and Sunday. A delightful and amusing party in the south Village last night.

FEBRUARY 19

I spent a happy night at 251 [East Fifty-First Street] just before John Stevenson departed to Texas and Florida conventions, interspersed with some sea and sun. Toward morning I dreamed of my grandmother, and an O-shaped knothole high up on a tree and wild bees in a continuous straight flight to it and honey overflowing down the trunk—a marvel.

FEBRUARY 21

Great mystery of time in old age: Time passing over my head, in and out of my mind, thought and heart; with no perceptible beating of wings, no very dramatic daydreaming or spinnings of narrative. Here I sit for an hour or two hours trying to figure matters of philosophical problems, spellbound by coincidences.

Coincidence can be adorable, like one of the lesser gods.

Poor Glenway's Almanac: Men and women do most of their reading in their youth, feeling the tides and undercurrents of their prime taking hold of them and bearing them they know not where; and once more, in the autumn years, when looking back on the mysteries, the miracles, the fortunes and misfortunes of their lives—and they seek in literature parallel life stories, insights of writers good and bad which may illuminate their own experience.

FEBRUARY 23

I feel that I now understand my fate; can I make use of my self knowledge?

FEBRUARY 25

Where is my dog-eared Renard? The one that *Book World* paid to have photographed? It's the limit. Nothing is going to do my mental health more good than to locate my essentials in this house, and exercise my ability to put my hands on them, and rejoice every time this happens.

MARCH 22

Desperate revulsion against, horror of, my old darling's concept of order: "Put everything in labeled boxes." But there are already so many of these, which is a good start, but there is no end to it.

My dream and purpose is to publish, to be published. He seems to me to have no dream except to keep everything, except what will make a suitable present for one of his loved ones, to sell when poverty catches up to us. For example, he has wrapped up, labeled and thrust into a corner the 1945 sterling silver with our combined initials "G+MW", devised by me, bought with *Apartment in Athens* money.

MARCH 29

"Memory is the great literary artist."—Maurice Baring.

[Re photo.]

Teenage Malraux, vulnerable and mean-spirited, with his mad-looking father who in due course took his own life.

It gives me cold chills to think that, however fervently one may dedicate oneself to memory, and to that record of the memorable of both first- and second-hand which is literature, more than half of the All is wasted on one.

One day Janet [Flanner] sat at the Ritz Bar with Hemingway, and she had been interviewing Malraux who had confided to her the fact of his father's weak and/or evil end; he had asked her not to write it. She and Hemingway then told each other that their fathers had done likewise.

One afternoon Janet and I gossiped tête-à-tête about some of the byproducts of friendship and sociability in the way of memory. And as we parted with a great hug, she said, "Glenway, the tales we tell each other are better than all the books our friends write, even the books we write ourselves."

～

How irregular, how precocious, how dilatory, how successful in improvisation, my book-learning and overall culture has been!

For example, when I wrote *Fear and Trembling* with tears in my eyes with a sense of its importance to me personally, my talent for fiction fallow all of a sudden—what next?—and historically, the resurgence of Germany's vanity and cruelty, I hadn't even heard of Kierkegaard's otherwise alarmist wondrous work, F&T, named after Goethe.

MARCH 31

Jottings by my dearest of all, rescued by me from his paper-recycle box. Why does he write them, or to be exact, half-write them—no headings or dates; the speakers not identified; as a rule not even quotation marks! They break my heart because I so long for his journal, prepared for publication by him (or by us together)—out of boxes and boxes of aide-mémoirs, a lovely small book—easy.

MAY 13

Today my beloved Monroe is to arrive in London from Florence on his way home. Every thought of him makes me weep; so strangely disabled, so ashamed.

JUNE 10

I attended the opening of Carson McCullers' "The Member of the Wedding" twenty-five years ago, with Carl Malouf and Tommy [Sullivan]. A quarter century has passed and I have a malfunctioning heart, I have aged considerably, and yet I think of myself as young; Carson has been dead for eight years and I think of her as young and I think of that first play of hers as touchingly true to life, at least to her life.

OCTOBER 12

[To Monroe re their household arguments.]

My dearest of all, I can't win—I've known that for a good while; haven't you? Let us promise each other not to blame ourselves in the hour of death, when it comes, however it comes.

OCTOBER 15

Maugham once said to Monroe, "If Barbara hadn't spoiled Glenway rotten by letting him have just enough money to eke out a bare living he would have buckled down to become a successful writer, and by this time he would have a little apartment in New York as well as a house in the country, and with a proper staff!"

DECEMBER

Asked one day what she was proudest of, Barbara answered, "I am not proud. I want to be remembered for what I have helped all of you to do."

1976

JANUARY 1

Just inside the cover of my long-habitual blue ring-binder, I have clipped and pasted a bright-colored three-line advertising slogan: "How to stop worrying and learn to love."

Worrying is not what I do.

If I were to love anyone more than I already do love my lifelong Monroe, it would destroy me.

Having written at 8:30 a.m. on a bench in the Trenton railway station, looking out at the shadowy graveyard surmounted by dark blue clouds, suffused with white sunshine, I cover my eyes and bow my head and weep like an old man.

~

Stop worrying and learn more about love than life has taught you.

JANUARY 9

Philippe telephoned once more: Pauline is in prostrate condition, with congested lungs, congested kidneys, the flu hanging on. [Dr.] Bernard Lown insists on her going to Santa Barbara around the 20th for about a month. The more often I write to her the better, Philippe says; it would be easier for me if I could be assured that he wouldn't be reading what I write. Not crocodile tears; his grief about her, and his love for her, in fact, couldn't be more genuine. But, oh, what crocodile endearments for my benefit.

JANUARY 11

Dear Tennessee [Williams]: How I have enjoyed your *Memoirs*! How glad I am of our old friendship! What a good example your present

health and ardor and dedication to production and reproduction of your
plays all over the place sets lazy, sentimental me!

JANUARY 14

Nothing bites so hard as the worm that turns.

My weakness as an aphorist is that I can't or won't stop when I am
ahead.

Like lyric poetry, the smallest forms of prose—aphorism, pensée, epigram, maxim, proverb—need not be true to be meritorious.

JANUARY 16

I am giving John Stevenson and Robert Phelps one of my care-
package meals in Bond Street tonight, before taping. The latter will put
to me a long series of factual questions that he has accumulated, or let
me try to narrate in brief or in outline some part of the memoir years
1914–33. It wants to be synopsis more than remembrance, and this technique may help.

JANUARY 17

Two young blacks: one a hustler trying to frighten me into jeopar-
dous intimacy; another, crowded close to me in the jam-packed subway,
cruising me—beautiful, elegant, with a small gold earring.

Do Me Evil—the long-awaited Toby Ross film with the visionary child
voyeur. Adonis Theater, Eighth Avenue.

JANUARY 27

[The *New York Times*, December 28, 1975: "Paul Robeson Dead at 77."]

Dorothy Smith [Lloyd Wescott's cook] longed to be accompanied to
Paul Robeson's funeral.

First meeting, 1924, someone brought him to a party of Betty Salemme's
in the studio overlooking Washington Square Park—I remember the way
he sang then, and at later stages of his career, but I do not see him in my
mind's eye as of that evening. I could tell by the soft pale flicker in our

hostess's eyes that she would joyously take him to bed if that opportunity presented itself. It did.

FEBRUARY

To think that, in 1976, the ones to beat are Capote and Vidal.

FEBRUARY 4

To John Stevenson: Since our afternoons and evenings together— a glorification for me as you listened to so much of my impromptu prose—everything has happened to me. I have worked hard; I have been damaged by anger; I have been ill again, though not alarmingly; I have had my heart not broken but eroded. Strangest of all was a series of mishaps: a furnace cracked open, a floor flooded, a shower of splinters of glass when the refrigerator door opened. I listed them on one of my worksheets which I entitled: "Weak old man visited by tireless poltergeist."

FEBRUARY 12

To Pauline de Rothschild: I can't stand my life. I am too ashamed of myself. If I can't work several hours more per day and complete more pages or at least more paragraphs per hour I shall take my life. Oh, in fact I can't do that while Monroe lives on, or while Barbara lives, because she has paid for my strange career of writing. I can't do it while you live, knowing you will wish to survive to help me to do likewise and to read what I may still write. There are certain younger persons to whom I must in honor set a good example: John #1, who was born the year of *The Grandmothers*, and John #2, who was born the year of *Apartment in Athens*.

FEBRUARY 19

[To Raymond Mortimer.]

I had a magical four days in Boston with Pauline, before Philippe arrived. His two or three lengthy calls on the telephone were pessimistic and pathetic; also a little antipathetic, from my personal point of view. I am afraid that her health isn't holding up as we had hoped. They are in California, and he is coming to New York for two or three days in a fortnight, on his way back to Europe. She will be in Boston for two or three weeks when of course I shall visit her.

FEBRUARY 20

Poor John! John R.C., calling me from his television studio, between acts of a soap opera. Hearing that I was taping tonight, with John Stevenson, along with Robert Phelps, he said, "Now, though not until now, I am jealous." And I shouted at him as I used to shout at my Monroe.

MARCH 3

I have been perfecting the sample of my Journals that I read at the Academy. Monroe returned from the Gulf of Mexico and Jamaica last night: twelve days on an archaeological cruise with Anatole. As he came in the door he said, "If I were you I'd turn that text over to the Academy tomorrow, just as it is; it is no matter." He made the same recommendation, word for word, a fortnight ago as he went out the door.

I responded, "If you were I, you wouldn't have written it at all. Much simpler!"

MARCH 7

[A telegram to Baron Philippe de Rothschild on death of Pauline in Santa Barbara that day.]

Thank you for two decades of care and devotion to our darling. Your heartbroken Glenway and Monroe.

MARCH 18

Every so often I find that my imagination is based on fear. My mind excels only at premonition. What a sad, bad inner litany that leads to, when things happen to go wrong.

MARCH 24

Photo of William Burroughs [in Tangiers, by Allen Ginsberg]. To think that this eminent sad personage is admired by my latest and perhaps last beloved!

Is it my duty, might it turn out to be my pleasure, to re-read *Naked Lunch*? One of the side-effects of love is to broaden one's horizons, to increase one's range of interest and feeling, is it not? Not always. There is a statute of limitations.

Is Burroughs, for everyone, as he is for me, aureole-ed with vague tragedy?

MARCH 28

Great saying of Gore Vidal: When asked whether he rewrote his work much, he said, "Oh, always, everything, a great deal. It appears apparently I haven't always very much to say, but I always find a lot to add."

The population of the world is expected to reach four billion today, having doubled in fifty years.

APRIL 15

I'm worried about Lloyd's health. It's always been based on neurotic optimism, overcoming ulcers, cancers, etc. Now his damned doctors, with ghastly timing, are crunching his courage away, breaking his heart. The point of this is that he may not get his retirement village [project] done. Barbara nibbling away at him. He is bored.

MAY 8

Dylan Thomas: A glimpse and a prejudice. I once saw Dylan Thomas, unappealing. He would have touched one to the heart if one had supposed him misbegotten, injured or sick. But I am one who is merciless about alcoholics—even alcoholics themselves are.

A great genius in both poetry and prose, but as a whole he writes too loosely and doesn't hold my interest.

JUNE 17

Inscription for Robert Phelps' copy of the Leete's Island reissue of *A Calendar of Saints for Unbelievers*: "For Robert, Aaron to my old Moses— holding up the arms of my self-esteem and my love of subject-matter and my belief in publishing and biography, as we both look down into our promised books."

Horror: Poor Earl, day before yesterday, wrote me a longish, plausible, rather convincing letter—a typed page, single-spaced—announcing that he is about to commit suicide and explaining why. Perhaps for the first time in my life, I felt like Victor Hugo.

Spring 76 Delight: Bill Maxwell is enraptured by *A Calendar of Saints for Unbelievers*—he had never read it, never even seen it. I am reading his *Ancestors*, which is exquisitely written.

AUGUST

Remembering: My mother's incessant feelings of farewell—the flowers, the autumn leaves. Having come to live with me, she wanted to live forever, and indeed did live two or three years longer than expected.

❧

John Stevenson rarely comments, but suddenly happened to say that the overall title [of the proposed journals] didn't please him: "The All and I." With no inclination to be influenced, without asking why not, I kept wondering, troubling. My lifelong trouble: not dilatory or procrastinational; indecisive!

NOVEMBER 3

I have been in a kind of almost incapacitating melancholy or melancholies of late, due in part to a cardiovascular slump.

The good news, or at least the reverse of very bad news: the election of Carter.

NOVEMBER 4

An order to myself: Write everything and anything plainer and larger—even the hastiest jottings. What a mercurial mind. . . .

DECEMBER 16

How I wish I could induce my Monroe to date and identify his jottings, and to use quotation marks.

It is one of my reasons for not wanting to survive him, when my loneliness will turn to curiosity about him, for creative and commemorative purposes.

As it appears now, he cannot teach me anything without unkind nagging, and I cannot teach him anything by any means whatsoever. It's too bad. We desperately need to learn, in both self-concern and altruism.

DECEMBER 24

Holidays are a matter of the past; literature likewise. On the one hand, nostalgia and the weight of embarrassments; on the other, a transposition of realities that fade and fade into language, which lasts.

1977

JANUARY 17

I stood at the kitchen door, half glass, looking out at the lawn and the upward-sloping cornfield, all plump with snow; furthermore the sky was gray with snow predicted. The paradox of not mentioning to my beloved brother that all the little birds have departed from my back door. Monroe is apt to attribute this to the presence of my three-legged cat.

FEBRUARY 19

In all my life I have only known two people to go mad from love. One was Louise Bogan who did it twice with the same protagonist and was treated at an interval of 25 years by the same psychiatrist in the same sanitarium. The other, as it seems to me now, was I myself.

FEBRUARY 22

When I first met Anaïs Nin in Paris in the twenties or the start of the thirties I did not know that she was a writer. I was told that she had a writer friend named Henry Miller.

Now many of us writers of Anaïs' generation may envy her in a way: with work in progress to the day of her death, like a phoenix high up on the tree with a host of young and old readers looking up to her, in a nest made of inspiration and experience, fiery with pain, singing her prose. She was amazingly beautiful.

MARCH 2

Lloyd almost pleads with me to dine as many nights a week as I can or will: not to leave Baba alone, not to leave him alone with Baba, not to leave him with the Clarks [Thane and Debo], outnumbered, dead-tired. Bringing me home, Lloyd said in his weakest voice: "Barbara's health is failing fast now. She has terrible pains in some ribs, and she realizes she has lost her fight."

MARCH 11

Day before yesterday, I lunched with Bill Maxwell in Gracie Square. He doesn't love me anymore, which embarrasses him and does something unbeneficial to me.

Yesterday I lunched with Ted Morgan at the Hunam restaurant on his expense account. He found a great file of Willie Maugham's business records at the Lillie Library. Who, Ted argues, who but Alan [Searle] could have had them and sold them?

Wasn't I clever to suggest his writing to Rebecca [West]? Two long answers from her. One of Willie's love affairs was with Violet Hunt, Ford Madox Ford's un-legalized wife, says Rebecca.

All very intimidating to me. A biography is an impossible form— everything has to be a fact, or to be made to seem so. Nothing is worth telling unless you can drop the name or names concerned.

MARCH 13, 9:50 P.M.

To Lloyd: I have just had a strange experience. I wanted to do some desk work but felt tired and incompetent, and lay down reading the *Times* magazine section, listening to the heavy rain on my flat roof and adjacent window, and fell asleep and slept for about an hour. Whereupon I had what I took to be a stroke—breathless, immobilized, struggling to get on my feet, just able to stumble into my study, into the kitchen, into the dining room. I took up the phone to ask the operator to call you—and then I woke up, in bed, that is, on the bed, holding the *Times*. No sign of it's having been anything but a bad dream. Pulse normal, eyesight clear, a little nausea, a little fear.

I heard the telephone ringing—thank goodness, it was John Stevenson. He will telephone me in the morning. I must remake my will. I am not afraid. If I were afraid I should write a page to thank you for all that you and Barbara have meant to me—your perfect love and care. I should ask you to remind Monroe that I have loved him exceedingly from 1919 until this day, and he has been able to give me inspiration to write, and may do so again.

Now to bed. I shall read myself to sleep.

[April 7: Barbara Harrison Wescott died in her sleep at Hunterdon County Medical Center.]

MAY 1

From my funeral remarks when we shoveled some of Barbara's ashes in front of the New Jersey State Museum:

Thankfulness was ever inherent in Barbara's life and nature. She reveled in projects, and sometimes conceived and started things large and long, beyond her powers of completion. She liked to be helped and she attracted helpers, and repaid them with affection and with praise.

I believe—credo—that the loving person, who has been loved in return, each for the other, and then is gone, not only leaves an eternal loneliness, but hallows the environment, the companionship and the activity, in which this love has taken place—the branch of government, the health center, the campus or museum or library, the painting, the writing, in which he or she or they have been engaged.

Goodbye for now, dear friend.

[The *Trenton Times*, May 2: "400 Celebrate Memory of Barbara H. Wescott."]

MAY 8

The soft upward whistle of the cardinal.
Baba's immortality.
The earthsick road and meadows of the farm.

MAY 18

Jane Gunther, more intensely fond than ever, and how lovely looking: her complexion like late winter fog over half melted snow. After dinner Jane told me the desperate story of her forcing John to adopt their
schizophrenic son (illegally, prenatally), which he didn't want to do
because of the agonized death of his own son (by Francis). The boy,
Nicholas, is in love with and treats her cruelly. What she mainly lives on
is John's morbid little masterpiece [*Death Be Not Proud*]: teenage cancer,
parental grief.

Last night I took John Stevenson to the ballet: A faultless production
of "The Goldberg Variations," which the youngsters have mastered at
last, to not quite enough avail. How I enjoy being with John Stevenson
when he is happy, which he almost always is.

The other day at the 55th Street movie, for the first time in my life, a
well-dressed man almost as old as I reached across two seats and very
gently groped my leg. I gave such a jump that it frightened him.

MAY 19

The Wescott-Thane Clark family crisis is worsening; some sort of
crisis is due or overdue.

JUNE 28

This is the second day of summer, isn't it? My parents were married
(and I was engendered) seventy-seven years ago. I fear the years ahead.

JULY 16

[Re an advertisement photo of a handsome mover in *The Advocate*.]

I have fancied that this might be the young trucker who brought Ivan's boxes from the pier to Haymeadows several years ago, with a husky small partner, whom he obviously was in love with, and by whom he was more deeply still, loved.

Excess of zeal on the small one's part—the bridge of his nose still half broken from having run into something, for example. Continuous, amused, but serious discipline by the older: "Stop grabbing more than you can hold, damn it!"

Haymeadows seemed heaven to them. I fascinated the elder. I wanted to keep them, at least for a few hours, and perhaps could have done so. Many a time I have kicked myself for my quietism.

AUGUST 19

[Re his journals.]

At some point in this huge patchwork of self-portraiture, somehow, I want to confess my strangenesses. Sorrows. Sexual incapabilities, dislike of my naked body, sense of failure and parasitism, willingness to learn but never being able to stand adverse comment/criticism by those whom I regard as my superiors, devouring nervous energy with underlying fatigue.

What I suffer from now is what my father made me feel when I was a boy.

≈

I suppose that this project of journals and remembrances as a whole is going to kill me. I doubt that I shall live to finish it as it has developed in the fateful influences and interchanges between Robert [Phelps] and me and Bob [Giroux] and Roger [Straus].

≈

Janet Flanner asked me to stay on after her cocktail party broke up, and like a fool I did—there was Natalia [Murray] and she also asked Connie Bessie to stay. All three talked me down, and Janet clung, and Connie clung, and Natalia said, "Now see to it that you don't drop me, when Janet isn't here for bait."

NOVEMBER 2

Monroe inherited a little money from Barbara and has insisted on spending most of it on a swift visit to the Europe of our youth. We shall be in Paris at the Hotel Calais from November 10 through the 15th, then Berlin for a few days—my first visit since Hitler came to power; and Amsterdam and London all the week of November 21–28.

NOVEMBER 7

Newspaper ad: "*White Trash*—the last gay production ever to be filmed by the Master, Toby Ross." What does this mean? The last gay production *ever* to be filmed by the Master. Perhaps six months ago I saw a squib in a newspaper stating that he had been convicted of something having to do with drugs. [Ross later resumed his career after having legal problems.]

NOVEMBER 10

Paris, Hotel de Calais. This room, number one on the mezzanine, which Monroe always asks for and gets, is pure Vuillard. Philippe [de Rothschild] has just sent two dozen pink roses and two dozen white fuschias. Paris spooks me.

Paris until the 16th, then the Museum Hotel, Amsterdam. On Monday the 21st to London, the Ritz, Piccadilly. The last weekend, the 25th to 28th, we have promised Raymond Mortimer: Long Crichel House, Wilbourne, Dorset.

NOVEMBER 14

Lunch and all afternoon with Jacques Guérin, scarcely getting a word in edgewise: his quarrels, his exploits of buying and selling, his treasures . . . After that, three grand meals with Philippe de Rothschild in thirty-six hours . . . I wonder if I have the time to see François [Reichenbach]—is our friendship restorable? Has either of us the time for it?

NOVEMBER 24

The Ritz, Piccadilly, London. To Raymond Mortimer's large but modest country house, shared with a music critic and an ophthalmologist.

The museums with Monroe—what pictures, what pictures, what pictures!

Homesick—home Tuesday. I pray for all, in my way.

NOVEMBER 29

Heathrow Airport, London, to Monroe: My dearest love, Thank you, from the beginning of our grown-up (or growing up) life, down to this date, and as far beyond as fate may determine.

Thank you for this holiday, on its last legs just now. There are ten minutes left before boarding and I can see the post office on the ground floor. Know that if by chance I failed to survive on the way back to you, my last breath, last thought, last gasp, last bit of mortality would amount to just one kiss, to you and by you.

1978

APRIL 12

The first day of my 78th year. Solemn resolve, broken as soon as made: at break of day, while waking up, read nothing not written by me. Then, immediately, write at least one readable page, allowing as much time as I have free that morning. And if I find that I have no talent, no memory, no sense of future—no matter. Then apply myself immediately to drudgeries of everyman's office or study: dating, sorting, stapling, pasting, filing, empty wastebaskets.

∾

The other day, aged 77, I reread my first novel, obscurely entitled *The Apple of the Eye*, and regretted for the umpteenth time the thinness of the characterization of Dan, the fictive me, and Mike Bryon, a little better, personifying my earliest love, or perhaps I should say impersonating my first beloved.

APRIL 24, 6:30 A.M.

"Crazy Days of Old Age."

My life with Monroe suddenly amounted to two lives in one—when did it happen, imperceptibly, six months ago? Now suddenly it has re-divided itself: his agony of arthritis and irrationality of drugs, his successful final sexuality—my blissfulness of body and great final romantic love with no sex whatsoever—his right to do or not to do what happens to please or displease him—my obligation to produce a masterpiece, more than I am capable of, broken on the rack, drawn and quartered. O shame! O vanity!—feeling the entire lesson of my life, the absolute uniqueness of my Self and Destiny. All this is a kind of madness—irreparable epiphany—but perhaps I can slip back out of it and give myself up to work, work, work at last—better late than never.

JUNE

Another twenty-five minutes hunting a fountain pen, with attendant self-belittlement, and blaming others (especially the dearest other of all), with damaging senescent indulgences and stupid grief.

JULY

An observation of myself, immature, aged seventy-seven. I don't like the taste of coffee, but it medicates me awake. Ideal breakfast: along with the hot, dark stimulant, a good-sized chunk of sacher-torte—my sense of taste is ecstatic for a few minutes with the summer sunrise streaming into my face.

And during this ecstasy what do I think? I think that I am failing heartbreakingly at all I undertake; not making a fool of myself—would that I were!—just fraudulent, just a disgrace to those who have loved me, those who have helped me, not wisely.

JULY 8

It is better in some ways to be a writer than a painter. One way: we don't have to share the word "literature" as they do the word "art."

JULY 19

To Raymond Mortimer: Do forgive Monroe for not writing to you. Every other day he blames himself for not doing so. Let me not suggest that he is "failing"; scarcely even changing, except from hour to hour—despite the arthritic anguish that I cannot even imagine and the really high-ranking analgesics that they have begun to give him. But, but, but—I am afraid that he is losing his epistolary ability. Might it not help if you complained of his not writing to you, sorrowfully, even indignantly? Nothing rusts so rapidly as inactive talent.

AUGUST 25

[To Raymond Mortimer re Baron Philippe de Rothschild.]

I'd like to try to tell you how I feel or what I think about him as of now; accumulated pettiness and finally the deathbed, the several deathbeds. I have always enjoyed him. Except tête-à-tête those obligatory morning walks. One morning he would complain of his wife, trying to get me to try to change her ways for his sake or to his advantage. The morning after, mood change, he begged and maneuvered and wheedled, supposed that I knew a great deal about Pauline before his time or by dint of her confidence. No such thing! I didn't even prevaricate, as I often do when pressured for secrets, mine or other people's.

I've never known anyone to cover her tracks so well, and she often told me untruths and denied truths, unaffectedly and as it were instinctively. Come to think of it, we talked about this as a part of the nature of womanhood—she brought it up—on our last day together, in Boston.

AUGUST 27

To quote Andy Warhol, dear, dull, ill, indomitable, cynically wise, sordidly successful, "Everyone is a celebrity for 15 minutes."

OCTOBER

Yesterday's arrhythmia, pulse, pain, sleep.
Horror, sorrow—not shame but a soft fatalism.

∾

One of my best and also one of my worst metaphors: my Titanic-like talent, my desk always inhabited morning after morning, by little donkey-like literary materials, jottings, sketches, commonplaces, clippings. Whatever my awakening eyes light on I irresistibly and disgracefully fall in love with.

OCTOBER 3

Exactly as the sun thrust up through neighbor Allee's trees, the great weeping sound of our wild geese circling up from the Wickecheoke Creek and down over the Delaware.

A little later, our cock pheasant, prophetic of frosty weather before long, shouted his way over the almost ripe corn into the spinney, the part of the spinney which hasn't been enclosed in the tiger cage.

OCTOBER 6

The other night I dreamt that I was Katherine Anne, uncontrollably garrulous. Last night I dreamt that I was Barbara, exhausting herself raising money for her Trenton museum while pneumonia and lymphoma devoured her. What next? I dread Pauline who will softly scold me for not writing.

NOVEMBER

My infancy was, or has become, a dream. Waking me up, lulling me back to sleep, mirroring my fate and my behavior and the choices I have made, and the potentials rejected or neglected, veiling things or confusing one with the other. Theme: fear.

NOVEMBER 7

[Re the death of Janet Flanner.]

This must not be, cannot be, an altogether grief-stricken occasion. In the deterioration of her great old heart, our beloved Janet has had to endure her share of suffering in the last year or two, with worse to come if she had lived longer.

The two large volumes, as edited by Mr. Shawn, are her masterwork, masterpiece. They have the unity and continuity of a great novel, and at the same time they serve superbly as a history of her half century, our half century.

DECEMBER

The great contemporary modern subject matter is the plight of women in love with homosexual men.

DECEMBER 14

Remembrance sometimes is like seeing and hearing ghosts, friendly ghosts. A number of my dead friends were gurus, which went unnoticed because of the energy, stir and originality of their everyday life style, and their sweet humility toward me. Now, dead, they have nothing to do for me except speak, re-speak.

1979

JANUARY 24

In childhood I saw a great comet. Was it Halley's? It had seemed to me a blunt thrust of celestial flame with a short bushy tail. What I remember is not the event but my effort to find descriptive words for it all the following week or two.

German proverb: "The eyes believe themselves; the ears believe other people."

APRIL 3, FIVE O CLOCK A.M.

My state of mind halfway between deep sleep and conscious-stricken reality, conscious failure, is like being a saint.

It isn't inspiration which would (should) lead to the day's work, as scheduled, bitten off, promised. It is vision, rotating, sweeping the very top of conscious awareness, the zenith, which leads to, or at least points to, again and again and again, what I find definable as god.

I can testify to the joy and spiritual sustenance of living with art.

If and when I move to a nursing home, I shall take a handful of post-cards of my favorite art around the world. If I lose my eyesight, my visual memory is so rich that I can summon up a museum in my mind, hang and re-hang, judge and re-judge. I could in the text list a hundred pictures, any one of which as I lie on my deathbed may bring tears to my eyes, tears of joy.

APRIL 16

I used to say (perhaps I simply believed) that Easter was the only holy day that touched me poignantly, helpfully, sincerely.

Serendipity: a detestably affected word—who invented it? Walpole? [The word was invented by Horace Walpole.]

JUNE 15

My dearest of all: There is a kind of surcease, at least for a few hours or a few days, when we part. It may well be that I shall feel it as I die, if you outlive me.

JUNE 16

I feel that I must communicate with someone (someone *not* Monroe) freely, frankly, and with some entirety, as to the scope and component parts of my fate and destiny.

JUNE 23

John Stevenson and I are going to a little party in Bond Street for him and Jerry [Rosco] and Terry [Tolkin], and Andrew [Faulk].

JUNE 28

Lincoln [Kirstein] at the ballet, on Balanchine's coronary by-pass: "It's like having your tonsils out."

JUNE 30

One should expect oneself to write efficiently in a room in which miscellany—the worst of all disconnected written or printed material—catches the eye. Some of it may inspire one, but that's the worst of it, inspiration in any direction, not in line with one's main work that day. A key-ring loaded with keys, fraught with emotions, and giving rise to anxiety, dread, shame, and waste of time and energy.

JULY 6

Poor over-age Monroe, divided between pain and pain-killers, has to deliver nine pages of promised manuscript to a rotten magazine as his contribution to the MoMA drive, rougher than ever this year, and as soon as he wakes up I must dictate from his scribble while he types it.

I don't believe in God. He is a killer and, worse still, he is a fool. But I seem to feel sure that there is an eternity, or at least immortality.

JULY 8

Could I provide my poor dangerous beloved with (in every room that we both have access to) a set of light-switches that turn themselves off in two or three minutes?

No. The word "no" in my deteriorated life is like Poe's crow's "Nevermore."

I had to put off writing this for three-quarters of an hour because I couldn't remember the word "light-switch." The least of my worries.

Word-consciousness, even negative, conducive to literature.

NOVEMBER 23

My Johnnie: I love him second (I suppose) to my old Monroe. And age is his advantage, with reference to me, as well as his handicap in general. In my case, perhaps only in my case, aged 78½, love consists mainly of gratitude and admiration.

∽

Forever is every hour.

1980–1984

D URING THE EARLY EIGHTIES, Wescott manages to add some
final journal material in a sporadic way. It is not a priority, and
bouts of poor health lead to a month or months of silence.
But he bounces back strongly, repeatedly, as some of these last entries
show. Correspondence with some of his favorite friends had bolstered
his journal writing in the past, and now those friends are gone. The most
recent losses are Katherine Anne Porter, Cecil Beaton, and Raymond
Mortimer. The journals book project weighs heavily on his mind, but
the motivation to add new entries fades, and then health issues make
the act of writing harder, until even some table-top notes to Monroe
become precious. After a single 1984 entry the effort comes to a close,
though he lives until early 1987.

As a public, social figure Wescott begins the decade in fine form. In
1980, Governor Brendan Byrne presents him with an award at the New
Jersey State Council on the Arts for his lifetime contribution to American Letters. He travels to San Francisco to address the Advanced Study
of Human Sexuality at the request of its dean, former Kinsey associate
Wardell Pomeroy. Frequent city trips, American Academy of Arts and
Letters meetings, and general socializing continue, including special
gatherings at the city apartment. In July 1980, John Stevenson arranges
a meeting between himself, Wescott, and *City of Night* author John Rechy.
Despite some periods of weariness and fatigue Glenway is often at his

best and very sharp, and some of his best recorded interviews and un-forgettable readings occur in the early eighties. One evening Nancy Rica Schiff photographs a handsome formal picture of Wescott and Wheeler together for her book of famous octogenarians. Monroe's overseas travel continues and Glenway's loneliness increases when John Stevenson—years from opening his own photo gallery—is transferred by his job to Los Angeles.

A few last Wescott pieces appear. To keep up interest in the long-delayed journals, Robert Phelps arranges for a long selection called "Paris 1938" to be featured in the premier issue of *Grand Street*, Autumn 1981. The melancholy but heartfelt account of Glenway's return visit to Paris includes his word portraits of Jean Cocteau, Janet Flanner, Nancy Cunard, and legendary entertainer Mistinguett. Drawn from lecture material, "A Succession of Poets" in the Fall 1983 *Partisan Review* is a fond reminiscence mostly of Marianne Moore, but also of Robert Frost and others.

Wheeler's health problems are the larger worry for years, especially after he has several serious falls. But in October 1983 they both notice when Glenway—for the first time ever—misspeaks while reading to Monroe. Circulatory problems begin making it harder for him to read, speak, and write. On December 2, he is supposed to introduce his friend Joseph Campbell at the Princeton Club, but to his surprise he can't get his little speech started. Campbell takes the microphone and gently covers over the awkward moment. During 1984, Glenway makes far fewer trips to the city, yet still manages to attend Monroe's March 14 party for Baron Rothschild, several lunches with Robert Phelps and other friends, and a December 7 dinner at the Academy of Arts and Letters. Sharing one of the white limousines bringing Academy members home, poet Howard Moss notices that Glenway stumbles badly when getting out of the car at Fifty-First Street.

It becomes increasingly clear that Wescott is fine in the first half of the day, but badly fatigued afterward, and in 1985 he stops coming into the city.

1980

JANUARY

A good deal of old age is error. Sorrowful wit, out of powerful useful mind, corroding away the great matrimony of Monroe Wheeler and myself.

JANUARY 31

How pitifully I wept last night, sitting alone in front of the TV, dismayed by my month-long physical enfeeblement—taken by surprise by the still sweet voice of one of the Andrews Sisters singing one of Richard Rodgers' best melodies—with the cowardly thought of not having Monroe here beside me for another crucial month.

~

Imaginary Letter: To Jill Krementz—"Let me alone. I am an old dropout. I can't be scolded."

MARCH

W. H. Auden: What exactly happened on September 1, 1939? Hitler's incomparable army invaded Poland.

Auden must have taken his facile, great timeless pen in hand immediately, as his "September 1, 1939" appeared in the *New Republic* on October 18, 1939. Rereading it now I am struck by its softly strumming music, its undressed vocabulary, its impact line after line, as it were a comforting, courage-giving hand, a touch of a loving hand, the slap of resentment or of self-criticism. Reminiscent, believe it or not, of "A Day for a Lay."

~

Enthusiasm was my attitude upon meeting Auden, soon after his arrival in the United States, and I expected real friendship to ensue. I have been as ashamed of my failure to like some admirable men and women as by their non-response to me: Sandburg, Hemingway, Stein. We did not spend many hours together.

I remember his pronouncing that I surely did not have the temperament to write the great novel—how did he know that?—and saying, perhaps to console me, that it was an overrated category of literature anyway.

MARCH 28

This great old house, Haymeadows, so-named by me when it was surrounded by hay (in recent years it has been corn); never properly divided between Monroe and me, the only theme we have ever fought about— now gradually ceasing to be home for us, naturally—is full of weird agglomerations, collections, abandoned pieces of prose, precious though not very valuable works of art, wonderful photographs of our very own departed photographer, great furniture provided by our departed female partner and benefactor. At the back door, lions and tigers.

MAY 8

Why am I cheered up by the designation of Senator Muskie to be Secretary of State? I remember his weeping when he was in the running for a still higher office and someone insulted his wife. And the way he drank too much at the fundraiser, then fell asleep at the long dais.

Elvis Presley died of coronary arrhythmia.

Is that what I am going to die of? I don't think so. Of losing my temper perhaps.

MAY 28

Memory, like inspiration, like belief, like eloquence and persuasiveness, has to be controlled and used, or it will run riot and hinder more than it helps.

JUNE 17

Memory is a long-term fairy tale. A good deal of the texture of existence is an interweaving of the present sensation with some part of the life gone by.

～

Melancholy at the task of boxing and labeling six boxes of my archives of the 1960s.

JUNE 28

Lincoln Kirstein's confession to me in the early thirties: that he was almost color-blind—hence his love of sculpture ([Gaston] Lachaise, [Elie] Nadelman, [Augustus] St. Gaudeus). Also his liking for realist and surrealist painting with 3-dimensional monochromatic under-painting, that of his brother-in-law [Paul Cadmus], for instance.

JULY 18

I am haunted by a great saying by Jules Renard, misquoted in my memory: Perhaps inspiration results from working. It certainly doesn't precede it.

AUGUST 4

My last (I hope) will and testament. M.W. reminds me to leave $5,000 to Anatole Pohorilenko. He has left that amount in his will to John Robert Connolly. Also, a matter of great consequence: As we now own jointly, half and half, apartment 8M, 251 East 51st Street, I must bequeath my half to him, as he has bequeathed his half to me.

Identity of my co-executor: John Stevenson.

AUGUST 8

Perhaps the worst thing that happens to me, sometimes more than once a day, is to lose my fountain pen.

I woke up at 2 a.m. and found myself too tired to go back to sleep. Leftover nightmare flowed around me. Fatigue of yesterday led to the fatiguing day ahead. Poor old fool.

AUGUST 13

I am afraid of the dark. Failing to find things, having to bring out and set up my little table and my tape recorder, and to pack and unpack my little luggage, makes me feel feeble-minded, acidic, self-conscious, Monroe-conscious.

AUGUST 29

The trouble with poetry is that, even in its futile mimicry of other poets, it aims at perfection.

Prose is free, free to be honest, to intermingle feelings, thoughts and emotions, free to change its mind.

AUGUST 30

An image of evil. For three days an unkillable large blowfly; presumably a side-effect of the carcasses that Thane Clark feeds his miserable tigers.

SEPTEMBER 9, 6:30 A.M.

My mind in the early morning is lined with mirrors of memory, unavoidably tormented with every sort of egocentricity and realization of myself, past and present and seemingly future.

Visiting with Angels. For days, no for weeks, there have been coincidences that others would think trivial—to my mind, in which superstitiousness and imagination mix, they have been like a coming and going of spirits in broad daylight, flashes of electric from my fingertips when I touch things.

When there is a streak of madness in me, is it possible to foresee what form it would take if it should happen? Sometimes when I think about myself, my inspirations, my sudden connections, my peaceful feeling of uniqueness, I am reminded of William Blake.

DECEMBER 9, 7:30 A.M.

My dearest of all: I am afraid that I am as mad as a hatter. No harm in that, if somehow I can manage to recall the last months or years of our unique life: a double portrait, in your honor.

1981

FEBRUARY 18

East 51st Street. Thoughtlessly at 7:20 a.m. I happened to turn on the desk lamp in Monroe's bedroom, rousing him from his last hour of sleep, his worst hour of arthritic torture. He reproved me and I begged his pardon. Then I told him, "I feel like a new man today."

How proud I was of his monosyllabic response. "Good!"

MAY 14

I might have gone to a new movie at the Jewel but didn't because Monroe said he might call. Then I fell asleep and the telephone rang and I thought it was Monroe, but at the same time believed that I was dreaming. It was John Stevenson, here for just 24 hours, with an early engagement with his big boss, and another engagement in Los Angeles tomorrow afternoon—too tired even to summon one of his playmates. Then Doris phoned to thank Monroe for a gift.

We're *all* separated; a funny feeling. This for Monroe with love and sorrow, and promise.

My family in our New Jersey abode has for some time been haunted by a criminal lunatic, divorced at last [from Lloyd and Barbara's daughter Debo] but still hanging around, threatening arson, and in fact a week ago attempting arson, and I, by my poor brother's miscalculation, have been cast in the role of the lunatic's chief enemy.

Haunted, haunted once more by the possibilities of arson.

JULY 4

Almost everything has happened to me in my long slow-moving life, now climaxing and coming to a close faster and faster and faster.

NOVEMBER 21

Said Saki, the author of cruelly funny stories which, strange as it seems to me now, I enjoyed reading in my mysterious youth, "Most writers are happy, if at all, only on the days that they write."

1982

FEBRUARY 11

Thomas de Quincey remark: "What luxury I lived in for half a century, writing well, and less well, reading all sorts of literature, and never having to keep house."

Elena Gerhardt [a famous German singer and early friend]: Elena had Greek goddess features and pulled her hair tightly up from her noble brow. Skirts were obligatorily short in 1923–24; she had shapely legs. She was beautifully corseted and when she sang her arms just reached around her full torso, so full of breath-control, and her fingers joined to hold open a little opera prompt-book that I never saw her look at. And just below the song book she wore a large round bouquet of orchids, slightly trembling with her soprano notes.

Note: My dearest Mon, Perhaps I will have fallen asleep before you get back. Make a noise in the library, unless you are too sleepy.

APRIL 9

For months and months, just before I wake up, I dream that I am myself and that I am about to die, and before that happens I must write something that Monroe hasn't already read, something as good as Kipling and Hardy and Henry James.

It was right and proper of me not to let Monroe ask Brooke Astor to include me in her dinner party—but damn it, I wish I had been wrong and improper.

MAY 30

It touches me how many indefatigable captions illustrated by the *New Yorker* cartoonists apply to me, as to my melancholy, apathy, my shame. For instance: "Most of Glenway's ideas never see the light of day."

"The press of my foot to the earth / springs a hundred affections, / They scorn the best I can do to relate them."—Walt Whitman, "Song of Myself."

No need, perhaps no possibility of explaining my many ill-starred enterprises, sorry abandonments.

JUNE 5. 2:45 A.M.

"Give me an old man's frenzy," Yeats exclaimed somewhere. Could it have been in one of the letters to Dorothy Wellesley, or perhaps *Dramatis Personae*? Would that I could plan, or even hope, to find time to read and re-read his never exactly collected works of prose and poetry. The greatest lyric poet—leaving out the playwrights and the epic narrators.

The moral of this fragmentary piece: Give me a reasonable and enforceable agenda, pre-auroral before daybreak.

DAY AFTER LABOR DAY, 5:20 A.M.

To Monroe: Have I told you what I want carved on my tombstone, if anything? "Always, in every way, I bit off more than I could chew."

OCTOBER 21

I got up at 12:30 a.m., tormented by John Stevenson having distanced me.

NOVEMBER 30

A good bit of the structure of my life and lifework caved in yesterday when my great Monroe gently, confidently, reported his nightmare about my publishing "The Glimpse Beneath the Door," that is, letting Ralph Pomeroy publish it.

1983

JANUARY 26

Monroe: Just lately, in his sickness, whereas he is faultlessly kind to great ladies and young men, he seems to look down on me. I dare say that it is mostly my fault. One of my most troublesome faults is getting my feelings hurt. Can I cure it?

I am afraid of the dark and I may say that it is afraid of me.

FEBRUARY 13

This is my lifelong Monroe's 84th birthday.

How we have suffered and made one another suffer for circa six months in the entire mysterious matter of David Rockefeller's commissioning him to write a brief but all too capacious foreword to the catalogue of his European pictures—his and his wife's—due to his inability to write any such thing and his wild determination not to give up writing, and due to my conceit and masochistic hope of helping him!

MARCH 23

It has always stirred my mind to notice what gaping distances that have taken place in the lifework of a good many painters.

I have invented certain forms: the family tree [*The Grandmothers*]; the Mozartesque opera without music [*The Pilgrim Hawk*], what the French know as *legende chorée*.

APRIL 28

Three or four times in the year gone by, Monroe has fallen face down and from head to foot. A seizure of some sort. On the eve of his departure for Geneva, Munich and Vienna, with his whirlwind International Council, it happened once more, worse than before, cutting his forehead, on West 54th Street in front of George Rey's restaurant. G.R. sent a waiter with a towel and put him in a taxi. His arrival at 251 frightened me indescribably. Anatole arrived and tagged after him to Lenox Hill Emergency Ward. They sent him home to New Jersey to the specialists in my brother's hospital and our good family doctor.

No one is desperate, not even I, least of all the sporadically bleeding octogenarian himself, and he persists in driving his old Cadillac to and fro.

I said to him, "Your optimism is so powerful that it amounts to heroism and frightens all the rest of us. You often fail to report truthfully, even to your own physician."

He replied, firmly, "I like the way I am."

Love in my case, at this phase of life, amounts mostly to gratitude and admiration.

JULY, 4:15 A.M.

Sometimes it seems in the morning darkness that I could seize and love the first glimpses of my latest small subject matter, and work with it word-by-word, play with it nonstop—until my elderly fatigue and physical weakness envelopes me.

SEPTEMBER 2

Good advice from a moribund great lady who asked, "Oh Glenway, are you as kind as you are courteous?"

~

I suffered what the French call "Un coup de vieux," translated by me as "a wallop of old."

~

[A note to Monroe.]

Dear—I didn't wake you because you need sleep. I love you and upon waking found myself happy thereby. Until this evening—G.

1984

MEMORIAL DAY

Is it possible that I may fail to ever write again? Again and again in the early morning I take a page of the pale pink paper that delights me, punched three times for my habitual three-ring binders, and then what?

Afterword

WESCOTT NEVER BELIEVED he would outlive Wheeler, even though Monroe had suffered with arthritis and other problems for the past two decades while Glenway remained relatively healthy. Now it was Glenway marooned at Haymeadows while Monroe kept up his city routine and international travel. To compensate, Monroe would report on their beloved New York City Ballet, the dinner parties, and museum news. Though Glenway's correspondence was over, Monroe sent cheerful postcards from abroad.

Looking to the future, John Connolly and Ivan Ashby bought the Haymeadows house from Lloyd and spent weekends there more often. At other times friends visited and found Glenway fairly well, speaking a bit haltingly but with clarity, wit, and humor—and with an excellent memory of past conversations and events. Nothing was getting resolved with the journals, and Lloyd and Monroe had most of the bankers boxes of material stored in the loft of the nearby garage, formerly a barn. In February 1986, Glenway experienced a mild heart attack and spent several days at Hunterdon Medical Center, at 2100 Wescott Drive. There he told John Stevenson, "I disgrace myself with loneliness and boredom and vexation." He'd like to come to the city and have a party, he said.

Wescott's last birthday was on Friday, April 11, 1986, and a local newspaper reported that he celebrated with family and friends at a restaurant in New Hope. The next day John Stevenson and I drove out to visit. At just that time Arbor House had published a handsome new edition of *The Grandmothers* with a cover illustration of Wescott's autobiographical character, young Alwyn Tower. Glenway had heard about it but not seen it and we brought a whole boxful, along with other birthday gifts. In jacket and bright lavender tie, Glenway was pleased by the attractive new book and—coming as it did, out of nowhere—seemed to put to rest any worries about the journals, though he knew they'd be posthumous. He took a phone call of congratulations about the book and replied, "I had nothing to do with it. It came through the trees, looking for me." When he was asked to sign a few books, his hand could only manage a shaky scrawl, which upset him. Then he went for a ride to see his favorite country lane, Laurel Road in New Hope. With a smile he said, "I dreamed of it last night, but I didn't think that would be enough to bring it on." He also enjoyed a visit to a public flower garden and lunch in Lambertville.

In May, Wescott's doctors gave him a pacemaker and he was stable through the summer, with the care of Lloyd, Monroe, and Anatole; John Connolly and Ivan; and Lloyd's faithful staff: Dorothy, Jerome, and Ethel.

In early October he suffered a stroke that affected his speech and mobility. He was home in two weeks and recovered slightly in the coming months. His bed was moved down to their library, by a window overlooking the fields. Still living in California, temporary executor John Stevenson visited in January 1987 for an emotional reunion. Then he met with Lloyd and a family lawyer to help settle affairs.

On Sunday night, February 22, Glenway passed away at home. Among the newspaper tributes, the *New York Times* referred to him as "one of the last of the major American expatriate writers who lived in France in the 1920s and 1930s," and the *Times* of London stated, "He will be remembered as long as fiction is read." On March 11, he was remembered at the American Academy of Arts and Letters, with speakers including Jane Gunther, Russell Lynes, and William Maxwell, and piano pieces performed by Ned Rorem.

Within forty-eight hours of Wescott's passing, Wheeler suffered a stroke. After a long rehabilitation he lived at his New York apartment and made his last trip to Europe in late July 1988. He passed away on August 14 and was honored by a large gathering at the Museum of Modern Art on November 3. Lloyd died at home on Christmas Eve 1990. *Continual Lessons*, Wescott's journals of 1937 to 1955, appeared shortly afterward.

At Haymeadows, a small, nearly hidden, centuries-old farmers' graveyard has a large marble marker, listing the names of the Wescott clan, including Glenway and Monroe.

～

Postscript: In his memorial speech for Wescott, William Maxwell said Glenway was wrong to punish himself about not publishing more. He should have finished more of his nonfiction projects, true. But no writer can produce more quality novels than he or she is able. Of his four novels, three are high art, and the other, *Apartment in Athens*, was a bestseller and is now an award-winning movie by producer/director Ruggero Dipaola. They are reprinted often enough, including in many foreign-language editions. And there are the journals. No writer could ask for more.

A Glossary of Glenway Wescott's Contemporaries

Cyrilly Abels (1903–75). Mademoiselle editor, later a literary agent.

Edward Albee (b. 1928). Pulitzer Prize–winning playwright best known for *Who's Afraid of Virginia Woolf?*

Joseph Alsop (1910–89). Played by John Lithgow in the 2012 play *The Columnist,* a powerful Washington insider who hid his homosexuality despite Senator Joe McCarthy and Soviet spies.

Lou Ames. Television show producer, including NBC's *Today Show.*

Louis Armstrong (1901–71). "Satchmo," the great New Orleans trumpet player and singer.

Brooke Astor (1902–2007). Socialite and philanthropist, especially favoring the Metropolitan Museum and the New York Public Library. She once saved the Jefferson Library in Greenwich Village after a phone call from Wescott. Monroe Wheeler used to accompany her to the ballet and visit her "Holly Hill" country estate.

W. H. Auden (1907–73). British-American poet, one of the century's greats. Wescott discusses one of his most important poems, "September 1, 1939," in a March 1980 entry.

Don Bachardy (b. 1934). American portrait artist and longtime companion to Christopher Isherwood.

George Balanchine (1904–83). Russian-American preeminent choreographer. Cofounder and balletmaster of the New York City Ballet.

Amiri Baraka (LeRoi Jones) (b. 1934). Poet, writer, critic, and educator.

Samuel Barber (1910–81). Acclaimed composer, twice awarded a Pulitzer Prize.

Maurice Baring (1874–1945). British poet, dramatist, novelist, essayist, and translator.

Djuna Barnes (1892–1982). Influential novelist, poet, and playwright.

Sir Cecil Beaton (1904–80). British portrait and fashion photographer, diarist, painter, and interior designer.

Ingmar Bergman (1918–2007). Swedish director, producer, and writer.

Connie Bessie (1918–85). Radio and television producer, then a *Newsweek* editor. She was a friend of Mary Hemingway and a favorite of Wescott at his 1970s readings of his journals.

Isabel Bishop (1902–88). Painter and graphic artist.

Louise Bogan (1897–1970). Poet who also reviewed poetry for the *New Yorker.* U.S. Poet Laureate in 1945.

Jorge Luis Borges (1899–1986). Argentine short story writer, translator, essayist, and poet.

Marie-Louise Bousquet (1886–1975). Paris editor of *Harper's Bazaar.*

Coburn Britton (1936–97). Poet, publisher, and founder of *Prose* journal.

William Burroughs (1914–97). Central figure among the Beats; novelist, short story writer, and spoken word performer.

Mary Butts (1890–1937). British novelist, modernist, and student of Aleister Crowley.

Witter Bynner (1881–1968). Santa Fe poet, writer, and scholar.

Paul Cadmus (1904–99). Influential American "magical-realist" artist. Brother-in-law of Lincoln Kirstein and a friend of Wescott, Wheeler, George Platt Lynes, E. M. Forster, and many more.

(Sir Thomas Henry) Hall Caine (1853–1931). British novelist and playwright.

Alexander Calder (1898–1976). American sculptor and artist.

Joseph Campbell (1904–87). Mythologist, writer, and lecturer. Author of *The Hero with a Thousand Faces.*

Cass Canfield (1897–1986). One of America's great literary editors and publishers, at Harpers.

Truman Capote (1924–84). American author best known for *Breakfast at Tiffany's,* the "nonfiction novel" *In Cold Blood,* the scandalous *Answered Prayers,* and many movie adaptations.

Henri Cartier Brésson (1908–2004). Highly acclaimed French photographer.

Willa Cather (1873–1947). Pulitzer Prize–winning novelist of the Great Plains.

Constantine P. Cavafy (1863–1933). Renowned Greek poet.

John Cheever (1912–82). Acclaimed novelist and short story writer.

Maurice Chevalier (1888–1972). French actor, singer, and entertainer.

Eleanor Clark (1913–96). Author and National Book Award winner. Wife of poet, novelist, and critic Robert Penn Warren.

Lord Kenneth Clark (1903–83). British author and broadcaster. As a museum director and art historian a friend of Monroe Wheeler.

Jean Cocteau (1899–1963). French artist, novelist, poet, playwright, and filmmaker. Best known for films such as *Les Enfants Terribles, Beauty and the Beast,* and *Orpheus.*

(Sidonie-Gabrielle) Colette (1873–1954). The French novelist inspired Wescott, who wrote essays about her and the introduction to *Short Novels of Colette*.

Padraic Colum (1881–1972). Irish poet, novelist, playwright, biographer, and children's book author.

Cyril Connolly (1903–74). Literary critic, author, and editor of the literary magazine *Horizon*.

Lady Diana Cooper (1892–1986). British socialite and actress, renowned for her beauty.

Bill Cosby (b. 1937). Comedian, actor, author, and educator.

Malcolm Cowley (1898–1989). Literary critic, novelist, and poet.

Josephine (Porter Boardman) Crane (1873–1972). Socialite and patron of the arts, co-founder of the Metropolitan Museum and a founder of the Museum of Modern Art. She was known for her literary salons at 820 Fifth Avenue, New York, and at Woods Hole, Massachusetts.

Aleister Crowley (1875–1947). British occultist, mystic, magician, and poet.

E. E. Cummings (1894–1962). Poet, playwright, and novelist. Longtime famous resident at 4 Patchin Place, Greenwich Village, New York.

Lady (Maud) Emerald Cunard (1872–1948). American-born London society hostess. An amiable favorite of the literary crowd.

Nancy Cunard (1896–1965). Daughter of Emerald Cunard; writer, heiress, and political activist. As one of the 1920s Paris expatriates she published The Hours Press deluxe books.

Mina Kirstein Curtiss (1896–1985). Author, editor, and translator. She was the sister of Lincoln Kirstein.

Marguerite D'Alvarez (1883–1953). British-born contralto, popular throughout Europe.

Jacques D'Amboise (b. 1934). Principal dancer and choreographer for the New York City Ballet.

Duchess de Gramont (born Marie Ruspoli) (1875–1954). French writer. Known for her long-term relationship with American writer, poet, and playwright Natalie Clifford Barney.

Sergei Diaghilev (1872–1929). Russian ballet impresario and founder of the Ballet Russes, which brought Vaslav Nijinski to fame.

Marlene Dietrich (1901–92). The popular German-American actress was Wescott and Wheeler's neighbor at 410 Park Avenue.

Isak Dinesen (Baroness Karen Blixen) (1885–1962). Danish author best known for *Out of Africa* and *Babette's Feast*, both also successful as films. She fascinated Wescott with her ability to narrate whole short stories from memory.

Laurie Douglas (b. 1915). Actress of late 1930s to 1940s fame.

Isadora Duncan (1877–1927). The key figure in modern dance. Her friends Wescott and Wheeler sat with her body the night after her tragic automobile accident.

T .S. Eliot (1888–1965). Major poet, playwright, and critic.

Suzanne Farrell (b. 1945). One of the great stars of the New York City Ballet, which Wheeler and Wescott often attended.

William Faulkner (1897–1962). Novelist and Nobel Prize laureate.

Peggy Fears (1903–94). Actress known for musical comedies, including the Ziegfeld Follies; also a Broadway producer. She later helped build up the Fire Island Pines and was a central figure of its gay and lesbian community. See the film *When Ocean Meets Sky*.

Edna Ferber (1885–1968). Pulitzer Prize–winning novelist, short story writer, and playwright. Films based on her books include *Show Boat* and *Giant*.

Edward Field (b. 1924). Popular and prolific poet and writer.

Janet Flanner (1892–1978). Writer and journalist who served as the *New Yorker*'s Paris correspondent for fifty years under the pen name "Genêt."

Lynn Fontanne (1887–1983). British-born actress of the American stage mostly. Wife of director and actor Alfred Lunt.

Charles Henri Ford (1913–2002). Poet, editor of the surrealist magazine *View*, coauthor with Parker Tyler of the controversial Greenwich Village novel *The Young & Evil*, filmmaker, collage artist, lover of artist Pavel Tchelitchev, and brother of actress Ruth Ford.

Ford Madox Ford (1873–1939). Prolific British novelist, poet, and critic. Editor of the *Transatlantic Review* and the *English Review*, and a friend of many American expatriates.

Ruth Ford (1911–2009). Actress of stage and screen, she was a member of Orson Welles's Mercury Theatre. Her first husband was actor Peter Van Eyck, her second was film star Zachary Scott.

E. M. Forster (1879–1970). British author of major novels such as *Howard's End* and *A Passage to India*. He arranged that Wescott and Christopher Isherwood would handle the posthumous publication of his gay-love novel *Maurice*. Monroe Wheeler brought the manuscript to America.

(Sir) David Frost (b. 1939). British television host, journalist, and writer.

Robert Frost (1874–1963). A four-time Pulitzer Prize winner for poetry, he first knew Wescott as a twenty-year-old poet.

Robert Gathorne-Hardy (1902–73). British poet and author of ten books on gardening, as well as *Recollections of Logan Pearsall Smith*, for whom he was a secretary and companion. His nephew is author Jonathan Gathorne-Hardy (b. 1933), biographer of Alfred Kinsey.

Paul H. Gebhard (b. 1917). Anthropologist and sexologist who succeeded Alfred Kinsey as Director of the Institute for Sex Research.

Felicia Geffen (1903–95). Longtime executive director of the American Academy of Arts and Letters.

Elena Gerhardt (1883–1961). German mezzo-soprano singer.

George Gershwin (1898–1937). Composer and pianist best known for orchestral compositions such as *Rhapsody in Blue, An American in Paris,* and *Porgy and Bess.*

Ralph Ginzburg (1929–2006). Author, editor, publisher, and photo-journalist.

Robert Giroux (1914–2008). Cofounder of Farrar, Straus, and Giroux; he was a publisher devoted to ambitious literary works.

Eric Goldman (1916–89). Historian, educator, and moderator of the NBC program *The Open Mind.*

Katherine Graham (1917–2001). Washington Post publisher who enjoyed many literary and social friendships.

Harley Granville-Barker (1877–1946). British actor, producer, critic, and playwright.

Jacques Guérin (1902–2000). French bibliophile and collector—he owned Proust's desk—who inherited a perfume company and was Wescott's Parisian lover from 1928 to 1934.

John Gunther (1901–70). Journalist and author known for his sociopolitical "Inside" books (*Inside Africa, Inside South America,* etc.) and for the popular memoir *Death Be Not Proud.* His second wife, Jane Gunther, was a mainstay at Wescott gatherings, especially readings.

Dag Hammarskjöld (1905–61). A posthumous winner of the Nobel Peace Prize and the Secretary-General of the United Nations; died in a suspicious plane crash. Wescott refers to Hammarskjöld's hidden sexuality in his October 15, 1963 entry.

Ernest Hemingway (1899–1961). Pulitzer Prize–winning novelist who, early in life, resented the success of certain homosexual authors and parodied Wescott in chapter 3 of *The Sun Also Rises.* His posthumous novel *The Garden of Eden* suggests his own unusual sexuality.

Jimi Hendrix (1942–70). Perhaps the greatest electric guitarist ever.

John Hersey (1914–93). Novelist and journalist who wrote the powerful account *Hiroshima.*

Hermann Hesse (1877–1962). German-Swiss novelist, painter, and poet. Awarded the Nobel Prize in 1946.

Karen Horney (1885–1952). The German psychoanalyst had the support of Wescott's sister-in-law Barbara Harrison. The Karen Horney Clinic remains today in Manhattan.

A. E. Hotchner (b. 1920). Author, editor, and playwright. Best known for his memoir of Ernest Hemingway, *Papa Hemingway.*

A. E. Housman (1859–1936). British poet and scholar. Best known for his *A Shropshire Lad* poems.

Richard Hughes (1900–76). British novelist, poet, and playwright.

Violet Hunt (1862–1942). British author and literary hostess. Known for her long relationship with Ford Madox Ford and her affair with W. Somerset Maugham.

Clement Hurd (1908–88). Artist and illustrator of children's books.

Aldous Huxley (1894–1963). British writer, humanist, and intellectual.

William Inge (1913–73). Pulitzer Prize–winning playwright and novelist. Wescott's companion John Connolly was his secretary.

Christopher Isherwood (1904–86). British-American novelist. Author of *The Berlin Stories,* on which both the play and the film *Cabaret* were based.

Juan Ramón Jiménez (1881–1958). Poet, writer, and Nobel Prize winner.

Philip Johnson (1906–2005). Architect associated with the Museum of Modern Art. Best known for the Glass House.

Matthew Josephson (1899–1978). Journalist, author, and literary scholar.

James Joyce (1882–1941). Irish novelist and poet—one of the most influential modernist writers. Author of *Ulysses.*

Edward MacKnight Kauffer (1890–1954). Avant-garde artist and graphic designer.

George Kennan (1904–2005). Historian, diplomat, and political advisor.

Alfred C. Kinsey (1894–1956). As the first director of the Institute for Sex Research, his study of human sexuality was scientific but compassionate, which led to Wescott's trust and close friendship.

Lincoln Kirstein (1907–96). A great force for the arts, he founded the school of American Ballet and eventually the New York City Ballet.

John Knowles (1926–2001). Novelist best known for *A Separate Peace.*

Jill Krementz (b. 1940). Photographer and author. Wife of novelist Kurt Vonnegut.

P. Lal (1929–2010). Indian poet, essayist, and translator.

Giuseppe Tomasi di Lampedusa (1896–1957). Sicilian writer whose only novel, *The Leopard,* was published posthumously.

D. H. Lawrence (1885–1930). British novelist, playwright, poet, and painter whose sexually controversial works were often censored.

Lieutenant Colonel T. E. Lawrence (1888–1935). British author and army officer who earned fame as Lawrence of Arabia. Author of *Seven Pillars of Wisdom.*

Paul Lèautaud (1872–1956). French critic, memoirist, and novelist.

Violette Leduc (1907–72). French novelist whose controversial *Thérèse and Isabelle* also became a commercial film.

Leo Lerman (1914–94). Writer and entertainment-magazine editor.

W. S. Lewis (1895–1979). Biographer of Horace Walpole (1717–79) and editor of Walpole's massive correspondence.

Anita Loos (1888–1981). Screenwriter, playwright, and author. Best known for *Gentlemen Prefer Blondes.*

James Lord (1922–2009). Author of biographies of Pablo Picasso and Alberto Giacommetti, as well as the posthumous memoir *My Queer War.*

Malcolm Lowry (1909–57). British poet and novelist. Author of the highly acclaimed *Under the Volcano.*

Clair Booth Luce (1903–87). Author, ambassador to Italy in the 1950s, and wife of Henry Luce (publisher of the magazines *Time, Life,* and *Fortune*).

Alfred Lunt (1892–1977). Stage director and actor. Married to actress Lynn Fontanne.

George Platt Lynes (1907–55). The influential portrait and fashion photographer was also known for his ballet photos and mostly—at least posthumously—for his male nudes. He was not only an intimate of Wheeler and Wescott but also a part of the circle of Paul Cadmus and many other artists and photographers. Among the photo books available is the recent *Male Nudes* (Rizzoli), text by Steven Hasse.

Russell Lynes (1910–91). Author, art historian, and managing editor of *Harper's Magazine*—he helped support the life and legacy of his mercurial brother, photographer George Platt Lynes.

Norman Mailer (1923–2007). Novelist, journalist, and playwright. He was awarded both the Pulitzer Prize (twice) and the National Book Award.

Carl Malouf (1916–91). New York artist who designed store windows and excelled in exterior design. He and artist friend Tommy Sullivan hosted gay parties in the 1940s and 1950s, once with Wescott's friend Dr. Kinsey as an observer.

André Malraux (1901–76). French novelist, art theorist, and Minister for Cultural Affairs. Author of *The Human Condition.*

Thomas Mann (1875–1955). Major German novelist, critic, and philanthropist. Nobel Prize laureate.

Jayne Mansfield (1933–67). Film, television, and stage actress, and sex symbol of the 1950s. Even her smallest cameo is notable, in Charles Henri Ford's short film *Poem Posters.*

Herbert Marcuse (1898–1979). German philosopher, sociologist, and political theorist who settled in America. "Father of the New Left."

William Somerset Maugham (1874–1965). British novelist, playwright, and short story writer, and one of the world's most successful authors for much of his life, thanks early on to plays and later to bestsellers and film adaptations. He saw Wescott often during the World War II years in America.

William Maxwell (1908–2000). Novelist, National Book Award winner, and longtime fiction editor of the *New Yorker.*

Mary McCarthy (1912–89). Political writer, critic, and novelist.

Anne O'Hare McCormick (1880–1954). Pulitzer Prize–winning foreign correspondent for the *New York Times.*

Carson McCullers (1917–67). Novelist and playwright, with such film adaptations as *The Heart Is a Lonely Hunter, Reflections in a Golden Eye,* and *The Ballad of the Sad Café.*

Henry McIlhenny (1910–86). Chairman of the board of the Philadelphia Museum of the Arts, collector, patron of the arts, and philanthropist.

Marshall McLuhan (1911–80). Canadian educator, philosopher, and communications scholar who taught "The medium is the message."

Lady (Elsie de Wolfe) Mendl (1865–1950). American-born actress, interior decorator, and socialite in London, New York, and Paris.

Charles H. Miller (1913–92). A poet who once served as Auden's secretary. Author of *Auden: An American Friendship.*

Henry Miller (1891–1980). Author best known for *Tropic of Cancer;* was a memoirist and critic, as well as an artist who worked in watercolors.

Sal Mineo (1939–76). Actor of film and stage, remembered best for the film *Rebel Without a Cause.*

Yukio Mishima (1925–70). Japanese author, poet, playwright, film director, and actor. He committed a sensational ritual suicide.

Jean Monnet (1888–1979). French economist and diplomat, and one of the early architects of European Unity.

Marilyn Monroe (1926–62). Actress, model, singer, and sex symbol of the 1950s and early 1960s, until her untimely death.

Douglas Moore (1893–1969). Composer, educator, and author.

Marianne Moore (1887–1972). The great poet knew Wescott from his early adulthood to his late years, but was closer to Monroe Wheeler.

Ted Morgan (b. 1932). French-American author, biographer, journalist, and historian.

(Charles) Raymond Mortimer (1895–1980). British writer, editor, and literary critic for the *New Statesman* and the *Sunday Times.*

Natalia Danesi Murray (1901–94). Italian-born author, journalist, publisher, radio broadcaster, and director. The American lover of Janet Flanner, she edited *Darlinghissima: Letters to a Friend,* correspondence organized as memoir. Her novelist son, William, followed up with the memoir *Janet, My Mother and Me.*

Vladimir Nabokov (1899–1977). Russian novelist, poet, and short story writer. His first nine novels were in Russian, then he rose to greater fame as a writer of English prose, including his masterpiece, *Lolita.*

Sir Harold Nicolson (1886–1968). British diplomat, biographer, diarist, and politician.

Vaslav Nijinski (1890–1950). Russian dancer and choreographer of Polish descent. One of the ballet greats of all time.

Anaïs Nin (1903–77). French-Cuban author, best known for her journals. Her novel *Henry & June* led to the 1990 film.

Frank O'Connor (1903–66). Prolific Irish author best known for his short stories and memoirs.

John O'Hara (1905–70). Author of thirteen short story collections and seventeen novels, including *Butterfield 8*.

Georgia O'Keeffe (1887–1986). A breakthrough artist of the American landscape, she became known as a painter and sculptor of the southwest, but was world renowned.

Dorothy Parker (1893–1967). Poet, short story writer, screenwriter, and critic. Her Hollywood success was cut short when she was blacklisted for her political views. A famous wit, she was a frequent contributor to the *New Yorker* and a founding member of the Algonquin Roundtable.

Isabel Patterson (1886–1961). Canadian-American journalist, novelist, and literary critic.

Bernard Perlin (b. 1918). Highly regarded painter and illustrator. Longtime friend of Wescott and a close friend of, and original executor for, George Platt Lynes.

Robert Phelps (1922–89). Distinguished literary editor who helped introduce the work of Colette to America and also edited works of Cocteau. His dedication to Wescott's work, especially the early journals, *Continual Lessons*, encouraged the author.

Rosemarie Beck Phelps (1923–2003). Artist, art historian, and educator. Married to Robert Phelps.

Donald Pleasence (1919–95). British actor who appeared in more than two hundred films, including the James Bond series.

Ralph Pomeroy (1926–99). Poet, artist, and intimate friend of Monroe Wheeler. An early collection of poems earned him the nickname "Faux Truman" because the book-jacket profile was even more attractive than the one the young Capote used.

Katherine Anne Porter (1890–1980). The Pulitzer Prize–winning novelist, story writer, and essayist struggled for notoriety for much of her life—until the publication of *Ship of Fools*, which was dedicated to Barbara Wescott. She was close to the Wescott clan, though her friendship with Glenway included thorns among the roses.

Elvis Presley (1935–77). One of the most popular singers of the twentieth century and a pop culture icon. Wescott, though a lover of classical music, listened to pop music on the radio.

Raymond Radiguet (1903–23). The brilliant, short-lived protégé of Cocteau, and author of *The Devil in the Flesh*.

Francois Reichenbach (1921–93). Academy Award–winning French documentary film-maker of forty films. He secretly contributed gay-themed films to Dr. Alfred Kinsey's archives, including his own *Last Spring* and Jean Genet's *Chant d'Amour*.

Cliff Robertson (1923–2011). Star of film and television, with a 1968 Best Actor Academy Award for *Charly*.

Paul Robeson (1898–1976). Concert singer, recording artist, actor, athlete, and civil rights activist. The black superstar knew Wescott in the early 1920s Greenwich Village years and during the expatriate years in France.

Richard Charles Rodgers (1902–79). Composer of more than nine hundred songs and forty-three Broadway musicals.

Ned Rorem (b. 1923). The prolific Pulitzer Prize–winning composer is widely known as the author of a series of tell-all diaries.

Philip Roth (b. 1933). Celebrated author of dozens of novels. Best known for *Goodbye, Columbus* and *Portnoy's Complaint*.

Baroness Pauline de Rothschild (1908–76). Wescott called her "My chief female friend." When she first met the Baron she flattered him by saying, "Oh, the poet." Before that, as Pauline Potter, she was one of America's top female fashion designers. She wrote a travel book about Russia, *The Irrational Journey*.

Baron Philippe de Rothschild (1902–88). One of the most successful wine growers in the world, he was also a poet, playwright, translator, and, in his youth, a Grand Prix racecar driver.

Helena Rubenstein (1870–1965). Polish-born Australian-American, she was a self-made millionaire after starting her cosmetics salon in New York.

Antonio Salemme (1892–1995). Italian-American sculptor, he and wife Betty were Wescott and Wheeler's Greenwich Village neighbors in the early 1920s.

J. D. Salinger (1919–2010). Reclusive author whose one novel, *Catcher in the Rye*, remains a classic of adolescent alienation. He also published stories and novellas.

Arthur Schlesinger Jr. (1917–2007). Author, historian, and social critic. Was a special assistant to President Kennedy and a Pulitzer Prize winner.

Zachary Scott (1914–65). Popular movie actor who turned back to the stage late in his career. His second wife was Wescott's friend, stage actress Ruth Ford.

William Shawn (1907–92). Longtime editor of the *New Yorker* who was famously indulgent with writers he believed in.

Isaac Bashevis Singer (1902–91). Polish-born Jewish-American novelist and short story writer and 1978 Nobel Prize winner.

Dame Edith Sitwell (1887–1964). A poet and critic, she had a frustrated devotion to Pavel Tchelitchev.

Osbert Sitwell (1892–1969). Author of six volumes of autobiography, plus novels, stories, and poems.

Sacheverell Sitwell (1897–1988). Prolific author on art and architecture, as well as poetry and autobiography.

Logan Pearsall Smith (1865–1946). American-born essayist and critic who became a British citizen. He was a perfectionist, known for his aphorisms.

Stephen Spender (1909–95). British poet, novelist, and essayist.

Maureen Stapleton (1925–2006). Actress of stage, screen, and television.

Sam Steward (1909–93). Novelist, short story writer, and a hero of sexual liberation. A friend of Gertrude Stein, he was a college instructor turned tattoo artist (under the name Phil Sparrow) and pornography writer (under the name Phil Andros). He kept records and images of his many sexual encounters and was an important volunteer for Dr. Alfred Kinsey at the Institute for Sex Research.

James Stewart (1908–97). Famed actor of film and theater, known for his distinctive voice and manner.

Lytton Strachey (1880–1932). British writer, critic, and founder of the Bloomsbury Group of authors. He was the subject of the 1995 film *Carrington*.

Roger Straus Jr. (1917–2004). Cofounder of the literary publisher Farrar, Straus, and Giroux. Considered one of the last of the old-time quality publishers.

Harold Strauss (1907–75). Editor who pioneered the postwar introduction of Japanese literature to America.

Graham Sutherland (1903–80). British artist known for landscapes who also worked in tapestries and glass design.

Bernadine Szold-Fritz (1896–1982). Journalist, screenwriter, and one of the first Paris correspondents for the *New Yorker*. She knew Wescott and Wheeler from the expatriate 1920s and later settled in Beverly Hills. She played herself in the Warren Beatty film *Reds*.

Allen Tate (1899–1979). Southern writer, poet, and critic. Married to the writer Caroline Gordon.

Pavel ("Pavlik") Tchelitchev (1898–1957). Russian-born artist who was the lover of American poet and artist Charles Henri Ford. Wescott hand-delivered a large collection of Tchelitchev's erotic drawings to Dr. Alfred Kinsey at the Institute for Sex Research.

Dylan Thomas (1914–53). Welsh poet and short story and screenwriter. His public readings made him very popular in America.

Virgil Thomson (1896–1989). Composer and critic who was awarded the Pulitzer Prize for Music.

James Thurber (1894–1961). Author, cartoonist, and wit. Associated with the *New Yorker*.

J. R. R. Tolkien (1892–1973). British writer and poet. Best known for his fantasy fiction: *The Hobbit, The Lord of the Rings,* and *The Silmarillion*.

John Updike (1932–2009). Novelist, poet, short story writer, and critic.

Paul Valéry (1871–1945). French poet, essayist, and philosopher.

Carl Van Vechten (1880–1964). Writer and photographer. A patron of the Harlem Renaissance, and literary executor of Gertrude Stein.

Gore Vidal (1925–2012). Novelist, essayist, playwright, critic, and political activist. Author of the controversial gay-themed *The City and the Pillar* in 1948.

Kurt Vonnegut (1922–2007). Novelist, essayist, and humanist. Author of the satirical works *Cat's Cradle*, *Slaughterhouse Five*, and *Breakfast of Champions*.

Diana Vreeland (1903–89). Fashion editor and columnist for *Harper's Bazaar* and *Vogue*.

Sir Hugh Walpole (1884–1941). British author of thirty-six popular novels. W. Somerset Maugham mockingly caricatured him in *Cakes and Ale*. (Not to be confused with Horace Walpole, 1717–79.)

Andy Warhol (1928–87). The key artist of the Pop Art movement. His unexpected death on the same day as Wescott's (February 22) captured the headlines before the writer was well remembered as one of the last of the 1920s expatriates and for *The Pilgrim Hawk*.

Peter Watson (1908–56). British art collector and benefactor who funded the magazine *Horizon* and was the main love interest of Cecil Beaton. Pavel Tchelitchev was also in love with him.

Denton Welch (1915–48). British writer and painter, known for the sensitivity of novels such as *In Youth Is Pleasure* and *A Voice Through a Cloud*, and his journals.

Rebecca West (1892–1983). British author, literary critic, journalist, and travel writer.

Alfred North Whitehead (1861–1947). British mathematician and philosopher.

Paul Whiteman (1890–1967). Big band leader and orchestral director. He sold Lloyd and Barbara Wescott the New Jersey farm that included Glenway's Haymeadows home.

Richard Wilbur (b. 1921). Poet and translator.

Thornton Wilder (1897–1975). Playwright and novelist who was awarded three Pulitzer Prizes. He warned Wescott during the expatriate 1920s that it was important to be mentioned on the news pages, not just in the book reviews.

Tennessee Williams (1911–83). Pulitzer Prize–winning playwright, with later movie adaptations such as *Cat on a Hot Tin Roof* and *A Streetcar Named Desire*. Also a novelist, short story writer, and poet.

Edgar Wind (1900–1971). German-born British art historian.

Yvor Winters (1900–1968). Influential poet and critic. He and his wife Janet Lewis, a poet and novelist, were original members of the Poetry Club with Wescott at the University of Chicago.

Thomas Wolfe (1900–1938). Major, influential novelist. Author of *Look Homeward, Angel* and *You Can't Go Home Again*.

Tom Wolfe (b. 1931). Popular author and journalist.

Virginia Woolf (1882–1941). Influential British modernist writer and central figure of the Bloomsbury Group. Author of novels such as *Mrs. Dalloway* and *To the Lighthouse*.

Herman Wouk (b. 1915). Author especially known for historical novels.

William Butler Yeats (1865–1939). Towering figure in twentieth-century literature, an Irish poet and playwright. Awarded the 1923 Noble Prize in Literature.

John Yeon (1910–94). Architect known for his work and influence in the Portland, Oregon, area. An intimate friend of Wescott.

Alexander Jensen Yow (b.1926). Artist and an intimate friend of Lincoln Kirstein. When he was unsure of what career to pursue, Monroe Wheeler suggested art conservator, and he went on to become an art conservator at New York's Morgan Library. Years later Wescott called him "the greatest cleaner of drawings and restorer of mediaeval miniatures in the country."

Index